★ HIGH BORDER COUNTRY ★

HIGH BORDER COUNTRY

AMERICAN
FOLKWAYS

EDITED BY ERSKINE CALDWELL

HIGH BORDER COUNTRY

by

ERIC THANE, *pseud.*

"Henry, Ralph Chester."

DUELL, SLOAN & PEARCE • NEW YORK

TO THE PIONEERS—

*Saints and Sinners—too few saints and too
many sinners, but for better or worse the race
that tamed the High Border. To the living of
them, honor; to the dead of them, the promise
that what they did will never be forgotten. To
all of them this book is dedicated.*

Contents

HIGH BORDER COUNTRY

1. Land That Is

DUSTY COUNTRY

THERE'S space that baffles the eye: peaks driving up until granite needles fade into cirrus-flecked blue; prairies green by spring, dusty by summer, frosty by winter, of a desolation scarcely equaled throughout the Americas; the mighty backbone of a continent described simply and altogether inadequately on maps as the Continental Divide, more commonly as the Rocky Mountains. And there are the headwaters and first hundreds of miles of a mighty river known to the twentieth century as the Missouri, to preceding decades variously and descriptively as the Wild Miz-zou-rye, Mizzou, Big Muddy, The Roarin' River, and other names of a type to brand the River for what it was and still is—wild mistress of the prairies, capricious, indolent, a fury and a lady of calm by turns, but immutably flowing from the depths of the Continental Divide first north and east, then south and east to join the father Mississippi.

This is High Border Country—the northern tongue of Idaho, called generally the panhandle; Montana, the third largest state in the Union; Wyoming, almost to its southern border; and Dakota, down into the region of its eastern boundary. This last is both North and South Dakota,

3

but you do not speak of them on the High Border as in·
dividual political unities; you say simply Dakota or, if
you must be specific, The Dakotas. All this is High
Border land, bounded on the north by infrequent stretches
of barbed wire, more often by an imaginary line drawn
across desolate prairie or mountain—the border between
the United States and Canada. It is "high" border both
in the sense that this is a country of high plains and high
mountains and because it is the northern boundary of the
United States—the high boundary on a map, as opposed
to the low border between Mexico and the south-border
states of Texas, New Mexico, and Arizona.

High Border Country may properly be divided into
two topographic areas—the plains region sweeping up from
Minnesota across Dakota into Montana and Wyoming,
broken decisively in only one place, and that the Black
Hills; and the mountain region, the Continental Divide
of western Montana and Wyoming, and the lesser hills of
the panhandle of Idaho. Relatively a new country, since
only in the last hundred years has civilization come up
the Missouri River to penetrate both plains and mountains, the land was one glossed over by eighteenth-century
cartographers, not from necessity but through ignorance.
It was called by them terra incognita—the Great American Desert, rolling up to the main chain of the Rocky
Mountains; beyond that lay a strange and fearsome region
of shining peaks that pierced the sky, of canyons deep
as the hells into which the actions of some of the pioneer
inhabitants, notably the mountain men, should have
pitched them.

Indeed, at the birth of the nineteenth century it was
a region believed to be inhabited by mastodons and other

creatures of that prehistoric kind. President Thomas Jefferson, seated at dinner with his bedroom slippers on his feet to show his contempt for the King of England, for whose representative the dinner was being given, told his guests that beyond the Mississippi, there on the upper reaches of the Missouri, the world was still primeval and fearsome creatures from the past were a reality.

Theodosia Burr Alston, daughter of Vice President Aaron Burr and a guest at the dinner, was practical-minded. "They'd be handy for pulling carriages through our Washington mud!" she said. She wondered what that country was really like.

She was the wife of a wealthy Carolina planter, and having leisure to dream, she thought about the vasty reaches of the great West of America, the unknown land. Not that she did any serious speculating; her thoughts were such as someone today might have about Mars. Terra incognita was unreal and had no link with her world; she could not foresee that in 1804 Lewis and Clark would head an expedition into the Great American Desert. But even at the beginning of the century President Jefferson seems to have hinted to friends that such was his intention, once the region had been secured for the United States.

Not even in her wildest dreams could any well-brought-up young lady like Theodosia Alston have visualized the cavalcade of the High Border: The fight of river men and mountain men, as hard a crew as has ever walked the earth anywhere, up the wild Miz-zou-rye for beaver pelts, during the 1810's and '20's and '30's and '40's. Discovery of gold in the Black Hills, in central Idaho, in western and southern Montana. The gold-boom country of the '60's, and the steamboat activity on the Missouri during the same decade. Indian wars of the '70's; concentration of the redskins upon reservations and the rise of the cattlemen and sheepmen during the '80's and '90's; the rush for free land at the turn of the century, up until 1910. Boom big-money years on the plains for wheat ranchers during the following decade and into the 1920's —big money for the copper barons in Butte, the silver barons in the Coeur d'Alenes, the lumber barons in the mountains. Depression in the '30's and the gradual ingrowth of a vast, dusty space where had once been fertile soil—the northern dust bowl—through the Dakotas into Montana, so that the seventeenth-century cartographers' Great American Desert became more of a reality than a vision.

High Border Country! You think of the vast plains of the Dakotas, frost-swept in winter, heat-swept in summer, an immensity of plate-flat continent that bewilders the senses. You think of the Black Hills and Gutzon Borglum's colossal granite-carved heads of Washington, Lincoln, Theodore Roosevelt, and the father of the High Border Country, Thomas Jefferson. You think of the Bad Lands—Hell Cooled Off the Indians called it—that area on the Montana-Wyoming-Dakota border where eroded rocks lift into fantastic nightmare shapes to haunt the imagination. Of the Yellowstone River, lodestone for the Texas herds in the '80's. Glacier National Park and Yellowstone National Park and Grand Teton National Park and the Rockies, and the valley of the Bitterroot in western Montana where Father De Smet brought religion into the High Border Country. Flathead Lake, and the Coeur d'Alene Mountains, where mines produce silver and lead and gold and where, in the two decades at the turn of the century, war between miner and silver baron raged as bitterly as it ever has between employer and employee. You think of Butte, Montana, the richest hill on earth, central city of a copper kingdom; Helena, built on gold-bearing ground and called not without justification the High Border's most historic settlement of gold and romance. You think of Powder River in southeastern Montana and in Wyoming. And always you think of the wild Missouri, gathered under the Continental Divide in Montana, flowing down through Dakota toward the Mississippi.

You think of the people who have made this land historic—the mountain men and river men; the Missouri River steamboat men, the traders, whiskey runners, prospectors, the redskins, soldiers, reservation agents, buffalo killers, wolfers, the lords of cattle, lumber, silver, copper—ruthless, avidly seeking wealth, hard as the hard land they lived in. You think of the dry-land emigrants from the East, storming in to seek homes upon the prairie and in the mountains, driving out the cattlemen by sheer weight of numbers. You think of these dry-landers in terms of their success, their hopes, their too-frequent defeats. You think of black blizzards of soil lifted from fields too eagerly tilled, scudding eastward under the thrust of the prairie's eternal wind. You think of the waste of the land and the waste of the timber; of conservation laws passed too late and of dams thrown up to retain run-off water—small dams and large, and that ultimate of them, the greatest earthfill in existence, which forces even the wild Missouri to calm down—the Fort Peck Dam. You are bound to think of all this when you think of the High Border Country, and you are a little appalled by the immensities of its prairies and mountains, and by the hardness of its men and women. Cruelty, lust, sweat, greed, tears, and passion went into the building of a region which even now is scarcely tamed except along the thin channels of civilization which are its modern highways.

This is High Border Country—buffalo country in the past, where those beasts were wantonly slaughtered off; Indian country, where a dozen tribes roamed, strongest among whom for personality, fury, and honor were the three branches of the Siksika whom white men named— soon after the redskins had been sighted walking over damp, burnt prairie—the Blackfeet. Mining country, where crude gold pans and hand-operated sluices have been replaced by modern floating dredges that capture the flakes which escaped the pioneer prospectors. Cattle and sheep country, both today and in the past, though the vast herds and the cattle barons of the '80's and '90's are dust, and smaller ranches—thousands of acres, some of them, yet small in comparison with the old days—furnish beef and wool to the East. Country of dust and heat in the eastern part, of high mountains and scenery and dude ranches and national parks in the West. And always, through all its yesterdays and todays, country of the wild Miz-zou-rye.

The northernmost part of the Dakotas and of eastern and central Montana is the home of Dark Hard Northern spring wheat, rich in protein. No loaf of bread is balanced without it. Inspecting a High Border map, you remember that during the first World War and almost to the end of the 1930's the little settlement of Scobey in northeastern Montana was the "wheat capital of the world"— and there was no bluff about the title. Wheat, which during the early '30's fell to two-bits a bushel, had brought over $2.00. Money flowed high, wide, and handsome in the wheat land then and the Swede wheat ranchers imported big-league baseball players and bet a thousand dollars a hand. There were hopes and more hopes and visions of vast fortune, but the wheat ranchers plunged their plows too eagerly into the prairie sod, tearing it up for wheat land, so that the eternal wind of the prairies got teeth into it and began to lift it into black blizzards. Today much of Dakota and eastern Montana lies sterile, and the only crop capable of existing upon that naked ground is the prickly, bushy, alien growth, imported as weed seed in wheat during the boom years—the Russian thistle.

The Russian thistle, squat, thorny, bleak, is emblematic of Dakota land, and eastern Montana land. Fields where ten years ago golden wheat grew forty, fifty, sometimes sixty bushels to the acre, now produce Russian thistle alone. It is ironical that wheat ranchers, wealthy ten years ago, now cut the Russian thistle and stack it like hay, feed for their lean cows and lean horses.

Dakota is either a land of dust and heat and blizzard, or land where growth from the soil is unretarded—depending upon whose viewpoint you accept. The truth lies between, with a strong leaning towards the former; neither the ebullient and optimistic outbursts from chambers of commerce of dusty settlements sprawled like collections of toy buildings on the immensity of naked plain, nor the pessimistic utterings of ranchers feeding dried thistle to their livestock gives the real answer. But the rancher has perhaps a more valid case. Not since the wheat-boom days has there been anything like a bumper crop or even a price for farm products that would justify continued endeavor. There is only necessity. The wheat rancher lives on the prairie because he has nothing else to do; in a sense, he is trapped, and such is the strength of the trap that only death, foreclosure, or conscription will release him.

This is Dakota to the Black Hills of South Dakota, and eastern and northern Montana up to the first upthrusts of the Continental Divide. Prairie and dust and blizzard, and settlements looming in unreal silhouette against the skyline of evening, the false horizon of mirage in the dawn, or in the hot or frosty noon. There is an occasional city of a few thousand or up to six or seven thousand, but most of the settlements are of three or four hundred, and up to fifteen hundred. They are centers for life on the High Border prairie, the trading points for the surrounding wheat- or cattle- or sheep-ranching regions, and their life and culture, while similar to that of most small towns in other parts of the United States, has a flavor peculiarly High Border.

It is a flavor created perhaps by the unceasing sweep of the wind, for eastern and central Montana and the Dakotas are flat country ideally situated to endure the down-flow of air from the high Continental Divide. There is wind most of the year. In the autumn it sweeps out of the West or Southwest with a faint, ominous whine of death; in the winter it screams down out of the Medicine Hat Country of Alberta where, say the Indians, the wind is made, though modern meteorologists explain that pressure regions, developing in the Arctic, follow the Continental Divide to swing off along the border eastward. In the spring it is still icy and so penetrating that it cuts through your sheepskin coat; and in the summer it is dusty and dry and so hot at intervals that you labor for breath under the vicious thrust of it. There are, however, moments in May and June with the unbroken prairie green and wheat coming up in the quarter-section fields, when the wind dies and the prairie lies beautifully breathless under the hot burst of noon or the bright orange of the Indian's night-sun—the moon—and life is worth living. You forget the hopes and the cares, and for a little while there is peace. Then the wind stirs again.

They say that the dusty sirocco of the North African desert, howling down out of the Atlas Mountains, forces cessation of all law among the nomad tribes, for the wise men decided long ago that no human being, his nerves worn thin by the hot whine of the wind, could then be held responsible for his actions. Along the High Border a sirocco blows more often than in Africa, yet such is the nature of the people that they have learned to endure it with a stoicism that is amazing until you learn that the majority of Dakotans and eastern Montanans are descendants of the Vikings whom no torrents, tides, or storms could affect. They are Scandinavians—Swedes, Norwegians, Danes. They came in during the free-land period, most of them from the old country. The blood of the past flows hot in their veins and in the veins of their children, and that such an earthly annoyance as wind should affect them is unthinkable. They tore up the prairie too eagerly and ruined much of it for nobody knows how long—though heavy rains during 1941 gave promise of possible reclamation of certain portions of it. They feed dried Russian thistle to their stock, figure on a good wheat crop one year in seven, live, love, die under the whine of the wind.

They send their children, and the children are beginning to send their children, to the schools in the little settlements that dot the land everywhere along the railroads— to the greatest extent, perhaps, along the high line of the Great Northern Railroad through North Dakota and Montana. Their life is an unceasing battle with the inhospitable country and their breed, molded in a furnace of wind and heat and frost and dust, is without equal.

CONTINENTAL DIVIDE

It is in central Montana that hills jut forth startlingly from the plains—the Little Rockies, where Kid Curry and his wild bunch held forth in the '80's and '90's; the Bearpaws, on whose base Chief Joseph gave up his unequal struggle with the white men; the Sweetgrass Hills, from whose tall spires the Blackfeet looked for buffalo or enemies. The Blackfeet, whose name is synonymous with blood and honor in the past, live today on their reservation up under the sudden cliffs of the Rockies of Glacier National Park. They live as do other tribes down in Dakota, in Wyoming, through Montana, on reservations set aside for them by their white conquerors—an old people clinging to old ways which have been modified by the necessity of obeying certain of the white man's admonitions; the young attend the white man's schools, learning as the white boys learn, playing much basketball and much six-man football. Original rulers of the land, they made their last bid for independence during the '70's and lost to a civilization stronger than theirs.

The Continental Divide sweeps up at an angle through Wyoming and Montana, and the people of this country

differ from the inhabitants of Dakota and the Montana
plains, for the mountains are a softer land, a more pleasant
land. Indeed, the whole span of the Rockies in Montana
and Wyoming, together with its offshoots in western Montana and Idaho, is year by year becoming more of a vacation land. "Montana–Wyoming–Idaho–Vacationland of
the West." Here are the dude ranches which cater each
summer to thousands of eastern visitors–where you live
in luxury in a cabin with bath, and ride on a modern
roundup. Here are playgrounds of unequaled beauty–
Yellowstone Park, Teton Park, Glacier Park, and, adjoining Glacier in Canada, Waterton Lakes National Park.
Here is a land of peaks and mountains, streams and forests.
The land of Butte and Helena and Coeur d'Alene–of
Father De Smet, Charlie Siringo, the Blackrobes. This
is a land of modern highways, where the wilderness is
usually only a few miles beyond–of mountain fastnesses
where only the hardiest venture, the primitive areas one
of which, on the south fork of the Flathead River, is said
to be the largest wilderness section left in the United
States.

Here, in the broad or narrow valleys between mountain
ranges, are farms and ranches where live the descendants
of the men and women who built the land–mainly immi-
grants from the East who crowded in after the opening
of the free-land era in 1890. Most of the elders still live,
as do many who came in during the times before 1890–
the miners of Butte and Helena and Virginia City and
Alder Gulch, the lumbermen of the mountains, the sheep
and cattle ranchers on the plains. Old-timer is a word of
peculiar significance in the High Border Country. There
are pioneer societies and societies for sons and daughters

of pioneers; everywhere the old-timer is looked upon with respect. His position is a glorified one, and too often it is forgotten that he was molded in the crucible of necessity, that his deeds were not always the result of an innate spark of nobility but rather the result of circumstance. He had to act or die. He is of the clan that evolved the saying, "The only good Indian is a dead Indian"—an axiom he put to work at every opportunity.

The old-timer is everywhere—the pioneer rancher, pioneer business man, pioneer lumberjack, pioneer miner, and always, in spots like the worn-out mineral camps of the past—the ghost towns—or lonely gulches, the bent, ancient breed known as the Old Prospectors. The pioneer breed and the old prospector breed is going fast; every few days High Border newspapers carry obituaries of those who have passed on, always reverently calling them Pioneers. The pioneer dies in bed, the old prospector usually drops off in his gulch, still seeking, as he has sought all his life, the elusive yellow gleam which will make him rich. For the golden lure is strong in the High Border mountains where there are untapped mineral resources, and on all sides you hear stories of big strikes, unbelievable successes, miraculous luck—even though for every success there are ten thousand failures, ten thousand sagas of men who did not win out.

In addition to the pioneer and the old prospector there is another clan of old-timer and that is the Last Survivor. He is the man who claims to have escaped Custer's last battle—who eluded the Indians—who rode with the outlaw Kid Curry. At least, to hear him tell it. He is the hero of sagas that drive historians wild because of patent inaccuracies provokingly interwoven with truth. He is the man who fought in the Big Hole against Chief Joseph. He is the man who concludes a story of escape from the redskins with the statement, "Yes, sir, I fought my way through fifty of them redskins—knifing and killing right an' left— Then they killed me!"

Pioneer, old prospector, last survivor—they are the old-timers whose actions, prosaic and usually revolting at the time, have taken on the aura of the years. They are the end of a race, a mighty race, truly enough, that conquered the High Border mountains and plains and made way for the twentieth-century civilization. They endured heat and cold and dangers and starvation and toil, and all honor to them for it. But they deserve no praise for their barbarities, the ways in which they subjugated the red man and cut each other's throats to gain fortunes, their callousness and their lack of human and social traits which made many of them misfits of the East and drove them West because they could not get on happily back home.

Pioneers! O Pioneers! A hard race and a noble race; builders and butcherers; men and women made strong by the mighty mountains and wide prairies. Hail them now, for they are going fast! Hail them but remember that these were the people who robbed the redskins and beat them down; who fought each other tooth and nail! And yet good, bad, indifferent, they were the race that built the High Border Country.

Blizzards of black dust and winter sleet; old redskins in blankets and young ones in store clothes; oiled highways going on forever in a straight line; tiny settlements like toy towns on the great prairie. Mountains in the sky; sheep on the hills; cowboys and dudes; the mines and the forests.

There are other signs of the High Border: Grain elevators, one, two, three, four towering above the towns.
W. P. A. schoolhouses, always the largest building of the
small community. Migrants working west from Dakota.
The chalets of Glacier National Park; the geysers of Yellowstone.

Space, space, space, and more space.

This is High Border.

Signs along the highway. A pile of junk, with the
Rockies beyond, and the bitterly worded sign of some
rancher gone broke, "Out Where the West Begins!" Another sign: "McGageville. Population, 14 dogs." Up in the
mountains the sign at every third service station: "Last
Chance for gas. Fill up here. Mountains ahead." And,
against a background of gorgeous scenery, a roadhouse
named "Dew Drop Inn."

The old prospector, bleary-eyed, bearded, with his sam-
ple of ore; the pioneer, speaking always with the authority
of the man who was there; the last survivor; the drunk
who sidles up to you in a bar and says, "I've got a million-
dollar mine, partner . . ."; the sheepherder in town for
a celebration, crooked staff in hand, dog at his heels as
he lingers in the red-light districts, while only a few blocks
away the modern barons gather to listen to the latest
lobbyist back from Washington, D. C., with defense-con-
tract information; the sign over a harlot's crib, "Indian
Trade Not Solicited"; stockgrowers' conventions when the
men of cattle and sheep whoop it up; the man who registered four months after the draft because he was out in
the hills tending sheep and knew nothing of conscription
until he came to town; oil fields on the prairie—Cut Bank,
Kevin-Sunburst, and Cat Creek in Montana, Lance Creek,

Salt Creek, Lost Soldier, Fannie, and Byron in Wyoming.
High Border.

The first tourist, back in the '70's, complained of road agents; the latest, glimpsing a branded steer, cried out, "See the monogrammed cow!" Here they buried a prospector who died of thirst, and wrote on his wooden headstone "Bill, he died dry." Here, too, a certain rancher sent one of his men to town for provisions and, when the cowhand returned with eight quarts of whiskey and a loaf of bread, asked unpleasantly, "What in hell are we going to do with the bread?"

Space, space, space. A rancher sent a young married couple down to his barn for milk; the barn was so far away that the couple's grandchildren brought the milk back.

It was in this land that an Easterner, newly arrived, saw three men rolling a fourth over a barrel. "Drowned?" he remarked. "I didn't know there was enough water around here to swim in."

"Nope!" one of the three said. "The damned fool took a drink of water by mistake!"

It is a land whose past is "smoky"—burnt gunpowder. There is a standard joke concerning the smoky days that goes something like this:

A citizen of Fargo (or Butte, or Bismarck, or Wallace, or Sheridan) returned home after an absence of some days and found a corpse in front of his house.

"He get shot?" he demanded of a stranger who was taking in the sight.

"Nope!"

"Too much whiskey?"

"No."

"Then I reckon he must be alive, because that's the only way they die in Fargo (or Butte, or Bismarck, or Wallace, or Sheridan)!"

Prairies and mountains. And always, somehow symbolizing the land, the wild Missouri River, flowing forever; the first road into the land, the historic river road into the Rocky Mountains; a hard trail, blocked by the "pesky" Blackfeet, but historic, for up the wild Miz-zou-rye they all came.

2. The Wild Miz-zou-rye

VERENDRYE

INTO the vast territory lying between the upper reaches of the Mississippi and the desert bordered on the west by the Columbia River the family Verendrye ventured during the middle years of the eighteenth century. They were lured by stories of the "Great Water Not Good to Drink"—the Pacific—and "Palefaces Who Wore Beards and Shining Armor"—evidently the Spaniards. They thrilled to hear of the Rivière à la Biche and the Roche Jaune, the stream of the yellow rocks. Yellow rocks to them meant gold. In later years the mountain men did find the river of yellow rocks, which they identified as both the Rivière à la Biche and Roche Jaune. But the yellow rocks were far from gold, though of sufficient color to christen the river the Yellowstone.

More than gold or Spaniards the Verendryes dreamed of that fabulous water connection between the Atlantic and the Pacific—the Northwest Passage. Somewhere west of the Mississippi must lie that passage, they reasoned, and neither heat nor cold nor hardships could stop them. Nor would the Blackfeet tribe—the scourge of the frontier, through fear of whom many an expedition had hesitated on the edge of the prairie country.

19

The Verendryes vowed that they would burn at the
stake before they turned back from seeking the Northwest
Passage. They did not burn at the stake, as it happened;
they met no Blackfeet; all the Indians whom they encountered were friendly. In peace, they buried on the
banks of the Missouri near Pierre, South Dakota, a leaden
plate inscribed:

"In the twenty-sixth year of the reign of Louis XV, the
most illustrious lord, the Lord Marquis of Beauharnois
being viceroy, 1741, Peter Gaultier de Laverendrye placed
this."

Then they headed westward, how far nobody knows,
but far enough to glimpse a faint saw-toothed line of
white—snow upon mountain peaks. The gleam fascinated
them, and it was with great regret that they turned back
due to scarcity of supplies. They named these peaks the
"shining mountains"; whether they were the jagged upthrusts of the Continental Divide or an outlying range
of the Rockies nobody knows, but the expression has
come down to the present.

The Verendryes planned more expeditions, but their
most illustrious sovereign, scheming with the viceroy of
Canada, revoked the land grants which had enabled the
family to carry on, and as a result the High Border Country remained as unknown as ever for half a century.

Expedition

In 1803 President Thomas Jefferson made the largest
real-estate deal in United States history. He purchased
from France for a sum amounting to a few cents per acre
the Louisiana Territory—a vast region fanning out from

the mouth of the Mississippi, roughly triangular in shape, with the base a line linking the headwaters of the Mississippi and the Rocky Mountains while the hypotenuse followed an erratic bird's flight from the present Glacier National Park to New Orleans. At the time of purchase it was country without a name, unpenetrated save by a few hardy fur traders who for the most part had never returned.

President Jefferson, finding himself with a territory almost equal to the original United States east of the Mississippi on his hands, decided that the first thing to do was send someone westward to see whether his purchase had possibilities of development or was merely a desert-wilderness foisted off on him by Napoleon Bonaparte. On June 20, 1804, he drew up plans for an expedition and issued explicit orders: "The object of your expedition is to explore the Missouri river, and such principal streams of its as, by its course and communication with the waters of the Pacific ocean, whether the Columbia, the Oregon, Colorado, or any other river, may offer the most direct and practicable water communication across the continent, for the purposes of commerce."

This letter went to two gentlemen, Meriwether Lewis and William Clark, captains in the army of the United States. Lewis was Jefferson's private secretary—a somber, morose young man much given to introspection but brilliant to the point of genius and wholly within Jefferson's trust. Clark was kin to George Rogers Clark, hero of the Ohio country, and a clever man among the Indians. They had dubbed him Red-Head Chief—a name he deserved unqualifiedly.

In 1804 the morose Lewis and red-headed Clark, and

twenty-six men who were in the light of later years the bravest of the brave but who in their own day were considered fools, poled up the Missouri upon an expedition which for fortitude and drama has no equal in all the history of the country north of the Rio Grande.

Congress had open-handedly appropriated the sum of twenty-five hundred dollars to finance the expedition. In addition most of the men were army privates, drawing their army wage of seven dollars per month. A special attraction for volunteers was a feature granting them 320 acres of land and six months' extra pay—if and when they returned to claim it.

The roster of the expedition included such names as Ordway, Proyor, Gibson, Howard, Willard, John Potts, John Colter, Patric Gass, Collins, and York, a Negro, the slave and personal servant of Clark, who soaped his hands in water but did not bleach, much to the amazement of the Indians. With French employees—*engagés*—they poled up the Missouri in a barge. They held councils with the Indians and presented solemn-faced and slightly bewildered chiefs, who had had the impression that this was their land, with dispossess notices in the form of metals bearing the picture of the new owner—President Jefferson. The red men, not quite aware of what the future held, allowed the party to continue, and the expedition beat its way upstream to a point twenty miles from the present Bismarck, North Dakota, where the lateness of the season forced the making of winter camp among the Mandan Indians.

In the spring they secured a guide, one Touissant Charbonneau, who for laziness and general inefficiency has no equal in all the annals of exploration. But Charbonneau fortunately had a wife, a seventeen-year-old Indian girl Sacajawea, a native of the three-forks region at the headwaters of the Missouri. Sacajawea, carrying a new-born child on her back and nagging her husband into something resembling usefulness, guided the expedition up the river, over the present Montana-Dakota line, through the Missouri canyon to the falls of the Missouri where the city of Great Falls, Montana, stands today.

Fear of the Blackfeet kept them all alert. At the falls they listened for the whoop of Blackfeet warriors, but heard instead only the thunder of falling water and faint, booming detonations resembling the noise of six-pound cannon. By some quirk of thought they decided that huge silver mines back in the hills were bursting.

The expedition pushed on. There was toil and misery and work for everyone. There were grizzly bears by the scores, buffalo by the thousands, dens of rattlesnakes, but most irritating of all something else, described day after day by both the captains in their respective journals: "Musquetors & Knats verry troublesom."

At the headwaters of the Missouri, the three-forks coun-try—where the Madison, Gallatin, and Jefferson Rivers combine to form the Miz-zou-rye—Sacajawea met Camea-whit, chief of the Shoshones, and, though many years had passed, immediately recognized him as her brother. As a child she had been kidnapped by the Minatarees from down the Missouri, and Cameawhit had given her up as dead. There was a family reunion with a roasting of the fatted buffalo, with Charbonneau none too happy by this turn of affairs, for he saw that he might lose a wife, not to mention the bonus promised to Sacajawea if she stayed with the party until it returned to the Mandan country.

Misfortune for one however meant fortune for the others. Cameawhit furnished horses and supplies, and the explorers pushed on. They pierced the Beaverhead Mountains by a pass too difficult for later travelers; they forced passage between crags of the Bitterroot upthrust on the present Idaho-Montana line; and toiled finally down the Columbia River to the Pacific, where they built a fort in which to live through the coming winter.

They were beyond the indefinite limits of the Louisiana Purchase now and in a land which was later claimed by both the United States and England—the Oregon country. Only a few ships, manned by "Boston Men" and "Long Knives" as the Indians of the Pacific called them, visited this coast for trading purposes. The expedition slept out the winter in their Fort Clatsop, named after a band of the Clatsop tribe camped near by.

On the twenty-third of March, 1806, they set out in return, retracing their trail of last summer. And now they encountered the tribe which had kept them alert from Mandan to the Continental Divide.

In western Montana, Lewis split the party, one group following the trail blazed in 1805, while he with a couple of men crossed the Continental Divide in the region just south of the present Glacier National Park. On the prairie east of the gigantic wall of the Lewis overthrust which is responsible for the ragged grandeur of Glacier, they met the Blackfeet. It was at the headwaters of a tributary of the Missouri which later generations called the Marias, but which Lewis himself designated as Maria's River, in honor of his cousin Maria Wood, though ". . . the hue

of the waters of this turbulent and troublesome stream but
ill comport with the pure celestial virtues of that lovely
fair one."

There was a brief dispute when the Blackfeet, peaceful
enough at first, attempted to steal the horses of the party.
Two redskins bit the dust—a very unwise killing, for if
the Blackfeet had been a surly lot before this, well deserving their ill reputation, now they became veritable
wolves especially where the white men were concerned—
indeed, earning the cheerful title of "scourge of the frontier."

Lewis and his party escaped with their scalps and rejoined Clark at the confluence of the Yellowstone and the
Missouri. Leaving Charbonneau, Sacajawea—who did not
abandon her husband, after all—and John Colter at Mandan, the expedition returned to a heroes' welcome in St.
Louis. Colter was afire with the dream of riches. He had
seen how thick the beaver were back in the three-forks
country, and a heroes' welcome held no fascination for
him. He headed back into the wilderness, to become the
High Border Country's first mountain man and to encounter the Blackfeet. . . .

Lewis and Clark, after St. Louis, made their reports and
delivered their journals into the keeping of the government; Patric Gass entrusted a crude personal narrative to
a Missouri schoolmaster who did his worst editing it. Of
the pair of leaders, Clark continued to administer Indian
affairs, while Lewis, presently governor of the territory he
had explored, accused of mismanagement of affairs, blew
out his brains in a little Tennessee cabin one stormy night.

But he and the expedition which bears his name had
opened the Missouri River country and the Rocky Moun-

tains to the white man. They told of the beaver—rich fur to be had for the taking, a fortune overnight, with nobody to interfere except the redskins. They opened the trail for the trappers, that hardy tribe which has become known as the mountain men.

MOUNTAIN MEN

They were trappers fundamentally, but they were traders, too, and thieves, criminals, sharpers, with but one purpose in mind—quick riches that the fur of the beaver made possible. They stormed into the High Border land, into Montana, Wyoming, Idaho, even to the confluence of the Spokane and Columbia Rivers in Washington. John Colter was representative of them, though more honest than the average; his great adventure with the Blackfeet gave evidence of the dangers that beset these mountain men and made them hard. These trappers followed no law, worshiped no god, knew they would probably die with their moccasins on and hoped it would be from starvation or arrows rather than from the torture of the Blackfeet, but really did not care. They lived life while they had it, they drank by the gallons whiskey strong enough to rot the insides of most men, they gorged on vast meals when they had them, they cursed with every oath known to man, they raped Indian women by the dozens and began a strain of red-white heritage that comes down to the present day. They are mountain and prairie dust now, but in the 1820's and '30's and '40's they were the wildest, toughest, most treacherous, and murderous mob of men that has ever existed anywhere.

All for the soft, sleek hide of the beaver.

John Colter, along the Wyoming-Montana border, was paddling downstream in company with one Potts, another veteran of the Lewis and Clark expedition, when suddenly he froze on his paddle, fixed his eyes on shore, and cleared tobacco juice from his throat long enough to ejaculate three words, "Them pesky Blackfeet!"

Potts turned to look. He never saw a warrior, for arrows feathered him as thickly as quills on a porcupine. Colter dived overboard, but the Blackfeet were swift swimmers and they presently hauled him, cursing and blowing, up onto the bank.

He stared around at the menacing faces of his captors, and cursed his Maker long and loudly in preparation for death. But this particular band had sporting blood in them; instead of burning their captive at the stake or otherwise ridding themselves of him as painfully as possible, they stripped him and turned him loose. They gave him a hundred yards' start. Briefly, the chief gave directions, "Run'um fast!"

Colter darted off. The lack of moccasins hindered him, but not too much. He was tough as wire rope and had the endurance of a strip of elk whang. He began to outdistance the band. Except for three warriors, who closed in on him stride by stride, until they were too close for comfort.

Colter began to conclude that he was, in the language of the mountain men, a "gone duck," but he dragged his wearying steps into a fresh heat and two of the warriors became also-rans. The third, evidently a champion foot-racer of his tribe, now also blew into his second wind. He overhauled Colter. He cocked back his right hand—not a formidable gesture, in itself. But there was a lance in it, and Colter's broad back was not far ahead.

Colter plowed to a sudden stop, swung to face the warrior, and before the redskin could control himself, let him have it right between the eyes with his tobacco, in the approved manner of wild-west fiction. Then he snatched the lance and drove it through the racer's heart, in a gesture familiar enough to him because he had done it before, except that upon other occasions the red man's back had been turned.

The rest of the band, trailing far behind, was maddened by the defeat of their best runner, and set up a howl. They redoubled their efforts. Colter knew his chances of escape were pretty slim and, sighting a huge trash jamb in the river, he dived headlong under it. He came up between an overhanging V of logs, where he clung until dark, regretting the loss of his tobacco and fervently hoping that the Blackfeet, who ran as thickly as crickets over the logs, would not discover him.

The Colter luck held, and the dark of midnight presently forced the redskins to give up their search. Colter waited until all was clear, then thoroughly chilled by the icy mountain water and appalled at the prospects of a hundred-mile jaunt naked and without weapons to the nearest civilization, the trading fort of Manuel Lisa, he set out.

In time, the mountain men at Lisa's Fort at the junction of the Big Horn and Yellowstone Rivers were treated to the sight of the original High Border nudist reeling into camp. They gave him a gallon of trade whiskey and as an afterthought a broiled half-quarter of buffalo, and listened to his story which had less to do with his escape from the pesky Blackfeet than with the region he had been forced to cross in order to reach Lisa's Fort.

"Yes, sir, I'm tellin' you there wasn't no water in that-there country, not a single spring of it! Jest bubblin' springs of mud! When I did find water it was jest bilin' hot, an' cross my lungs an' liver, if some of them-there hot water springs didn't go a-shootin' away up in the air, jest as reg'lar as nothin'—"

He gulped down another half-pint of trade alcohol, belched a fiery breath that singed the bark of the log wall along which he squatted, and went on devouring the half-quarter of buffalo.

"There was a fall of water higher'n any mounting I ever seed, an' there's a lake that's a sight bigger'n any durn water I ever paddled onto! There's a sight of bubblin' pots plumb full of mud jest the color of the noses of some of you trappers—an' blue as them corpses yuh run across in the spring—"

"A hell of a country!" a listener said, winking at his friend.

"Colter's hell!" the friend returned.

And so it became Colter's Hell. Later decades found he had not lied, and today the "Hell" bears the more dignified but less descriptive title of Yellowstone National Park.

The majority of the river men, who seldom penetrated beyond the three-forks of the Missouri, were French-Canadians, but the mountain men were a motley lot—Canadians, half-breeds without sympathy for their red brothers-under-the-skin, Scotchmen, a few Irishmen, Englishmen, Iroquois from the Atlantic coast, Scotch-Irishmen from Virginia, Carolinians, and even a few Hawaiians. The Coriacan Defile, more usually known as O'Keefe Canyon, through which the main highway runs north from

Missoula, Montana, is named after Koriaka, a Sandwich Islander who left his soft life for the hardships of the High Border—and died there from the thrust of Blackfeet arrows.

The beaver quest was not allowed to remain long in the hands of the free-traders and trappers who dealt with the Hudson's Bay Company of Canada and its rival outfit, the Northwest. Neither the Northwest nor the Hudson's Bay —so ancient a company that the initials H. B. C. on its buildings led trappers to identify them as "Here Before Christ!"—attempted to invade the High Border Country. But other traders and trading companies did enforce monopolies by blood, murder, and price-cutting. First was Manuel Lisa of Lisa's Fort fame.

Lisa organized the Missouri Fur Company with the intentions of cornering all the beaver in the Rocky Mountains. If it had not been for the general unrest of the Indians following the War of 1812 and, specifically, the hostility of the Blackfeet, he might have succeeded. As it was, this organized pursuit of the beaver failed, and it was not until 1822 that a powerful organization did succeed. The Rocky Mountain Fur Company it was, based in St. Louis and headed by William H. Ashley, Andrew Henry, and Jedediah Smith.

They secured the services of a number of promising, tough young men among whom were Thomas Fitzpatrick, Milton Sublette, Henry Fraeb, Jean Baptiste, and Jim Bridger. The company was an instant success. It established no trading posts, but organized a rendezvous each year to which the mountain men brought their furs for purpose of trade. The great rendezvous was on the Green River in western Wyoming. Here Ashley sent trains of trade goods, whiskey, and ammunition—trains that months later returned to St. Louis, coasting down the Missouri in boats laden to the gunwales with beaver purchased for a song.

Rendezvous. Here came mountain men who had not seen a white face for a year. They trailed in from far and near, to camp in the valley. Dozens of them, then scores and more scores. Indians from all the High Border land flocked in, with their squaws and papooses and the furs which the mountain men had been unable to get either by trade or robbery. Even the sullen Blackfeet came down from the North, seeking the white man's powder and firewater and chewing tobacco.

Where had been only a lonely valley there was, in the early summer of 1825 and during subsequent decades, the greatest assemblage of lawless men the West has ever seen.

One Bill Williams, a roamer of the whole mountain country between the high border of Canada and the low border of Mexico, was there. Kit Carson may have been there. Jim Bridger certainly was, as was John Colter. And many, many others.

Mountain men all—bearded, unshorn, covered with vermin-infested buckskins. They charged into the rendezvous from their headquarters a few miles or a hundred miles away. They made camp, they piled their skins before the sharpers who commanded the trading wagons. Beaver passed in exchange for powder and shot and sugar and salt and Boston-man clothes and trinkets—and whiskey stronger than sin, for sin was the usual thing with the mountain men, and tobacco so hard you had to chew it a

day to moisten it and even then it was like a sledgehammer in your head.

The Indians, lodges pitched beyond the white men's
section, swarmed around the wagons too, and were easy
prey for the traders. Half a tincup of whiskey would
deaden a brave's senses to the point where a single red
bead—or another drink of whiskey—seemed fair payment
for one beaver. Deliberately the traders saturated the Indians with alcohol, and half the time when the redskins
were dead to the world the traders deliberately stole the
furs.

Velvety nights of Wyoming descended, but they were
never peaceful and silent nights during a rendezvous.
For the mountain men had been without companionship
and whiskey and tobacco for months, and this was their
time to howl. And howl they did. Latter-day cowboys,
riding into border towns to paint them red, were pikers
compared with the mountain men. Amateurs. Their pint-
drinks of whiskey were mere sips compared with the drinks
of Green-River Jones who used to tilt a gallon jug of
trade alcohol and let it pour down his throat. . . .

Then and there began the thirst which has made citizens of High Border states, especially Montana, the greatest consumers of liquor per capita in the United States.
Green-River Jones, legitimately speaking, had no children
—though in many an Indian lodge throughout the mountains there were light-skinned papooses—but he gave a
heritage to the High Border land. He gave alcoholic
thirst.

Green-River Jones, soaked to his toes in alcohol, brought
up a hand to rub his bare head—bare in the sense that
it had no scalp. A Blackfeet had lifted his hair a couple

of years back, but Jones was too tough to die from such a minor operation. He had sworn to "get" the amateur surgeon and, lacking knowledge of this particular redskin's identity, he got as many of the tribe as he could. Maybe fifteen, maybe twenty, he could not tell. He had lost count. Tonight, scratching his scalpless head, he decided the time was ripe for fun. Reeling to his feet, he charged down among the Indians. A score of mountain men raced at his heels, for they were both sympathetic and intent upon an evening of celebration—in the mountain man's way.

They cut, slashed, shot, strangled. When the Indian bucks were dead, they attacked the squaws. In the dawn they reeled back to their cold fires and a fresh jug, several of them missing but the rest satisfied that this had indeed been a large night.

The wagon tenders, the traders who remained sober, went out to their wagons in the dawn, dismissed the guards, and uncovered their goods. They looked down into the Indian encampment; they saw three smoking heaps where lodges had been; they saw a couple of mountain men lying stiffly, and a dozen or more Indian bucks; squaws, who had been battered unconscious, roused to the hot thrust of the sun and crawled away to the lodges of their relatives. A mountain man, hair untouched by water so long that it coiled out from his head like the snakes of Medusa, reeled by, hiccuping a song, "We shoot our Injuns one by one! We do it all jest fer the fun!"

He tottered, then screeched out, "Hi! Ho! The wild Miz-zou-rye!" and as if the effort had finished him, huddled down into the dust, snorting like a steamboat. One tender spat casually and turned to a companion.

"Right quiet last night, wasn't it? But things'll pick up an' we'll have real celebratin' before this rendezvous is over with!"

Hugh Glass

Mightiest of the mountain men, mightier even than John Colter, was a certain trapper by the name of Hugh Glass. His bear adventure, colored naturally by the years that have passed, is a feat of survival that cannot be matched by any other saga of the High Border land. Odds for his existence stood at 10,000 to one, but Hugh Glass won.

In the 1820's, in company with a small expedition under the leadership of Major Andrew Henry, Glass penetrated the High Border Country in search of furs. There were other members in the party whose names illuminate the history of the land, if not altogether gloriously—Jedediah Smith, the scalpless explorer; Jim Bridger, liar and guide; Thomas Fitzpatrick; and Etienne Provot, of Utah fame. There was also a certain Gordon, always laughing, whose laughter stilled but twice—when he died, and before that, when Hugh Glass reeled back from the dead.

Entering the High Border Country, the party briefly encountered the Arikaras; nothing serious, a few redskins killed and scalped. It was in the region of the Wyoming-Montana border that the adventure of Hugh Glass first began. Glass was scouting with a companion in advance of the party, and surprised a grizzly she-bear with cubs. Meat uppermost in his mind, he sighted and let fly; his shot failed to kill. It merely wounded.

The bear charged. Glass' companion fled. Glass trailed, but tripped, and before he could rise, the bear overwhelmed him, and when Glass did fight up it was right into the fury of fur and three-inch fangs and eight-inch claws.

This was even worse than capture by Blackfeet, and Glass fought as he had never been called upon to battle before. He wrenched out his pistol and fired once, and then the bear knocked it away from him. He managed to unsheath his knife, and with monotonous regularity but little effect he plunged it into the animal's side. He had given himself up for lost, when the bear released him to rush to her squalling cubs.

Glass' companion, with considerable presence of mind, had begun to belabor them with a club, but now that he had distracted the mother's attention, he fled again. The bear almost reached him, before the wounds Glass had given her with knife and bullet took effect; she sprawled forward dead. When the rest of the party arrived it was a toss-up which was the more lifeless, the bear or Glass. The mountain men leaned on their guns and regarded their former companion with considerable sorrow, for he had been an inveterate borrower and owed most of them tobacco. Jedediah Smith spat casually, rubbed his scalpless head, and made a remark the rest of them were thinking, "Don't he look right nat'ral now, if 'twarent fer them scratches all over him. Why, that b'ar near tore all his clothes off. An' I'm a buffaler killer if them ain't his innards stickin' thar out of his back!"

Then someone, more ambitious than the rest, bent over Glass and discovered that he still lived. Major Henry made camp and they laid Hugh Glass out beside a fire and tried to choke him with whiskey. There were no medical supplies of any kind, of course, since each man was responsible for his minor wounds—and such injuries as laid Glass low were regarded as beyond medical attention of any sort. The men lingered for a few days, hoping Glass would either show signs of recovery or die; when no change took place, they moved on. Major Henry offered a reward to any person who would remain with the near-corpse until he passed on, as they concluded he eventually must, and two men, one of them young Jim Bridger, offered to hold the wake.

Bridger and the other man, Fitzgerald, found time hanging heavy on their hands after their companions trekked away. They held a conference, decided that Glass was as good as dead, took what possessions he had—overlooking, to his great fortune, a razor—and hastened after the Henry party. They reported Hugh Glass dead and buried. And promptly forgot all about him.

But in a day or so Glass opened his eyes and discovered his position. His mental reactions are of no moment, being those of any trapped and wounded person whose odds of life are infinitesimal; in a blind, instinctive manner he rolled down to the spring of water beside which he lay, drank to cool his fever, afterwards as instinctively crammed his stomach with chokecherries and buffalo berries that grew all around. Then he slept.

When he awoke the second time, however, his mind had cleared, and after cursing his companions, he settled himself to decide what to do. Fort Kiowa in the Dakotas lay more or less a hundred miles away and looked like the best bet. So Hugh Glass, on hands and knees because his back had been injured in a manner that prevented any upright action of his body, crawled away—at an average rate of two miles from sunup to sundown.

The wounds in his thighs and stomach and chest he could wash and care for, but he was unable to reach the deep gashes in his back. These filled with dirt, filth, everything that might breed disease—and worms, that were a blessing in disguise, for though they burrowed and pained intolerably they cleaned away the putrefying flesh—a medical principle not discovered until a hundred years later. Glass went wild with them until he became accustomed to them—and by then he could endure anything.

There was, fortunately, plenty of water and Glass drank a great deal to augment his diet of berries and such small lizards as he was able to capture. But his terrific exertion took toll of him, until at last starvation faced him if he failed to secure food more nourishing. Strength drained from his arms and legs, and he slumped forward upon the point of total collapse.

"Glass, you old —— —— ——!" he said to himself, "looks like yo're a goner, fer sure. Mebby you ought to make your prayers. They do say if you make your prayers you rest a danged sight easy after the coyotes hev et you up. But dang me, ef I kin think of a prayer!"

So Hugh Glass, instead, cursed with every invective known to the mountain men—and there were many of them, all luridly and obscenely descriptive. He took in the sun, the moon, the stars, his expedition, his life, death, mother, father, relatives, and most of all the men who had left him for dead—Jim Bridger and the other who had robbed him and abandoned him, Fitzgerald. Then, comforted, he filled his belly with water and buffalo berries, and slept.

Not for long. A noise roused him—a buffalo calf pursued by three wolves. Glass sat up, wheezing with hope when the wolves closed in upon the calf. One of them hamstrung it and when the animal collapsed, they all darted in to dig fangs into the live body until it died. Then they settled themselves to gorge.

Drooling so that little rills ran down his beard, Hugh Glass waited. He hesitated with a purpose—waiting for the wolves to satisfy themselves, that their ferocity would not lead them to attack Glass when he frightened them. When they lay down, gorged, Glass crept forward. The wolves roused, snarled, but their full bellies dulled their ferocity. They slunk off, the mountain man shrilling curses after them.

"Anaaahhh!" Glass, no longer a man, screamed as he dug his mouth into the entrails of the dead calf and began to tear.

In time he paused, refreshed. And, hope rising now, he cut up what he could pack of the animal and crept away. This meat kept him in strength for many days, and formed many a delicious tidbit though eventually it became "high." This was prairie country, hot, dry—not the cool mountains where, as Jim Bridger said to Father De Smet some decades later, when the priest expressed astonishment that two redskin arrowheads which had been in Bridger's back for three years had not infected and killed him, "In the mountains, Father, meat don't spoil!"

Hugh Glass crawled on and on, hands bruised beyond the semblance of the hands of any being, human or otherwise, knees no longer the knees of a man. He lived on borrowed time—by all rules of life and death he should be dead.

The time came when he downed the last of the meat and then once more tried to live on berries and lizards.

Again desperation forced him to make his peace, in his own way, by cursing. And, as before, his luck changed, for upon the horizon he saw a dozen or more inverted V's —redskin lodge poles from which the coverings had been taken. A deserted village, but surely here he would find a little something to keep him alive. Foot by foot, yard by yard, Hugh Glass snaked forward, until he lay in the village.

It sprawled absolutely deserted. Nothing here at all. Except—and Hugh Glass' eyes lighted—a dozen or more wolfish dogs abandoned by their masters but faithful to their village.

They were wild, gaunt, huge of fang and wary of eye. They were carrion-fed and carrion-fierce, but not so brave as to attack this curious creature that writhed towards them, calling out with cracked, pleading urgency. They backed off, howled, and then fled, but returned to squat on thin haunches at a safe distance.

Glass was not dismayed. He expected wariness. And set himself to overcome it, each hour making the spectacle of himself more familiar to the animals, so that they began to overcome their fear of him. They crept closer and closer—while Glass waited, open razor between his teeth.

It took several days. Then, once, a thin beast ventured to sniff at Glass, and the mountain man's hand gripped like the jaws of a trap around one foot, while the razor in his other hand whipped like light through the air. Red, hot blood spurted, and Hugh Glass, crying sounds that were neither human nor animal, drove his mouth to the slashed jugular and drank and tore. He feasted himself into exhaustion and then, what was left of the dead body under him as he might cover a horde of gold, he slept. Again he possessed the strength to continue.

He went on, dragging the remains of the animal after him; holding his razor, his sole weapon, between his teeth. On and on . . . and then he saw Fort Kiowa and knew he had won. He crawled to the stockade; traders found him, took him in, marveled that this thing with worms in its back should be a man. It had undergone tortures beyond the imagination of any mountain man. Yet it had lived; it was alive now; and it had a name.

Hugh Glass. Six weeks later, strong and well again, he set out for the upper reaches of the Missouri to find Jim Bridger and Fitzgerald.

He rejoined, presently, his party which months before had been convinced of his death. Gordon was laughing when he came up, laughing at a story he told, "An' I took them three Injuns, one by one, an' cut off their heads. The last one wiggled an' I had a hard time with 'im. Haw! Haw!" Then he saw Hugh Glass. His laughter gurgled to silence.

"Hugh Glass . . . it can't be! It's a ghost thing!"

But Hugh Glass was no ghost. He was flesh and blood and pretty tough flesh and blood at that. He continued in pursuit of Bridger and Fitzgerald, who had left the expedition, and months later when he overtook Jim Bridger there occurred an incident which lends a further element of wonder to an almost incredible saga:

For Hugh Glass said simply, "You're a young 'un, Jim. You're not even eighteen yit. You didn't know what you was doin'. Tell you what—you fetch me back that rifle you robbed me of when you left me, an' we'll call this matter squar'!"

Jim Bridger returned Glass' gun and lived to become the greatest trailblazer and greatest liar of the West. Glass' intentions concerning Fitzgerald, however, were more elemental; he intended to cut off his ears and kill him by bits. But Fitzgerald joined the army and thus placed himself beyond Glass' vengeance. Before Glass could get to him in later years, Glass found himself one day on the ice of the Missouri River, with Blackfeet guarding both shores. The ice offered no protection. Again the odds for life stood at 10,000 to one.

This time Hugh Glass lost.

REDSKIN TRADE

Where the Yellowstone River joins the Miz-zou-rye there was constructed, in the later years of the 1820's, a stockaded group of buildings known as Fort Union. The American Fur Company thus daringly invaded territory from which furs might have gone to the Hudson's Bay trappers north in Canada. Here one Kenneth McKenzie, an astute and unscrupulous trader, was set up as factor to exchange whiskey, beads, calico, tobacco, smooth-bore rifles, and black powder for beaver, mink, and martin. So clever a hand with the red men did Kenneth McKenzie become that presently he gained the title of King of the Upper Missouri—the High Border's most successful trader, hated far and wide for his sharp methods but possessing a singular power over the redskins. His power was no black magic but whiskey.

United States law, theoretically in force in this new territory, forbade the selling of alcohol to the Indians. But Kenneth McKenzie knew no law, save that set by his em-

ployer's urgent demand for vast profits. He built a dis-
tillery at Fort Union and dispensed the raw, water-white
liquid.

According to writings of a later period, he evolved the
High Border's first cocktail, for the redskin trade—known
as a Redskin Cocktail, for which the ingredients were
somewhat as follows: 1 qt. alcohol; 1 lb. tobacco; 1 handful red peppers; 1 bottle Jamaica rum; 1 qt. black mo-
lasses.

The mountain men were great drinkers, swilling it
down from tin cups and jugs, but they were able to hold
their liquor and confine their impulses to the reasonably
gentlemanly business of cutting off ears. The red men on
the other hand became downright mean when inflamed
with trade alcohol and went on strictly personal warpaths
without provocation. They lacked humor. They yearned
to kill. Kenneth McKenzie doled liquor to them carefully
and cleverly—just enough to make them half-insane for
more.

There was method to this, of course. The less satisfied
a redskin was, the more whiskey he wanted and the harder
he would work to secure furs to trade for it. The result
was that McKenzie corralled the country's fur trade, for
beads and smooth-bore rifles and black powder, offered by
the Hudson's Bay Company traders to the north, were
nothing when compared to whiskey strong enough to make
a Gros Ventre think he could manhandle a Blackfeet. The
Gros Ventres were an indolent lot; they were called Gros
Ventre, or Big Belly, in tribute to their feasting ability.

Kenneth McKenzie became the most successful trader
on any frontier. He was the first to make systematic use of
alcohol on the redskin. Living in the open, the redskins

seemed peculiarly susceptible to alcohol, not so much as a stimulant but as a drug powerful as opium. All else paled beside the desire for the pale liquid, which was far more satisfactory as a creator of visions than the conventional Indian means of starvation and exposure to winter blizzards. Starvation took days, exposure hours, whereas liquor, a few minutes after it had burned into the stomach, made the visions walk around.

Kenneth McKenzie, in a rough country where soap was not to be had casually and the color white was always associated with snow and never with cleanliness, nevertheless lived in a style befitting his title of King of the Upper Missouri. The factor demanded that his meals be served to the accompaniment of linen and silver, and he himself appeared bathed and in white shirt. Guests at his table were asked to wash and comb, though at times the task involved such painful and uncertain labor that, rather than taste McKenzie's wine and carefully prepared food, many declined his invitations and swilled their liquor and chewed their own jerky in a corner of the fort, grumbling meanwhile. Since when was it that an honest trader —well, practically honest, counting those two men killed and the three caches of furs he had raided—must smell like a prairie posie when he came to do business with the representative of a fur company? And weren't onion and garlic the best preventive of scurvy—?

McKenzie's personal popularity did not detract from his managerial ability, and John Jacob Astor, organizer of the American Fur Company, grew richer. He rewarded his faithful vassal accordingly. McKenzie piled up a fortune in St. Louis. Nevertheless he continued as Fort Union factor, running his alcohol still overtime except during those periods when the United States government investigated. McKenzie was always warned in advance and would dismantle the still and bury the whiskey kegs down by the river. Government officials, sometimes searching too diligently, always found a cache of gold before they reached the evidence. Taking the hint, they would give Fort Union a clean bill of health.

Fort Union continued after the end of Kenneth McKenzie; it boomed until the beaver had been cleaned out and the fur trade ended, until the river men and the mountain men were no more and their descendants with the big thirsts had become miners or freighters or settlers or, still later, cowmen. During its time, however, such was its fame that it entertained some important personages, among whom were Jim Bridger; Prince Paul of Wurttemberg; Maximilian, Prince of Wied; Audubon, the naturalist; and Father Pierre Jean De Smet, the Belgian Jesuit who first stirred the undeveloped soul of the High Border Country and brought Christianity to the red men.

It was at Fort Union that Jim Bridger arrived one autumn with a band of men of whom Bridger boasted, "My boys kin lick twict their weight in catermounts! We ain't scared of man ner beast, an' as fer them pesky Blackfeet—jist let some of 'em show up here an' I'll skelp 'em myself, jest like I'd cut up a buffaler—"

Later in the season, after the river had frozen over, Bridger wandered across to low bluffs opposite. A band of Blackfeet appeared, and to the great delight of spectators on the Fort Union side of the river, Bridger was compelled to play hide-and-seek among the cutbanks and wind-worn hoodoo rocks for half an hour before he could

get a good run for the river. He raced across the ice, bullets and arrows flying after him, but unpursued because
the Blackfeet were afraid to come within reach of the
weapons of the fort. Blown and sweating, Bridger reeled
up to the watchers.

"I figured you'd scalp them pesky redskins," an onlooker
remarked. "That's what you been tellin' us, Jim. But from
the way you was duckin' around them bluffs across the
river—"

Bridger drew himself up and fixed the doubter with a
terrible eye.

"Sure it looked to you as if them pesky critters was
chasin' me. But fact was, I was huntin' 'em instead! 'Twas
only when I found out that my gun was wet an' my knife
broken that I headed back fer the fort—"

Father De Smet, gentle and strong in his faith and as
conscientious a man as ever trod the High Border Country,
halted briefly at Fort Union. One of his charges, lately
converted, reported the presence of gold in the country
north and west of the fort. The father feared gold, as
he had a right to, as the instrument of the devil, and he
sought to hush the rumors. But they persisted and the
convert began to show a decided interest in the white
man's lure. Presently he disappeared, obviously in quest
of the metal, and the father gave him up as lost.

But in time the redskin returned, coming up to Father
De Smet, obviously highly discouraged, but with a touch
of bravado to conceal his feelings.

"Your dreams of gold are false, my son?" the priest questioned.

"But I have brought gold, father!"

The convert indicated a large bale of trade calico he had been carrying. The father's heart fell. Gold meant that there might be a rush into this country, and the beginning of a wave of godlessness even worse than that which he fought so valiantly against. Fingers a-tremble, he began to unwrap the trade goods. Yard after yard of it came away. At last there remained only a single fold.

"Gold!" exclaimed the convert, pointing.

Father De Smet smoothed the calico. There lay a white man's coin. The convert's whoop of glee boomed out. He was having his joke to cover his failure as a prospector. Relieved, the father refolded the cloth. He smiled.

"It is good to know that you have not found gold!" he said.

The convert, thinking only in terms of earthly wealth and not spiritual salvation, did not understand. But he continued to whoop on and on, almost as if he were filled with white man's firewater.

A certain Major Alexander Culbertson, succeeding McKenzie, refused to employ the former's still for trade purposes, though he himself, like most men of the period, drank whenever he could possibly secure the liquor. But he was a good trader; Fort Union flourished even without the potent urgings of liquor. In later years, however, the major found himself unemployed, and it is related that at Fort Belknap up the Missouri he fell in with the agent of the post, one Fenton, who permitted him the use of a cabin over winter. Fenton, a moralist of sorts as long as it did not concern himself, took such an interest in the major that he vowed he would break Fort Union's former factor of the drink habit. Accordingly he began to enforce a strict prohibition as far as concerned the major.

But day by day the major appeared in a state certainly not normal. Fenton, wrinkling his brows, decided it must be the amount of alcohol the major had soaked up through former years; he subsisted now camel-like upon a reserve. The whole affair assumed an air of mystery, and it was not until spring that Fenton was able to solve the situation.

The autumn before an Indian had brought in the head of a two-headed calf which Fenton wished to preserve in order to present it to the Smithsonian Institution in Washington. He had dropped it into a keg of alcohol and had stored the keg in the cellar of the cabin where the major lived. When spring came, it was discovered that the keg lacked weight; investigation proved where the major had been able to accumulate his eternal drunk. All left in the keg was a pair of dried buffalo heads.

Andrew Dawson, like Culbertson, was one of Fort Union's best factors, known best perhaps for his novel solution of a peculiar problem. A less harsh trader than most of his contemporaries, he had become known to the Indians as a man who could do practically anything. And anything meant *anything*. His particular problem was that of a young redskin who wanted Dawson to turn him into a white horse.

A white horse, or an Indian horse of any kind, could not by any stretch of imagination be thought of as the acme of desirability; nevertheless, this particular Sioux insisted upon becoming a white horse and it was up to Dawson to consummate a bit of magic or lose face. And to lose face at that particular time might prove a serious matter. Dawson's reputation as a big medicine man must be upheld or he might lose the respect of the redskins—and their trade, for Dawson did not use firewater and his success depended entirely upon his ability as a trader.

"You mak' 'um me big white horse!" insisted the brave.

"Now, look here!" Dawson argued, "a white horse would be out in the cold and rain. He'd get a beating from his master all the time—"

"Me want 'um be white horse!"

Dawson studied the situation. Presently he told the brave to come to the fort upon a certain date. Luckily, the day was stormy; a blizzard howled down out of the Northwest, and the redskin came into the factor's office shaking snow from him.

"Bad day. Me want 'um be white horse!"

"Don't worry, you'll be a white horse when I get through with you!" Dawson proceeded to make various motions and utter words without meaning. The redskin did not demur when the factor commanded him to strip. Dawson then put a halter around his neck, led him out on the snow-swept prairie, and staked him there.

"You stay here for a couple of hours, and then you'll become a white horse!" Dawson promised. Then he returned to the comfort of his fire, to wait. He did not wait long. Presently the door burst open and the redskin dashed in, to throw himself against the heat of the stove.

"Me no want 'um be white horse!" he chattered. "Never want 'um be white horse."

Dawson, as host of Fort Union, entertained some eminent personages, among whom was Count Kosciusko, grandson of the Polish patriot. Count Kosciusko was more

familiarly known to Westerners as Count Cask of Whiskey
for good reason. Dawson himself, while not a drinking
man (he had his quart after each meal, but only to keep
off the chill), nevertheless eventually passed on from the
effects of liquor, indirectly, for in his later days, after
an accident had somewhat disabled him, he fell down
the steps of the fort's whiskey cellar—a loss both to his
company and the redskins, for he appears to have been a
just man.

Fort Union, through the '30's and '40's, even to the
beginnings of steamboat trade on the Missouri in the latter '50's and early '60's, held its place as the High Border
Country's foremost trading post. But there were others,
scattered throughout the territory; many of them harassed
by the Blackfeet, always a thorn in the side of the traders,
for the Blackfeet did not trade and, what was worse, did
their best to keep others from trading.

A certain Chardon, assisted by a certain Harvey, probably the blackest pair of traders along the frontier where
traders were black, one day decided to rid themselves of
the attentions of the pesky Blackfeet and accordingly
opened the gates of their post, Fort McKenzie, to the
Blackfeet temporarily encamped just outside the walls of
the stockade.

All the Blackfeet warriors were gone on a hunt—as
Chardon and Harvey probably knew—and it was women,
children, and old men who responded to Chardon's invitation to enter the fort. Chardon dumped beads on the
ground just in front of a small cannon concealed inside a
cabin, and while the redskins quarreled and scrambled,
he emptied the contents of the gun into them. The resulting pile of dead gratified Chardon and Harvey highly,

and the post's attachés applauded, though some of them were appalled by the deed—not so much from feelings of humanity as from fear of Blackfeet reprisal. The wounded, Chardon and his sympathizers quickly dispatched with knives. Then they hauled the bodies out on the prairie where they left them, scalpless and in some instances mutilated.

WIJUJON

"The white man's world is very big!" said Wijujon, in council with his red tribe on the upper Missouri. "Their lodges are as tall as the tallest tree, and the white men are as thick as flies around carrion!"

His compatriots nodded politely but stared at one another. Wijujon, they had concluded after listening for many evenings to his stories of the marvels of the white man, could only be lying. He had been a powerful medicine man when he first returned from the land of the white man, but he was plainly going too far now. Nevertheless, he probably retained sufficiently strong medicine to stop a bullet; something stronger must be devised. Accordingly, a young brave devised a weapon that would without doubt overcome even Wijujon's magic—the handle of a kettle, beaten straight and fitted into the muzzle of a gun. Someone put the loaded rifle against the back of Wijujon's head and pulled the trigger, and Wijujon abruptly died, a martyr to truth. Every word he had ever uttered about the white man was true.

Wijujon—in the white man's tongue, Pigeon's Egg Head —lived on the upper Missouri in fur-trade days, just at the beginning of the beaver boom, so that neither he nor his compatriots had come to gaze upon a white man without awe. The presence of a single paleskin was a matter of great moment, and when the chiefs selected Wijujon, the most intelligent of his tribe, as good-will ambassador to the seat of government of the United States, upon request of army officials, the excitement was overwhelming. The solid element of the tribe solemnly charged Wijujon to remember everything about the white man and report to them upon his return, that they might understand more of this curious race.

"I will remember everything I see, and I will speak with a tongue of truth, and never with the snake's forked tongue of deceit," Wijujon promised.

The army, through some official more far-sighted than his contemporaries in sensing that the Indian problem would become one of the army's main perplexities of the future, had concluded that Wijujon's knowledge of white man's ways and manners of thought would benefit his tribe.

Wijujon, painted to the ears and dressed in his newest breechclout, boarded a mackinaw boat as the guest of the United States government and headed downstream, with Washington, District of Columbia, his destination. He carried his war club. After a few days, while squatted on the deck watching the shore, he called a paleface and pointed at a low log structure on shore.

"What is that?" he demanded in sign language, and the paleface readily explained that it was a white man's house. Wijujon solemnly listened, then reached for his knife and war club.

"They tell me that there are many of these palefaces," he said. "And in order to tell my tribe how many there are, I shall put a notch in my war club for each home of a paleface I see!"

All went well for a few days, cabins being few and far between. But down the river, nearing civilization, cabins and frame buildings appeared in greater numbers, and Wijujon's amazement grew.

"There are indeed many white people!" he said, nicking away at his war club. He cut industriously, day after day, and presently when the handle remained as only a corrugated sliver, he went ashore for a sapling.

"There will indeed be many white men if I but half fill this!" Wijujon now spent most of his hours carving. A worried frown creased his painted brow. The white men were very, very numerous indeed, but surely they must soon become less, for his tribe would never believe the existence of so many human beings anywhere.

Then St. Louis appeared, which even then was a sizable settlement—and Wijujon, with a groan, threw both notched sapling and remains of his war club overboard.

In Washington, Wijujon was feted, for no painted savage from west of the Mississippi, especially one with Wijujon's apparent intelligence, had ever trod the muddy thoroughfares of the nation's capital or slipped on moccasined feet through its gilded halls. Wijujon, impassive, inscrutable, apparently drawn within himself, yet, as evidenced by the stories he took back to his tribe, observing all, became a standard attraction at Washington's soirees for several weeks. Then the army decided that enough hospitality was enough and sent Wijujon back to the upper Missouri.

There was a council the night of Wijujon's return and all the sub-chiefs and super-chiefs gathered in a smoky

lodge to hear the emissary's words, "The white men are
as thick as flies about carrion!" Wijujon said truthfully,
for he was not one to stretch the truth. "They live in
houses as tall as the tallest trees on the plains along this
river—houses that have not one ground, but two and three
and four. They have all the salt they want to eat. Their
squaws do no work at all. They sit around and wear something about their waists that makes them look as thin
as a wasp, and they have great trouble when a papoose
comes into the world. The men wear hats that stick above
their heads and all have long hairs on their face, and never
once in the village where the Great White Father lives did
I see one cut off the ears of another. . . ."

The sub-chiefs and the super-chiefs lifted eyebrows at
each other. Was Wijujon lying? Things like this could not
be. They were not of the world. They were so patently
absurd that Wijujon must be deceiving them. Obviously
he had broken his trust to speak only the truth.

Wijujon talked on and on, not only that night but
the next day and the day after and for weeks after. Such
was the power of his words that he presently stepped up
in rank and became a medicine man. This dissatisfied
those whose power he unwittingly usurped, or at least
threatened, and they went into conference. Their tribunal,
like so many tribunals since the world began, because
their imaginations could not encompass the truth, decided
that Wijujon must die.

The Blackrobes

Ad Majorem Dei Gloriam

Back in 1521 a certain Spanish grandee, Ignatius of Loyola, had his dream of military glory shattered by a French cannon ball which took off one leg. While recuperating he read *The Lives of the Saints*. So impressed was he, a man of the world, that upon his recovery he became a man of Christ. With a certain Francis Xavier he formed a religious order which grew and flourished in spite of the opposition of the Roman church, which did not acknowledge it as legitimate until 1540—the Society of Jesus.

From Ignatius of Loyola to a certain valley of western Montana is a long distance and a long time, yet between Ignatius and that valley, roamed by certain redskins known as the Ootlashoots, more familiarly called the Flatheads, there is a real connection. For it was the Jesuits of the Society of Jesus who brought religion into the High Border Country.

No man knows why the Flatheads were known as Flatheads; certainly nothing in their physical makeup suggested the name. Flatheaded redskins there certainly were, but they lived on the Pacific coast, where they shaped the heads of the babies by compressing them in V-shaped boards so that the adults appeared wedge-headed—certainly not a spectacle to be observed unemotionally by a drinking trader. The Flatheads of the High Border Country lived in the broadest and most fertile valley of western Montana, hundreds of miles long and dozens of miles wide, of which today Missoula is the largest settlement.

They were well-formed redskins, calm enough, and what was important to their future, of such a decidedly peaceable disposition that they were willing to go to great lengths to secure themselves from harm.

Their main article of food, the spetlemen—the bitterroot—is today the state flower of Montana.

In the 1820's and '30's the Flatheads found themselves sorely harassed by the raiders of the plains—the Blackfeet. It was the custom of the Flatheads to trek east each year, crossing the Continental Divide in search of buffalo, which did not roam the valley of the spetlemen. But east of the mountains were the Blackfeet, who lay in wait along the usual trail of the Flatheads and frequently ambushed them. It did not occur to the Flatheads to select another trail and thus avoid the wolves of the plains; they followed the footsteps of their ancestors, through the most convenient pass of the Rockies, traversed in later years by Mullan's Road, in still later years by the Northern Pacific Railroad, and now by U. S. Highway Number 10. Because they had traveled this way for generations they would not change, and they died at the hands of marauding Blackfeet as generations before them had died. They were resigned to their fate.

In later years French-Canadian trappers named the narrow pass where this trail joined with the valley of the spetlemen, Porte de l'Enfer—the Gates of Hell. Significantly.

But there came a time when unrest stirred. Among the Flatheads arrived an Iroquois redskin, Ignace La Mousse, christened thus by the Jesuits in St. Louis. Ignace had religion—not only did he have it, but he was a fanatic, and when he settled among the Flatheads he continued to follow the customs prescribed by the order. He scorned the heathen gods of the Flatheads utterly. He made his prayers, observed Sundays, which he called *S chazéus* as religiously as if he were still in the St. Louis mission where he had received initiation into his faith.

"The white man's religion is very strong!" he told the Flatheads, not once but a thousand times. "It is much, much stronger than your weak gods!" But he added, "Not all the white man's religion is strong. Only that of the men who wear long black robes, those who call themselves Jesuits. The white men have other religions, but it is no good—no good!"

"Our own poor gods are no good; we pray to them and still they do not deliver us from the Blackfeet," the chief of the Flatheads decided. "Perhaps the god of the Black-robes is strong enough to save us from the Blackfeet. We must send for the Blackrobes to teach us about their strong god!"

A council decided that a deputation should go east to St. Louis to call for the Blackrobes, that order which weaves itself all through the history of the High Border Country like the black thread with which the robes were sewn, yet with the bright, bright thread of faith. In 1831 four Flatheads set out over the mountains, buoyed by hope and perhaps confident that upon their naked shoulders rested the fate of the Flathead nation.

"Good-by to our old, weak gods. With the one god of the Blackrobes, we will destroy the Blackfeet—"

Two of that deputation did not return. They died in St. Louis, were christened posthumously Narcisse and Paul, and buried there. The others returned, with word that the Blackrobes would arrive in due time. There followed jubilation among the Flatheads.

But Blackrobes failed to arrive. White men did come, but they were not the Blackrobes. They were not Jesuits. They were Methodists and Presbyterians, and Old Ignace had said that their medicine was not good. The Flatheads turned away from them, and in discouragement they went on to Oregon. Briefly one whose name is glorious in the annals of the Pacific, the Reverend Jason Lee, attempted to found a mission, but failure thwarted him and he fled to the Columbia country.

Then there came a day of joy when a messenger announced that at last the Blackrobes were at hand, resting this moment in the vicinity of the great rendezvous of mountain traders on the Green River, Wyoming. A certain chief Insula hastened there, fighting his way furiously through a band of Blackfeet—to receive, when he reached the river, the crushing disappointment of discovering that these men of God were not Blackrobes.

Again the missionaries attempted conversion, but the Flatheads resisted. There were whispers and scandal among them to discredit the Blackrobes. At Lapwai in the Oregon country a certain Reverend Samuel Park had broken the cross, the symbol of the Jesuits, which an Indian had placed at the head of his red child's grave. The only proper burial, he had insisted, was a stone at the head and foot of the grave. The cross was not emblematic of the true god. *His* god, not the god of the Blackrobes, was the true god. If the cross were so powerful, some of the more radical Flatheads wondered, why had not this desecration resulted in his destruction? But these doubters were in minority; the Blackrobes must come. And, not having come yet, they must be sent for again.

So, in 1835, Old Ignace, his son Charles, and another later christened Francis, headed for St. Louis. They received promises. They returned to the valley of the Bitterroot. They waited eighteen months.

No Blackrobe came.

The Blackfeet depredations became worse. In 1837 five persons, including Old Ignace again, once more headed east. On the South Platte they fell in with a certain W. H. Grey, Protestant missionary, also eastward bound, and the two parties joined forces. But not for long—presently they were surrounded by a horde of Sioux, who demanded the blood of the red men though they determined to spare the white. The Sioux, confronting the two parties, ordered the white men to stand to one side that they might not interfere with the massacre; Old Ignace, clad in cast-off clothes given him by the whites, appeared to be one of them, and so the Sioux treated him until he forced his way among his brethren to die with them.

When he and the rest of his party did not return to the valley where the bitterroot grew, the chiefs decided to send forth still another expedition. In 1839 the son of Old Ignace and a certain Flathead later christened Peter Gaucher set out. They reached St. Louis, petitioned the Jesuits, received the usual promises, and returned to their people. There were murmurings of unrest now. Too long had the Flatheads waited for the strong medicine the Blackrobes would bring. Too long.

But this time the Blackrobes did come. The first of them was one whose name must forever ring immortal in the annals of the High Border Country—Father Pierre

Jean De Smet. He sent word ahead, received at the Green River rendezvous a lukewarm delegation which, seeing that at last the Blackrobes had come, went wild. He baptized them and then returned to St. Louis. The following spring he returned with two priests and four lay brothers to found St. Mary's Mission in the valley of the Bitterroot. He went on, into what later became the Idaho panhandle, to establish another mission—notable in High Border history because to it was sent in 1871 the only Papal brief ever addressed to an Indian tribe.

Thus ends the saga of the Flatheads who would have strong medicine. Father De Smet found willing converts not only among that tribe but among all tribes in the mountains. The plains tribes did not evidence the same desire for his white god; the good father concentrated his attentions upon the mountain redskins, and did such a good job with them that his name has come down through history with the reverent title, Priest of the Rockies.

3. From Head of Navigation

M. R.

IN the East of the earlier 1800's there was born a lad
who dreamed of being not a soldier or a sailor or president of the United States, but the builder of a road. And
because he hoped hard enough and worked hard enough
and the High Border Country had need of such a road,
John Mullan was able to realize his dream. His road ran
from the frontier settlement of Fort Benton at the head
of navigation on the Missouri River, across the Continental Divide, through the present state of Idaho into
Washington, to Fort Walla Walla at the head of navigation
on the Snake River. It was subsidized by the army and
built as a military road, and the marks cut into trees along
the way were "M. R." Later generations called the M. R.
Mullan's Road, a harmless inaccuracy and a tribute to
the builder, who has also been honored by a dozen or
more statues along the highway which today follows what
in the '50's and '60's and '70's was a bumpy, rocky wilderness trail.

John Mullan was disappointed that no soldiers ever used
his military road. But the wheels of emigrant wagons
headed into Washington Territory and the whole Northwest wore deep ruts in it. Mullan designed his road with

horsemen and not wheels in mind, and it was not an easy trail. But easy or not, it speeded the opening of the country and brought civilization, which in the 1850's had halted reluctantly at the Dakotas for want of named trails into the wilderness, into the farther West.

John Mullan studied roads and maps throughout his youthful years; in military academy he specialized in road-building. As one of the chief aids of General I. I. Stevens he helped survey the northern route to the Far West in 1853-54. It was logical that he should be authorized by Congress to build a military road into the Northwest when it was decided that such a road might some day become a necessity. He began his task in 1857, and pushed his wagon road through the rocky wilderness to completion in 1861.

It was a difficult assignment for Mullan and his workers. Not even the military guard gave them real protection. There were mosquitoes, snakes, bad food, cold and heat to contend with, and there was toil and sweat, toil and more toil. But above all there were the ambushing and murderous redskins, slipping quietly through the brush with gun and tomahawk, quick to kill any man careless enough to relax his vigilance . . . at least, until one Fourth of July, when the builders rested from their labors in what today is known as the panhandle of Idaho.

Independence Day, and the men and soldiers alike took time off to celebrate. Celebrate they did, with cheers and songs and a flow of liquor which sent them dancing out into the cleared space around their camp. They limbed a tall tree, ran a flag to the top, cheered until the narrow canyon through which they were building echoed like thunder. They executed wild and wooly dances, they stripped themselves and whooped, they aped the redskins who, as they knew, were watching from the brush. This was Independence Day, and they made the most of it. The men went berserk and they kept it up until after dark, defying the somber wilderness and taking a riotous holiday from the monotony of toil. After nightfall they lined up in military formation and fired volley after volley into the sky—their substitute for fireworks.

Back in the forest the redskins held council. It was a solemn, decisive affair. And brief. The head chief delivered his verdict: "Crazy men. All of them crazy! We cannot harm crazy men, for they are favored of the Great Spirit. From this moment on, we leave them alone!"

And never again did the redskins harass the builders, though work on the road continued for almost two more years.

John Mullan left as his memorial in the High Border Country a road. When he returned to the wilderness again he found no wilderness, even if the land still lacked any signs of advanced civilization. In 1883 Mullan attended the ceremony of driving the golden spike which united the eastern and western thrusts of the Northern Pacific Railroad's transcontinental route, at Gold Creek, Montana. The rails followed the Mullan trail for many miles, and it was Mullan's pride that expert engineers for the railroad had been unable to improve upon the route he had surveyed so laboriously and with cruder instruments many years before.

MOOSE

Strangest of the sights along the Mullan Road during its lifetime was undoubtedly the one seen by a certain

Missourian, of whom history has the following story to tell:

The Missourian, surprised in the thick timber by a creature as weird of form and feature as ever he had seen, swiftly swung his gun up and took aim. For a moment, while he tried to identify the animal, he forgot his troubles, and he had plenty. At the moment he was vainly seeking gold near Blackfoot City, a gold-boom camp up under the Continental Divide on the Mullan Road. Some time previously he had been forced to flee from the war currently raging between the states east of the Mississippi River, both because he didn't know which side his sympathies were on and because he did not particularly care to be killed. Like many another, he had sought refuge in the High Border.

The Missourian, unacquainted with the fauna of the Continental Divide, found himself in the grip of an excitement beyond anything he ever experienced. For suddenly he identified the creature. A moose. Obviously. In the Ozarks a moose was a creature of far lands, as fabulous as tiger or lion. A man who killed a moose was a mighty hunter indeed. All this happened more swiftly than he could tell it. At any rate, he pulled the trigger and the moose, with one great leap of agony, crashed down dead.

Presently the Missourian staggered into camp with the moose on his back. Blackfoot City, with its motley shacks and tents, men, gamblers and Indians, had gold-boomed until it was an inferno. The Missourian waded through its noise and dust to the largest slab-and-canvas drink emporium to celebrate his exploit.

"A moose!"—he exulted to the miners at the bar, and added—"Shot it myself. First bullet, too!"

"Moose, hell!" remarked an onlooker, spatting casually. "That's no moose. That's a camel!"

The Missourian, though he knew nothing about the habits of the camel, knew nevertheless that something was wrong. Vaguely he seemed to recall that camels were more at home in Africa or Arabia or somewhere. He took a swig of red-hot alcohol to help him think. He took a second and was ready for his third when a commotion broke out in the street. The Missourian swung from the bar just in time to face the irate owner of the camel.

The owner was irritated in a manner to command respect—he had a gun. The Missourian did too, but he was so obviously in the wrong that any attempt to use it would bring down on him not only the wrath of the owner but also that of the interested onlookers. The camel lay there —plain evidence of the shooting. The owner stood there —declaring loudly and profanely that this was his favorite animal, his best among the dozen now herded out on the edge of Blackfoot City where the camel caravan had gone into camp for the night. The Missourian had but one choice, and that was to make amends. Which he did, by parting with his none-too-promising gold claim, his gun, and his watch.

The driver, still waving his gun, tromped off with the deed and the other spoils. He was secretly relieved, for the camels which he had purchased from the army had turned out to be a nasty lot of beasts almost unmanageable and certainly worse smelling than anything he had ever endured. . . .

In the middle of the 1800's the United States Army had decided to make an experiment—to employ camels instead of mules and horses for military maneuvers and campaigns throughout the High Border Country, especially in the mountainous sections of Montana and Idaho. Military traffic experts had noted the success of the native tribes of central Asia in using the camel in country similar to the High Border. Camels, they felt, were a great solution. Whereupon the army imported a score of camels and set them down in the High Border Country, deciding with a fatalistic serenity of which only the army of that day was capable that all their transportation troubles were ended.

But the beasts were difficult to manage, and treacherous, and so untrustworthy that an army mule, synonym of stubbornness, became the dream of every camel-skinner. The mistake of the army, of course, was in assuming that a soldier accustomed to mules and horses could care for camels; with proper handling by imported camelmen from the camel country the experiment might have been a success. It was a dismal failure. Some of the camels were sold into private hands; these died, or like the moose, were killed by mistake. Others were sent to Arizona, where for many years the army used them with some success to transport water and supplies to military outposts in the desert.

ITEMS

There are several stories of the middle period of the 1800's—which marked the decline of the mountain men and the fur trade and the rise of gold and steamboating—worth recording. Foremost of these, perhaps, is that of the Blackfeet Treaty, by which the scourge of the frontier pledged themselves to keep to the prairie north of the Missouri and Sun Rivers in Montana, and agreed to make peace with neighboring tribes upon whom they had preyed so mercilessly.

Credit for the treaty goes to Isaac I. Stevens, a Mexican War hero and the then appointee to the governorship of the new Washington Territory which ranged from Puget Sound and the Pacific coast to the Continental Divide, who in 1853 was directed to make a survey from the headwaters of the Mississippi to Puget Sound for railroad possibilities. Congress further empowered him to make such treaties with the Indians as he thought necessary to preserve peace. They were thinking particularly of the Blackfeet. Stevens laid the groundwork for a grand council cleverly, and did not rush matters; indeed, it was almost two years after his first efforts that he eventually called the grand council at the confluence of the Judith and Missouri Rivers. Present on that day were some ten thousand redskins, mainly Blackfeet. The chiefs ranged themselves in a semicircle before Stevens, bucks of more modest rank and braves behind them. Stevens, somewhat startled at the size of the assembly, nevertheless spoke boldly of the wars which the Blackfeet waged not only against the white man but against all their neighbors. He recalled former talks with influential chiefs.

"It was Low Horn who, two years since, said to me, 'Peace with the Flatheads and the Nez Perces.' The Little Dog, Little Grey Head, and all the Blackfeet chiefs said, 'Peace with them; come and meet us in council,' and here we are. Here you see them face to face. I met them the same year. I told them your words. They said, 'Peace also with the Blackfeet.' And the Great Father has said, 'Peace with the Crees and the Assiniboines, the Crows, and all the neighboring tribes!' "

The Blackfeet expressed a thorough willingness to make peace with the Crees, Crows, Assiniboines, Flatheads, and Nez Perces. Further, they agreed to confine themselves to the north central part of Montana, in the region up under the frowning Rockies of what is now Glacier National Park. They solemnly promised never to make forays against the white man in organized war parties. They kept their word. What the white man did about the treaty is another story; and in the general Indian uprising of the 1870's, in which the Blackfeet did not participate, the white man took it upon himself to see that the Blackfeet were so thoroughly vanquished that there would never again be any danger from them.

A group of Indians floated down the Missouri from Fort Benton and dropped in on a trader. They were friendly redskins, so he permitted them to camp in his post. They were excited, and when the trader asked why he got a reply that astounded him:

"For many moons we have seen white men but never have we seen the mother of a white man. Three sleeps back we saw at last the mother of a white man. And she is queer. . . . She is of strange color; she has great ears and horns over her eyes and she walks on four legs. Her milk is not in the same place as that on the mothers of the red men. A curious mother to have. . . ."

Indeed a curious mother, the trader reflected, and though it was some decades since he had seen his own mother, he was sure she had possessed neither big ears nor horns. He took a swig of whiskey, while he cogitated. He took another swig and another, and by the time he finished cogitating it did not matter to him what his mother looked like.

"Foursh legs!" he hiccuped. "Earsh! What the hell—" and reeled to sleep.

"A curious mother!" the redskins repeated, pondering among themselves. . . . They had seen the first cow on the upper Missouri.

The tribesmen floated on downstream and fell in with some traders who, in an effort to diversify trade, were issuing hundred-pound sacks of flour on which the trade name of the company was stamped in bright, crimson circles. The Indians knew little about flour and they wasted it, but the sacks they esteemed highly. They cut holes in the top and sides, and slipped them on. The Dakota Sioux especially favored these sack suits, for some medicine man started the rumor that the crimson circles brought good luck.

The Sioux were always a bit erratic in their dress, with a leaning towards the flamboyant. At a later date a frontier parson, named Colwell, so anxious to secure a congregation that he set up a barrel filled with whiskey and promised all whites who would listen to his sermon a cupful afterwards, was appalled one morning when his flock, momentarily almost one hundred per cent Sioux, appeared unconventionally clad. Because some official in the Indian department in Washington, D. C., had decided that the red children should sleep warm and decently and accordingly had ordered an issue of the slumber garment he himself used, every member of the congregation was attired in a nightshirt.

For many months thereafter Sioux braves and squaws

strutted around in the latest from the nation's capital. Colwell had the satisfaction of knowing, at least, that the savages in his district had covered their nakedness.

Liver-eating Johnson must receive mention. He ranged the Missouri from Fort Benton to the Dakotas, and is said to have esteemed Indian liver as a delicacy. Whether he actually ate it is a question, but his interest in dissection is definite. The frontier expression of threat, "I'll cut out your liver," was no bluff in his case. The Indians feared him and avoided him, and he was none too popular among his white companions, who restricted themselves to pot-shooting redskins and removing the hair for display in their belts. Liver-eating Johnson upon several occasions removed the livers of dead Indians and made a pretense, at least, of eating them raw.

During steamboat days on the Missouri the Liver-eater would stand along the river and watch the boats. His costume generally consisted of one shirt, ballooned up by the wind, and a whiskey-soaked, burr-matted beard. When larger boats went by he donned his Sunday clothes—moccasins. He never acknowledged the necessity for trousers except in winter. He gaped at the river boats and the passengers gaped back, sometimes thumbing their noses, sometimes laughing—to recoil at the hurricane of vituperation launched at them. Their laughter died quickly for another reason. There before them stood thirty whitewashed poles in front of Liver-eater's place—atop each pole the skull of an Indian bleached to leper whiteness by the dry air of the high plains.

4. Days of Gold

LUCKY MEN

THE man, huddled under the frame of a shack, put a pistol in his mouth and pulled the trigger. He slumped forward into the grave he had prepared for himself in the dirt floor. It was a scene of the most abject poverty. The man killed himself because he had no longer the wherewithal, either physically or spiritually, to live. His name was N. T. P. Comstock—the man who discovered the Comstock Lode in Nevada, one of the richest ore finds on earth. He had discovered millions—perhaps billions.

His end, here in Montana, paralleled the fate of other discoverers of bonanza. Lewis and Clark, hearing sounds like thunder in the mountains, attributed them to "bursting mines of silver." The mines were there—but not bursting out into the open—and prospectors and miners, especially during the '50's and '60's, searched doggedly to discover and open up the vast deposits of gold, silver, and copper all along the mountains of the High Border. Too often the discoverers themselves profited little. Or, profiting, threw their gains recklessly to the winds.

Bill Fairweather, for instance. Bill was a rough, tough, rootin', tootin' hombre who, to impress the redskins, snatched up a rattlesnake and bit its head off before the reptile could strike. Captured by Crow Indians somewhat later and doomed to death at the stake, he watched the redskins dance around their holiest of holies, a sacred bush. He managed to rip loose from his bindings; he tore up the sacred bush and beat the chief over the head with it. Awed, the Crows withdrew, and Bill Fairweather went his way, to become a prospector along the foothills of the Rockies in western Montana.

With a certain Edgar and two other men he came stumbling down into a gulch along the foothills one dusty evening of summer, 1863. The party, disappointed in their prospecting venture, was headed south. They made camp in the gulch and both Edgar and Fairweather dropped their gold pans into a little stream in hopes of making tobacco money.

Edgar swirled his pan for a minute, then held it up to the light. He blinked. The sand gleamed almost pure yellow. He bellowed out, "Pard, I've found a scad!" A scad was then the colloquial term for a small amount of gold.

Fairweather screamed back, "If you've found one, I've found a hundred!"

Thus Alder Gulch, probably the wildest gold strike in the West, had its start. Meanwhile to the North a prospector from Georgia, at the end of his trail and taking his last chance, dropped his pan into the stream of a dry, god-forsaken gulch, and gasped at the sight of heavy yellow. And Last Chance Gulch came into being, a narrow, triangular cleft in the hills that tails out in a wide fan into Prickly Pear valley. In the cleft and from it has grown up the capital of Montana, Helena, called by proud

citizens the City of Gold and Romance, where in the older
districts the Chinese still pan in their cellars for gold dust.
Construction of the city's most prominent hotel is said to
have been financed by gold excavated from its basement;
and out in the valley well within the city limits, a gold-
dredge worked during the 1930's and '40's. The city is
literally built upon gold, and dredge men bite their fingers
in futile wish that they might take their dredges up Main
Street.

Neither Fairweather nor Edgar cashed in to the ultimate, but they became comfortably fixed. Both passed on
in poverty. Edgar lost his money in the butchering business. Fairweather used to drive through Denver streets
in his open carriage, scattering handfuls of gold coins and
laughing at the way the Chinese and the children scrambled for them. He died without wherewithal for a cup of
coffee. The men who came after, smart and sharp, were
the ones who made the big fortunes in gold. It is the
history of the High Border that discoverers never grew
rich from their discoveries.

There are exceptions—Tom Cruse, who located the
Drumlummon Mine up under the Continental Divide,
for instance. In an age when placer-mining—the taking of
loose gold from the streams—was almost universal, Tom
Cruse believed in the metal that might lie deep embedded
in quartz rock. His partner, a certain Bill Brown, scorned
hard-rock mining and as a result, though he provisioned
Cruse, failed to profit from Cruse's discovery. Cruse eventually struck the Drumlummon, named it after his home-
town in the old country, and presently sold out to a British
syndicate for several millions of dollars. Whereupon he
lived high for the rest of his days, washing his insides with

good Scotch liquor, enjoying women and song to his lusty
fullest, and contributing with such generosity that he has
never been forgotten. He provided money toward a cathe-
dral then rising in Helena. It is a magnificent mass of
architecture, equaled by no other man-made structure in
the High Border anywhere, a twin-spired monument
staring serenely and a little superciliously out over a city
and a land from which the elemental rawness has not all
vanished. When Cruse died, they built him a mausoleum
and there he rests today, smothered in stone.

High Border prospectors first struck gold during the
latter 1850's in the Elk City, Oro Fino, Florence, and
Warner Creek regions of Idaho. Hundreds of men from
east of the Mississippi, thousands from the California
strikes of 1849, which had begun to peter out, stampeded
in. Gold flowed as freely as the red-eye liquor; hurdy-gurdy
and honky-tonk houses crowded the saloons for choice
locations on camp corners. And of course there were outlaws of the most vicious sort, at this time headed by an
urban gentleman named Henry Plummer, who with his
men congregated in hangouts they called "shebangs" where
they plotted raids upon the more conventional citizenry
of the camps.

Within a few years the Idaho mines began to play out,
money ceased to flow so freely, and some of the more law-
abiding individuals banded together into Vigilante groups
for the purpose—a simple one—of hanging evildoers. They
did stretch the necks of several and the rest escaped over
the mountains into Alder Gulch. Settlements under the
Continental Divide, in the present Montana, first Bannack
and then Virginia City, mushroomed into life, and Alder

Gulch, with Virginia City the center, became probably the wildest gold camp the world has ever seen. Men by the dozens of thousands swarmed in, and all up and down the gulch, suburbs as it were to Virginia City, smaller settlements sprang up. None of them, however, excelled Virginia City for size and general all-around hell.

"I name this yere place Varina, after the wife of our president, Jeff David!" yelled a Southerner, at the mass meeting convened for the purpose of naming the settlement. "We southerners came here first, an' we're aimin' to name the place—"

The Civil War raged then, and both northern and southern sympathizers had stampeded into the gulch. There was an immediate expression of dissatisfaction upon the part of Northerners—a certain Dr. Bissel particularly. "I'll see everybody here damned first, before this settlement's named Varina!" he roared. A committee of arbitration, hastily formed, compromised on the name Virginia. So Virginia City it became, where gold flowed and gold lay everywhere, and Chinese launderers panned the dirt they washed from the miners' shirts to recover gold dust.

The largest percentage of the miners had emigrated from California, and though laborers were in great demand, commanding as high as one ounce of gold for a day's work, often a laborer who was not from California found difficulty in securing employment. One man from some eastern state, new to the gulch, drifted from working to working, each time rebuffed curtly, "Better try the company above!" But at last, wits sharpened, he decided to get a job by the simple expedient of saying that he was from California.

At the next working he hailed the red-shirted boss.
"Where you from?" the boss demanded. "Right from California!" said the job-seeker.

"Get out of here!" the foreman snapped. "You're a liar.
Why, you can't even pronounce Californy!"

A woman from the East, of the more respectable sort,
went from camp to camp soliciting cooking. The miners
were not overly dainty when it came to food; and the lady,
angry at last, said to one camp boss, "Why, you miners
are—are filthy! You need a woman to keep your food clean.
Why, you never even wash your hands when you bake
bread!"

The camp boss was quick to defend his honor. "That's
not true!" he exclaimed. "Sure we wash our hands! How'd
we get the dough off 'em otherwise?"

The mines at Bannack—most often pronounced Bangup
at the time—to the west of Alder Gulch harbored rats to
the point of a plague. Bunkhouses and camps suffered.
The miners impressed redskins into service, but they
proved ineffective rat exterminators. They meandered
around, grunting their habitual wonder, and only occasionally
did they make a kill. The miners held a camp
meeting and decided there could be but one solution to
the situation.

Cats.

The miners never washed their plates, simply turned
them over after swabbing them with bread; and it was
the custom at meal time to put them right side up with
a terrific bang. Rats scampered across the tables, sniffing
the downturned edges of the plates. They had become so
bold they dashed around the miners' feet at the tables.
A miners' meeting of Bangup called for a Pied Piper or

at least cats. In vain. There was not a cat in camp; none anywhere within three or four hundred miles.

Then two entrepreneurs of a sort, John Thompson and Jeff Blevins, sensing big money, took a fling at the cat business. In the spring of 1863 they trekked over the mountains, through the camps of Idaho where they found no cats, into Oregon; presently they were on the way back, their wagon filled with wailing cats. Deep in the hills they met with an accident—their vehicle slipped from the narrow road, went plunging downhill to the accompaniment of a great outcry from the cats and a greater cry from Messrs. Thompson and Blevins, who saw their profits disappearing as the cats, one by one, escaped through the shattered sides of the wagon box.

The situation was not hopeless, however, and Thompson and Blevins, who had jumped at the moment the wagon overturned, went scrambling down the slope. They reached the wagon in time to prevent the escape of a part of their cargo, and after righting the vehicle they continued on to Bannack. There the citizens hailed them with great joy, and at the auction which followed immediately as much as seventy-five dollars in gold was paid for each cat. Even after deducting their losses on the road, Thompson and Blevins had made a large profit.

The cats proved a civilizing influence. In cabins where cats patrolled the men no longer upturned their plates after each meal. Not only did the felines wreak great destruction among the rats, but they kept the plates clean.

Pie Eater

In Bannack, after the arrival of the cats, things went boomingly on, as they did in Alder Gulch and in the now discovered Last Chance Gulch to the north. There was gold everywhere—at least, for a few men—much hilarity, much misery, and always a shooting or two to liven things up. Prominent on the scene was the gentleman commonly known as the Great American Pie Eater because of his enormous mouth and his strong teeth.

It was the Pie Eater's boast that he could bite completely through seven pies, laid one on top of the other. A stranger, drifting into the settlement one day, was skeptical about this and ready to back his skepticism with gold. The bet was made, with the stranger agreeing to furnish the pies.

The stranger was one of those fellows who liked to have the cards stacked his way, so he went to a baker and ordered several pies baked according to his specifications —which is to say, in loose-bottomed tins. When the pies were piled up for the great test of skill, the stranger carefully removed the tins but neglected to peel off the bottoms. The Pie Eater gathered up the stack with both hands and took a bite. He had almost reached for the bet, placed in plain sight of both betters according to the custom of that time and place, when a look of bewilderment shone suddenly in his eyes. He champed hard on the tins, without result.

"Well, well!" the stranger remarked casually scooping in the stakes. He walked away, rather more swiftly than would be expected.

Defeated, the Pie Eater muttered, "Toughest pie crust I ever bit into." He muttered again, "That's damn tough crust!" and then he spied the tin bottoms.

He promptly went for his rifle, but the stranger had fled. The Great American Pie Eater, disgruntled, wandered down to his favorite hurdy-gurdy. They say he was never quite the same again.

A certain theatrical troupe, playing the tougher camps of the West, held a performance in Bannack. This was years later, when population of the camps had ceased to be exclusively male. The name of the play doesn't matter. What does matter is that the troupe was one which, for full effect, was accompanied by an orchestra. At the high point of the show the orchestra wailed out a shrill accompaniment to the heroine, whereupon a baby in the audience began to scream. The orchestra leader and the actors, annoyed, cursed freely as the instruments made a vain attempt to drown out the infant.

Then from the rear of the room there strode a whiskered miner, just in from the hills. He clapped a hand to his gun in warning, and called out, "Stop that there orchestra an' let the little one cry! I ain't heard a sound like that in ten years!"

Rich as some of the mines were, there were more mines that yielded nothing—causing futile stampedes and high hopes on the trail which led to the end of the rainbow. Up along the Sun River a prospector who had dropped into the settlements remarked quietly to a friend, "I've got as good a thing up my way as I can want!" An eavesdropper, seeing the small poke of gold the prospector tendered in payment for supplies, concluded that here was a strike. He informed a friend, swearing him to secrecy, but the friend also had a friend, and within a couple of days the stampede was on.

The weather was bitterly cold, the mercury at minus forty. It was so frosty as to "freeze the legs off a heatin' stove." Miners perished by the score, but the stampede persisted until someone discovered that the prospector's "good thing" were a warm cabin, supplies, and, last but not least, a new and comely Blackfeet squaw.

Down along the Dakota-Montana line someone discovered traces of gold in a coulee, and there was a rush which caused the overnight growth of a settlement, Alexander City. But it seems there was some slight hitch. Traces of gold were very faint, the story of a strike having been based upon the discovery of a supposedly ancient coffin containing a body and a poke of gold. The coffin, in fact, stood on display day and night as prospectors worked patiently up and down the gulch and the gamblers, saloon-keepers, and madams waited impatiently for business.

Then someone discovered that the coffin had been constructed with wire nails—a fairly recent invention. Alexander City vanished as quickly as it had been born. Within a day the gulch was deserted. On a tree somebody nailed a sign: "I hereby located the right-of-way up and down this tree!" In the general exodus the gold-seekers passed an old Dutchman who had arrived just in time to leave. He plodded along, pack on back, and when he was offered a ride he answered, "Nope. I'll learn this damn Dutchman something! Walk away, you feet!"

In the camps where gold really existed, there was constant trouble and bickering. "Skookum Joe" Anderson located a good claim in one of the myriad of gulches between Alder Gulch and Last Chance. Fat Jack Wassem coveted the claim, took steps to secure it in a direct manner. At the local store he threw some gold on the counter and called out, "Give me all the powder you got, an' a short fuse. I'm aimin' to blow up Skookum Joe an' jump his claim!"

The storekeeper refused to sell and Fat Jack sulked. Skookum Joe, hearing of the incident, got out his gun and promised Fat Jack that he'd land in hell if he ever appeared near the claim in question. Peace was established.

The Way They Hit It

In Virginia City Bummer Dan lived up to his name. No manual labor had ever calloused Bummer Dan's palms, though they were sufficiently soiled. But he appeared a genial enough character, harmless and ingratiating, and the camp tolerated him and fed him and gave him smokes and an occasional drink. He lived the life of Riley, effortlessly and peacefully.

But in time grumbling was heard. Most of the miners were a hard-working lot, and the fact that Bummer Dan could exist without labor seemed to them, or some of them at least, a bit unfair. So when, one day, Bummer Dan turned plain thief, robbed a cook-shack of a pie, and was apprehended in the act of stuffing himself, they decided that he must, in some small measure, pay. Accordingly, they handed him a pickax, carried him out of camp to a section of the gulch which had been untouched be-

cause the formation appeared unlikely to yield gold, and
set him forcibly to work.

"Now dig!" the No Work-No Eat committee ordered,
and Bummer Dan, beginning to sweat honestly for the
first time in his life, wielded his pick half-heartedly. His
lack of ambition roused the anger of the party, and they
showered him with curses and threats that stirred him to
the point of—what was for him—strenuous activity. He
picked away for a few minutes, excavating a hole about
the size of an egg. The party, mollified, withdrew—threat-
ening to return.

They came back presently, to find Bummer Dan sitting
on the edge of a sizeable excavation, his hands full of
gravel. He had dropped his pick; nor, when the party
came up and caught him idle did he show the least panic.
He merely stared at the gravel—gravel crossed with yellow:
nuggets and dust. Of all the discoveries ever made in Alder
Gulch, Bummer Dan's Bar carried the highest percentage
of gold—a find of unparalleled richness. It was as close
to the mother lode—that fabulous bonanza which is the
source of supply of all gold strikes—as possible. Bummer
Dan's theft of a pie paid big dividends.

Up in the country around Last Chance a group of Confederate soldiers found color in a gulch which they christened, properly enough, Confederate Gulch. There followed a minor rush and a settlement was swiftly built
up. They called it Diamond City, and most of the inhabitants, though able to get a living out of the gulch,
were disgruntled because the yield was so small. They
turned envious eyes towards Last Chance to the west, but
all available ground there had been claimed long ago.

They refused to abandon their small claims, however, cursing their lives but making little effort to better themselves.

Then one day a stranger drifted in—a rank greenhorn in store clothes, new outfit on his back. He dashed eagerly into Diamond City's largest saloon, informed the crowd that he had come West to discover the mother lode, and demanded to be shown "the best place to pan for gold!" A hard-bitten miner took him by the arm, pointed through the open door to a gravel bar long considered worthless, and said, "Thar you are, partner! Jest dig that an' you'll git plenty of gold!"

Eagerly the greenhorn dashed out and began to dig. . . . In later years they named this stretch of gravel Montana Bar. It was only a little less rich than Bummer Dan's Bar. At Montana a miner's goldpan—a shallow affair something like a dishpan but of heavier construction—often yielded above a thousand dollars.

Bummer Dan's Bar, Montana Bar, Alder Gulch, Bannack, Last Chance Gulch, Virginia City, Elk City, Florence, Oro Fino—golden names in the history of the gold region. And they are concrete names, mines that actually produced. But for every mine from which gold flowed, there are a thousand that never existed except in the imagination of the old prospectors or, during the '20's of the present century and even in the money-starved 1930's, upon the ornately printed paper of stock salesmen. Tales of lost mines, lost gold, are legion. In Bannack in the earlier days Olaf Gustaferson vanished at intervals, to return with leather pokes full of gold dust. Parties which set out to trail him and ferret out his strike failed. Dying, Olaf Gustaferson refused to reveal the location of his claim, but his story did not die with him, and even today there are old prospectors who will whisper to you, "Pard, fer a drink I'll tell you about Olaf Gustaferson's mother lode. I know jest where it is. . . ."

From Montana to Wyoming, down into Dakota, there are scores of Lost Chinee mines, the sagas of which invariably run something like this: In the early days a group of Chinese worked a mine with more or less success—enough at least to fill a baking-powder tin or some other receptacle with gold dust. Each deposited his day's take in it according to the communal system in force in most Chinese settlements of the day, and they kept it carefully hidden. The time came, however, when white men drove them from the gulch, so suddenly that they had no opportunity to reclaim their treasure. Nor were they ever permitted to return, with the result that the cache of dust still rests today in some hiding place unknown to the white man but eternally sought by old gulch-rats or prospectors.

CHINEE

The Chinese are inextricably a part of High Border history. They came in with the miners, following the gold rushes—as laundry operators, low-class laborers, doing any task the white man found beneath his dignity. In later years they helped build the railroads, and white bosses threw them into the more dangerous and unpleasant jobs. Every cow town had its Chinese; every railroad camp swarmed with them; only the dryland settlements, where there was little money and all tasks were unpleasant, were shunned by them.

Low as they were, they inspired the term "Chinese"

luck which was sometimes widely used. There is the case of Sin Louie, resident of the Alder Gulch gold diggings, whom angry miners accused of robbery and brought to trial at the big, flat Pulpit Rock where ordinary trials were held—some earlier self-appointed law having seen in this rock, balanced on the lip of a gulch, a dramatic place for enforcement of justice. The jury gave Sin Louie what was then the "benefit of doubt" and decided to hang him. A dry thunderstorm had been raging; now the rain broke in a deluge and the jury prepared to seek safety.

But the judge had other ideas. "This yere's a law court!" he called. "An' I'm a-goin' through the fomal'ties jest like they do back in the Confederacy. I'm sentencin' the prisoner formal-like. Stand up, Sin Louie, you ——, while I tell 'em to put a rope around your yaller neck!"

Just then Pulpit Rock, which had tottered for untold years there on the lip of the gulch, began to quiver. A flash flood right under the base of it had weakened the few clay pillars which still supported it. The judge and jury waited no longer, but dove for safety, while the rock went landsliding down into the gulch. There was a minute's silence while judge, jury, and prisoner stared solemnly through the rain at the emptiness where they had stood a moment before.

Then the judge, groping hastily for a bottle, made an observation stopping just short of wisdom, "Sin Louie, you're the luckiest yalla son-of-a-gun I ever did see! Why, if you'd 'a' stayed on that rock, you'd be a gone duck right now. You'd be dead!"

Sin Louie, warily eyeing the rope in the hands of the jury, swallowed.

The judge took another drink, then goggled solemnly at his prisoner. "Damn me, Sin Louie, ef I don't figger this is an act of Prov'dence! Mebby we're wrong in hangin' you. Mebby we ought to let you go. How about it, boys?"

The foreman was handed the bottle, took a quick one —about a pint long—and coughed. "Wall, seein' how we'd be kickin' in the teeth of Prov'dence, we find Sin Louie not guilty!" he decided.

And the judge concluded, "You're free, you yalla —— Now get out of Alder Gulch an' stay out!"

During the gold-rush days—and, indeed, even today— every settlement of any size had its "Chinee-town." The Chinese always belonged to tongs, and at times they fought bitterly among themselves—so viciously once, in Butte, that posters in Chinese characters on every street corner of Chinatown offered a reward for the murder of three members of an opposing tong. As recently as the 1920's there were sporadic outbreaks of tong feuds in Butte, Bing Kong vs. Hip Sing. But the greatest battle of them all, the acme of Chinese tong war, occurred in Alder Gulch during the latter part of the gold-mining period. It is known as the "Chinee War."

Virginia City, in Alder Gulch, and all of the gulch, swarmed with Chinese—washermen and day laborers, although a few had been able to accumulate a bit of gold ground and, what was really marvelous considering the day and age, had managed to hold it against the white man to whom the Oriental was rated just a shade above the redskin. In every small settlement of Alder Gulch, Chinese made themselves generally obnoxious or useful, according to the viewpoint of the individual white man. There was, however, one laudable quality about them—they were quiet and peaceful. Until one morning. . . .

Certain tongs claimed most of the Orientals, and for some reason which has never come to light, private quarrels broke into open war. From every small shack and settlement, from the more metropolitan area of Virginia City, the yellow men gathered at double quick, rifles in hand. Presently, at a point, two small armies drew up, face to face, and shooting broke forth with a vigor that more than made up for the marksmen's lack of accuracy. Many of the Chinese fired into the air, apparently more interested in the noise than in the death of their adversaries, but a certain percentage seemed to be in earnest. Thousands of shots passed back and forth, but only two men lay dead when the firing ceased and the tongs concluded a formal truce.

The whole battle was endowed with a quality of unreality, from the way in which it began to its conclusion. The two dead men were not killed by bullets—they had been knifed to death.

For many years Chinese avoided the city of Great Falls, Montana—a boycott that had its grim reason, for in the early days it is said that a group of citizens, disguised as cowboys, rounded up the Chinese in the city, put them on a raft, and shoved the raft out into the Missouri River, which at this point breaks over cliffs in the series of great falls from which the city takes its name. No attempt was made to recover the bodies when they were presently cast up below the cascades.

If Chinese were everywhere in Alder Gulch, so was trouble. Supplies came in from Salt Lake City, freighted over mountain passes which deep snow sometimes blocked in winter. News arrived early one spring that a freight team, enroute to the gulch with flour, had been held up by drifts—a serious situation because of the dwindling food supply. Bread with beans was the staple food of the miners. Certain merchants saw a chance to make a killing and accordingly boosted prices on the flour they had —up and up to as high as $2.00 per pound. This naturally aroused discontent, which presently grew into a howl of protest, which grew louder as miners tightened their belts and dieted on beans, plain.

A miners' meeting, the universal court of justice in the mining country, convened and decided that prices must come down. More excitable—or hungrier—members of the meeting urged instant action, and when the merchants refused flatly to sell their flour at more reasonable prices, the men of action found listeners. Presently a mob, somewhat more orderly than most mobs, formed and marched on the merchants.

There was a formidable display of guns; the mob seized all the flour in Virginia City and in the smaller settlements, and brought it to a central point where the sacks were piled in a wagon and divided up by a committee. The merchants received what the committee thought was a just price for their flour; the committee then rationed out the flour, more or less honestly, and the mob dispersed.

Among the famines of the High Border, flour, food, whiskey, and plain water, there was the tobacco famine at Fort Benton on the Missouri, in the '60's when Benton lay at the head of the Missouri River steamboat traffic.

The river boats did not travel by winter, because of ice. Bentonites in the fall used to buy enough tobacco to last until the first boat came up from St. Louis in the spring, but they left no leeway for emergency—to their great dismay, for the first boat up the river this particular spring battered her nose on a sandbank and then froze in. Almost a month passed before a thaw enabled her to float; in the meantime the sufferings of the male population of Fort Benton were terrible to behold.

When their tobacco played out, they experimented with a mixture of redskin smoking materials, which neither satisfied their craving nor gave them any of the deep spiritual satisfaction which nat'ral twist appeared to offer. Tobacco shavings boomed in price, took the place of gold on the gambling tables. One enterprising storekeeper tore up the rough, plank floor of his establishment and panned the dirt beneath to separate tobacco tailings, which had fallen between the planks, from the dust. He did not draw too careful a line, but nobody cared. This dust-tobacco mixture brought a price that made the storekeeper (strictly a non-smoker himself) beamingly happy.

In time the supply boat hove in sight, and men were injured in the rush.

Mines got their names in various usual and unusual and sometimes downright weird manners. The Algonquin, for instance: Quinn and Casey, owners of the mine at the turn of the century, had gone into the town of Deer Lodge for a bit of night life. They returned next day, with the ubiquitous bottle. The mine consisted of a single shaft in the side of a hill, over which the owners had constructed a winch-and-bucket rigging to raise ore and dirt. Quinn in the morning got into the bucket and Casey dropped him slowly to the bottom of the shaft, where Quinn pecked away with a pick and shovel to fill the bucket, which, loaded, Casey would hoist to the top of the shaft and dump.

Casey retained possession of the bottle and took a comforting nip or two to keep green the memory of the night in town. He took three and four nips, and five. Quinn meanwhile developed both a sweat and thirst, and presently called up, "Send down the bottle, Casey!" When no action was forthcoming, he added, "Send down the bottle, you ——!"

Casey's red nose appeared in the square of light at the entrance to the shaft. "Shorry!" he explained, "All gone, Quinn!" Thereafter that was the Algonquin Mine.

THE INNOCENTS

From the Idaho gold fields, into the Bannack and Alder Gulch diggings, came an urbane gentleman with a bullet in his right arm, lodged against the bone. This affected his deadly accuracy with a pistol not at all, for he had taught himself to handle a weapon with his left hand. He was soft-spoken, pleasant, and kind in manner; he won as his bride one of the most beautiful girls on the frontier —yet he hanged, and when they took the bullet out of his arm they found it polished as shiny as a new silver dollar by constant friction with the bone.

He traveled under the name of Henry Plummer, and he headed a band of outlaws who for out-and-out cut-throat bloodthirstiness had no equal anywhere in the High Border or for that matter anywhere in any period of the West.

Plummer was no rough-mouthed desperado. When he set out to murder and rob, no red neckerchief masked his face, and there was no gun in his hand. That rougher work he left for men without imagination, men of limited intelligence. Plummer did the planning.

Bent upon robbery—and murder, its inevitable corollary—Plummer got himself elected sheriff of Alder Gulch. Thus protected, he organized his desperate crew—Boone Helm, Joe Slade, Cyrus Skinner, George Shears, Whiskey Bill Graves, George Ives, Red Yeager, Buck Stinson, Ned Ray, and a dozen others who acted as informers, spies, or road agents. Henry Plummer stayed in the background, never soiling his own hands, yet he was the master mind behind the wave of murder and robbery that began.

The band called themselves the Innocents; they wore a distinctive knot in the neckerchief at their throats by which to identify each other; they had as password the expression, "I am innocent!" They stalked the streets of Virginia City, Bannack, and the other settlements by night, and by day they overhauled the gold-laden stage coaches headed for Salt Lake City or Last Chance. The time came when they were in complete command of the gold fields, and no man dared raise a voice against them. They murdered, robbed, blackmailed, until at last it was said that in Virginia City no honest miner with an ounce of gold on him dared set forth a foot after dark.

The gold fields of Idaho had run most of these desperadoes out. It is the history of gold booms that lawlessness flourishes at first, until a more settled citizenry arrives. Then there is inevitably a struggle between the forces of law and the forces outside the law. In the Idaho fields the settled citizens had arrived; there followed hangings and banishments, with the result that the desperadoes, no longer in command of the situation, fled to newer, greener fields, just as they had fled from California to Idaho. Bannack and Alder Gulch were the next stop. And it was the last stop for most of them.

To balance their lawlessness there lived certain individuals who had faith in law and order. X. Beidler, for instance—a stocky, perpetually drunken man, who cursed both his fellows and God, but played fair with both. When he was a lawman, the newspapers chronicled his activities generally in three terse sentences, in successive issues: "X. Beidler left yesterday for Bonanza Gulch after horse thieves." "Yesterday a man was found hanging in Bonanza Gulch. He is believed to be the horse thief who has been annoying ranchers of the vicinity." "Yesterday X. Beidler returned to town, after a trip to Bonanza Gulch."

Drunkenly reeling from side to side, but in perfect control of himself, Beidler drove stage frequently. He argued with his friends, of whom he had few in the gold camps because it was almost suicide to be seen with a man hostile to Plummer. He held book larnin' in contempt, though he knew well how to read and write; indeed, he kept a diary. He had no use for maps, finding his way through the wilderness by instinct.

He loved to tell a story about the United States Army, for whom he served as guide: An officer, inspecting a map, suddenly called out to the wagon men to brake the wheels of their wagons, though before them stretched the level prairie—not a grade in sight. Beidler remonstrated, whereupon the officer swore and shook the map in his face. "There's a grade shows here on the map!" he snapped. "And by God, we're going to block the wheels if it kills the mules!"

X. Beidler went his way, defying the desperadoes with such carelessness that they swore he bore a charmed life. Conditions had become so bad that he had secured a following among the more lawful men. A general uprising took place, with the formation of a group of Vigilantes who swore never to retreat until the desperadoes swung. They exposed Henry Plummer, hunted him down, and hanged him with all his crew. They sent Vigilante posses out in fifty-below weather to round up suspects; a posse plowed through the snow across the Continental Divide to the settlement of Hell Gate, later Missoula, whence some of the outlaws had fled at the first intimation of vengeance. They hanged these men, to the great relief of a certain storekeeper upon whose safe, supposedly empty but in reality filled with gold dust, one of the outlaws had liked to sit.

Joseph A. Slade

Joseph A. Slade was not called Joe, even by his intimate friends, of whom he had few. A rattlesnake is not greatly liked outside the rattlesnake clan, and a bad rattlesnake is presumably disliked even by his companions.

Joe Slade was a bad rattlesnake.

One day Mr. Slade bargained with a rancher for a stack of hay. The rancher, unacquainted with Mr. Slade, attempted a ruse, stuffing the inside of the stack with green brush. Mr. Slade paid his money. Presently, how-

ever, he tested the feed which he had purchased for
horses on the Overland Stage route, of which he was a
division agent, and discovered the trick. He then took
steps to prove to the rancher that crime did not pay.

Joe Slade ran the rancher down, dragged him to the
stack, and chained him there. Then, very deliberately,
he set fire to the hay.

Joe Slade was a rough, tough hombre, even for that
era of the '50's, '60's, and '70's. Joe was so tough that he
did not die a natural death. As division agent for the
Overland Stage, he had to be harder than the average
man, for the Overland Stage was the Big Business of the
time and obvious game for criminals. In a wild country
where they did not call it murder when you did away with
a fellow man through violence, Slade was able to handle
the troubles of the Overland Stage in a manner highly
satisfactory to his employers.

But in time he fell out of grace, partly because of a
terrific thirst he developed and partly because of a somewhat less desirable habit of helping himself to the company's loose change. He drifted from the Overland route
north to the Alder Gulch diggings where he fell in with
a band of cut-throats.

This is getting ahead of the story, however. While still
an employee of the stage line, Slade had developed a feud
with Jules Reni, a French-Canadian who appears to have
been anything but pleasant. Jules, something of a power
along the stage trail, met Slade when the latter resented
certain things Jules had done. Both Jules and Slade were
hot-headed and terrible when roused. Jules swore to get
Slade. Mutual threats were exchanged. But at the next
meeting Slade greeted Jules cordially, and they fell into

amiable conversation. Jules possessed a slick tongue, and his words lulled Slade's suspicions, for when Slade turned to leave, he made the error of the frontier which has been fatal to so many men—he turned his back on his adversary. Jules pulled a shotgun from hiding and pumped eighteen buckshot into Slade's back.

"I'll get you for this!" Slade promised, and fell unconscious.

"He weel las' one houiare!" Jules said, to friends. "And theen you can put heem on a packing box. The g-great Slade. Pah!" He spat on his unconscious victim and left.

A doctor would have given Slade the same length of time to live. But Slade was tough. When he was able to move, he rode the stage to St. Louis for treatment. Some months later he returned to Wyoming, packing eight slugs the medical men had been unable to remove.

To certain persons who knew Slade, Jules Reni was now as good as dead. Jules, however, did not think so, and boasted at many bars that next time his trail crossed the trail of Slade, there would ensue a final reckoning, with Jules Reni the certain winner this time. Jules, so great was his confidence, even purchased a special gun for Slade's death. He wore it next to the regular weapon in his belt and fingered it significantly.

"He weel die!" he promised ceaselessly.

Jules proved an excellent bluffer, so good that Slade decided to seek expert counsel. He consulted the military authorities at Fort Laramie, in Wyoming. Lest it be thought that Slade welshed, remember that the Reni-Slade feud had acquired fame all along the line and the killing of Reni might bring on an investigation injurious to Slade. Slade reasoned that if he accepted the advice of

military authority, there could be no blame attached to
him, nor would there be any investigation. He was pretty
certain what the officers would say.

The only honorable course, in view of Jules' attack
upon him, was to kill Jules, they said. Whereupon Slade
whet his knife and put it in his boot, cleaned his pistol
and put it in his belt, and went out for Jules Reni. He
appears to have been a little shaky—so much so that he did
not go alone, but recruited four companions.

The four men preceded him. At a place known as
Chansau's Ranch, they captured Jules and tied him in
the corral. In due time Joe Slade arrived, well equipped
with guns, pistols, and knives. He inspected a pistol to see
that it worked properly, rushed to the corral, and took
a pot-shot at Jules.

The bullet may have been intended for a quick kill.
That would not have been like Slade, however. At any
event, it shattered Jules' mouth. The French-Canadian
sagged as far to the ground as the ropes around him
permitted and gave every look of death. It was a possum
gesture, which Slade recognized at once.

"Get up, Jules. You ain't dead," he said, and added,
"But you will be afore long! I'm a-goin' to have your
will made!"

And make Jules Reni's will he did; he then forced
Jules to sign it. Then, ordering that he be left alone
with Jules—an order which nobody challenged, for when
Joseph A. Slade made a request, it was instantly heeded
—he proceeded to do away with Jules. Specific details
of the death are lacking, but those we know include such
cheerful items of torture as nail-pulling, gut-shooting, and
eye-gouging. Whatever happened, when Slade came back

among the men after a considerable period of time, Jules Reni was dead and Slade carried his two ears in his pocket.

He carried the pair of ears with him to the Alder Gulch diggings. There, as mentioned before, he fell in with that organized band, under the leadership of Henry Plummer, calling itself the Innocents.

Slade, being reasonably intelligent, not only ran with the Innocents but joined the Vigilante group. He reasoned that he would thus be wholly safe to carry on his villainies, which included such innocent pastimes as taking an occasional poke at a miner's head with some blunt instrument and raiding the sugarbowl safes of poor washerwomen. His pilfering activities during his later years with the Overland Stage had not yielded him any great amount, and he was constantly pressed to secure money for gambling, drinks, and to gratify the whims of his wife Virginia.

Eventually the Vigilantes, tiring of his escapades which included much fighting and gouging of eyes and tearing off of ears, investigated his sub-rosa activities and discovered that he was not what he appeared upon the surface. They thereupon decided to deal with him. A companion ventured warning.

"Watch yourself, Slade. The Vigilantes are after you!"

Slade, too sure of himself, grinned in amusement. He sought out the leader of the Vigilantes, Judge Davis. "I hear you're out gunnin' for me!" he said, and drew a derringer pistol from an inside pocket with the evident intention of crudely and openly doing away with Judge Davis.

The psychology behind this move is a bit beyond comprehension, for intelligent as Slade was, he must have known that such an action would sign his death warrant. The quick action of a friend of the judge's saved the judicial life and thereafter Slade tried to pass the whole thing off as a joke. But circumstances had gone beyond his control. The Vigilantes, six hundred strong, later surrounded Slade and hoisted him on a box with a rope around his neck and over a corral-beam above.

Slade, the bold, bad Slade, was a coward at the last. He fell to his knees and prayed for release. Failing, he screamed and raved, promised and threatened. He clutched the dried ears from his pockets and threw them to the ground. He grew almost insanely violent. But inexorably the Vigilantes put the California collar around his neck —just as inexorably as they had thrown it over the heads of other outlaws during those few red months when law and order for the first time came to the High Border Country. They had had enough of Slade. There was no stopping them.

Presently the bad man became composed, and sent a messenger for his wife. He asked as a favor that the execution be delayed until she should arrive. But the executive committee of the Vigilantes was wary, for there were men among the Vigilantes themselves who sympathized with Slade, degenerate though he was. One man in the audience fell on his knees before the packing box, prayed long and fervently; when this failed to soften the executive committee, he jumped to his feet and threw off his coat, screaming that he would stop the hanging by force. A hundred gun muzzles brought him to his senses, and he retreated into the crowd.

The presence of a woman could easily incite a riot,

the committee feared. They whispered among themselves.

They did not consult long, for they were stern men. "Sorry, Slade, we can't wait for your wife!" someone said, and another man kicked hard at the packing box. It collapsed under Slade. The rope around the corral beam straightened stiffly as an arrow, and Joseph A. Slade's neck tilted curiously to one side while he pendulumed back and forth.

VIRGINIA SLADE

Virginia Dale, wife of Joe Slade, had beauty, intelligence, and passion; also a desperate affection for this abominable murderer. Joe's public life has been described; his home life was something quite different. That he loved Virginia beyond all else in life cannot be doubted. He built for her, some twelve miles from Virginia City, a small stone house, where he kept her as a queen in lonely grandeur—not against her will, for she was as much of a lone wolf as he.

Virginia Slade had beauty—not just ordinary beauty; frontier writers who knew her invariably grew rhapsodic in their descriptions of her. Of all women, good, bad and indifferent, who have left their mark upon the High Border, she possessed the greatest physical attraction.

Virginia was at her house when news came of the Vigilantes' vengeance. She saddled a horse and rode fast to the scene of the hanging, sparing neither the horse nor herself. When she raced into the settlement, she was white-faced but dry-eyed, nor did she weep when she saw the frayed end of the rope.

Someone told her that the body of Joe Slade lay in the hotel. Virginia dropped from her horse and went forward.

She was quite calm, according to eyewitnesses. But when she saw the body she sprang upon it and burst into such a torrent of grief, mixed with bitter curses, that it was hours before she calmed down.

"Cowards! Why didn't you shoot him down, instead of torturing him on the gallows—"

In time Virginia dried her tears and bethought herself of the future of her beloved. Evidently she could not think of planting him underground at once, so she decided upon a way of keeping him temporarily in view. She ordered a tin coffin, filled it with alcohol, and placed Joe in this— preserving him until the next spring when she took him to Salt Lake City.

Here she bade her husband a last good-by. She placed a granite slab at his head and a rose at his feet. The rose withered but the slab endured for decades.

Virginia Dale Slade, the most beautiful woman of the High Border, then passed out of sight. Romantics might suggest that she killed herself or wasted away for love of Slade. More likely she joined the occupants of some bawdy-house in remote regions or teamed up with some gambler as his mistress and come-on. It is illogical to assume that she married some respectable miner and settled down. But nobody knows.

BOONE HELM

Of the bloodier characters of the High Border probably the worst is Boone Helm, whom the Vigilantes also hanged. Boone's story begins simply. He was camped in the snow. He carried his food with him. It consisted of one human leg, rolled in an old red flannel shirt.

He fed steaks to an Indian, Mo-quip, and Mo-quip,

not knowing whence the meat had come, said, "This is *bueno* game—very, very good." But when Boone Helm unrolled the red flannel shirt, Mo-quip turned deathly sick—even though his own food for the last two weeks had consisted of toasted ants, and tobacco plant.

That was one winter of the '50's. In a later decade, during the '60's, Boone, a fugitive from justice, was seized on the Frazer River in British Columbia. Too weak to travel, he allowed himself to be captured without a fight. The lawmen asked him one question, and received an answer anything but pleasant.

"Where's your companion, Boone?"

"D'you reckon I'm damned fool enough to starve when I can help it? I ate him up, of course!"

Boone Helm came from Kentucky. His life there had lacked color, having been made up of fights, drinking, and attacks upon the colored girls of the community. His first brush with the law was ordinary—the judge of the circuit court ordered his arrest, and Boone rode his horse into the courtroom and demanded what the hell they wanted of him. A companion, Littlebury Shoot, more of a cautious soul, managed to smooth the matter over, and later promised to go West with Boone.

Shoot, however, changed his mind and when the moment came to depart, he refused to go. Boone treated him in characteristic fashion. He put one massive arm around Shoot's neck and with the other thrust a Bowie knife into his heart. Boone Helm believed that other people should keep their promises.

Littlebury Shoot's brother, considerably irritated by the killing, organized a number of men who packed a rope with them. Boone Helm fled. Eventually they overtook him, though much to their disappointment representatives of the law, who had joined the pursuit, claimed him. The law took him back to Monroe County for trial. Boone was convicted of murder, but because his actions raised doubts concerning his sanity, the authorities committed him to an insane asylum—where he did not linger too long, just long enough to gain the confidence of his guards.

Boone sought sanctuary in the West, where justice was more lax. He killed several other men without punishment. This was chiefly because of his skill in evading authority; several of the law officers sent after him never returned. Others, however, made things so hot for Boone that he drifted, for the good of his neck, north into the lawless camps of Idaho, and later into Montana. In Idaho he turned organizer and ventured to band a group of Snake Indians into a raiding party with the aim of stealing horses from the peaceful Walla Wallas. A partner of Boone's foiled the plot by warning the chief of the Walla Wallas.

Boone made furious threats, and headed eastward into the mountains over which, five hundred miles away, lay Camp Floyd. He traveled with five companions, cut-throats like himself, and without apparent fear plunged into the high passes where snow of winter lay twenty and thirty feet deep and the thermometer, even by day, seldom registered less than ten or twenty below. All wild game had retreated to the lowlands. The party carried few supplies.

Boone Helm was the sole survivor. In gold-mushroomed Florence, Idaho, Boone established headquarters. The second or third day there he came into violent contact with Dutch Fred, chief of the settlement's rougher element. Bystanders interfered and disarmed the men. Calmly, Boone looked at his opponent, then grinned.

"I reckon I've been a mite hasty," he said apologetically. "An' if you gents will gimme back my gun, I'll be on my way. I'm plumb sorry, Dutch—"

"Wall, if you take it that way, I reckon I'm sorry, too!" Dutch Fred remarked, reaching into his pocket for his pipe.

He was in act of lighting it when one of the bystanders handed Boone his gun. Still smiling, Boone walked up to Fred, pushed the muzzle to his chest, muttered an oath, and pulled the trigger.

This was a bit too much, even for the tough citizens of Florence, and some of the more solid element decided that Boone must stand trial for murder. Things began to look black indeed; quite possibly Boone might have swung had not a brother, Tex Helm, appeared at this moment with a well-filled poke which thinned out as he made secret visits to star witnesses of the killing. When the day of trial dawned, not a single witness came to testify against Boone. The court released him promptly, in the manner of one who holds a rattlesnake by the tail.

Boone and Tex cried in their liquor at the Last Chance saloon. They downed several quarts, swore eternal fealty to each other, declared blood would forever be thicker than water, and Boone promised Tex that he would return to the states, currently involved in civil war, and join the southern army.

Army life was furthest from Boone's intentions, however, as he said farewell to his brother and rode away on a cayuse provided by his brother. Over the mountains Alder Gulch, richest and wildest gold camp on the face of the earth, boomed furiously and here should be rich pickings for a man who used his head. Boone drifted into Virginia City, currently run by Henry Plummer. Boone met up with Plummer, and thereafter he lived upon the fat of the land.

He began by lopping off a few heads and wringing a few necks, just for practice, and presently he advanced to the post of chief gunman of the band. Robbery and road-agenting were underhand work, but his acts of violence also took place in the open; by day Boone Helm swaggered along the streets of Virginia City, guns swinging on his hips, his progress a bit unsteady from drink. His name became a by-word of unsavory import.

"Boone's coming!" rang out, and the streets cleared of the more timid, while the rougher men moved warily away.

But the day of reckoning came. The power of Henry Plummer broke, and Vigilante groups took him into custody from which there was no appeal. Boone Helm, scoffing at the word that the Vigilantes were up in arms, stood in front of the Virginia Hotel one day. He had just had a couple of drinks and now he dried his whiskers with a red sleeve on his forearm.

"Vigilantes!" he boasted. "I can lick the whole passel of 'em—"

But he calmed down when three men surrounded him and three gun muzzles poked into his sides and back. "Shut up, Helm, and come quietly with us!" someone ordered. Helm burst out laughing. He went, nevertheless, his face a little ashy. In a dark room he faced the judges of the Vigilantes.

"If I'd only 'a' had a show, you would have had a gay time taking me—" he blustered.

"Wall, Helm, you're took now. Don't forget that!"

Someone pushed Boone down on a bench, from which he stared defiantly at his captors. The judges shifted uneasily. They knew Boone as one of the Plummer gang, as red a killer as had drifted into the Alder Gulch gold mines, yet they hesitated to take human life. They were not in this cleanup merely for blood. They were agents of law and order. It might be better to banish him, they were thinking, as one of the judges said, "We've proof that you belong to Plummer's gang. You're guilty of road-agenting and murder. What have you got to say to these charges?"

"Wall, it's this way!" Boone Helm returned, making the fatal mistake of his career, "I'm innocent—innocent as a babe unborn. I never killed anyone and I never robbed or defrauded a man!" Then he added, sealing his doom, for these men, of all the rough men who thronged Alder Gulch, held more or less devoutly to religious principles, "I swear it on the Bible!"

Someone handed him a Bible; clasping it in his hands, unwashed for a week, Boone Helm repeated, "I swear it on the Bible!" A Vigilante leaped forward, tore the book from him, and retreated, rubbing the covers as if to wipe away something filthy.

Boone Helm stared around him and knew he was lost. And so, though his cheeks were grayer, he spat casually on the floor when another prisoner, Jack Gallagher, was brought in and began to plead. Boone said to him, "Don't make a fool of yourself, Jack. There's no sense in being scared to die!"

With five of his partners in crime, he was lined up. One by one Boone Helm watched them, gurgling as each dropped, "There goes another one to hell!"

Presently only Jack Gallagher remained. Gallagher screamed, "Forked lightning will strike every strangling —— —— —— of you!" and then someone kicked the box out from under his feet.

"One more in hell," Boone Helm said, and added, "Kick away, my man! My turn is next!"

Then he shouted, "Every man for his principles! Hurrah for Jeff Davis!" and his rope twanged harshly.

X. Beidler, who had no liking for Boone, officiated as adjuster of the ropes and later took the bodies out for burial. Boone was the last whom he rolled into his grave. He hesitated a moment, chewing on his quid solemnly. Then he spat into the opening in the ground, groped for his penknife, and remarked, "Pard, I feel fer you. Yep, I'm feelin' fer your left ear!"

He made the amputation and rolled Boone Helm into his grave.

CYNTHIA

She was "the cause of more personal collisions and estrangements than any other woman in the Rocky Mountains"—to quote the words of a writer of the period. She seemed to have had beauty of a kind, intelligence of a sort, and the High Border remembers her because she was probably the most consummate bitch ever to stalk the mining country during the boom days of the latter '50's and '60's.

Cynthia married young, obscurely; but presently her husband died and left her penniless.

After a joust with honest toil as a chambermaid in a hotel in Lewistown, Idaho, the girl learned quickly. She came into prominence when she threw her lot with one Bill Mayfield, whose presence in the gold diggings of Lewistown was not approved. He was a thief and not a particularly high-class one at that, and his companions, including Cherokee Bob, were of the same sort. He had money and a certain air. Cynthia marked him for her own the moment he flashed a poke of gold.

Mayfield made a proposition to Cynthia, and presently the two headed for Florence, in the heart of the gold country, where pickings were great. Cherokee Bob trailed along, much to Mayfield's disgust. Cynthia's admiring glances at Bob, who flashed a heavier poke than Mayfield, troubled him. But he felt reasonably certain of Cynthia's affections, and confident that if ever a showdown came, Cynthia would choose him.

Things did not go smoothly. Cynthia began to giggle too much when Bob brought her trinkets, and her eyes sparkled too much when he displayed his well-filled poke, which increased each night that he went forth on black-jacking expeditions. At last Mayfield rebelled. He burst in on Cynthia and Bob, sitting on a couch in an informal manner, and laid his hand on the gun in his holster. The two men had the following conversation:

"Bob, you know me!"

"Yes, and Bill, you know me!"

"And now, Bob, the question is, are we goin' to make all-fired fools of ourselves?" Mayfield said.

"Just as yuh say, Bill. I'm al'ys ready fer anythin' that turns up!" Cherokee Bob replied.

The conversation became more intellectual. Mayfield

said, "Now looky, Bob, if Cynthia loves you more than me, take her. I don't want her. But if she thinks most of me, there ain't no man livin' ought to come a'tween us. I call that right squar'!"

"Wall, I think a heap of Cynthia, an' she's got no strings on her. She ain't married to you," Cherokee Bob said, whereupon Mayfield turned to Cynthia and asked the fatal question, not in the least fearing that she would leave him.

"Choose for yoreself, woman!"

Cynthia's answer was devastating. "Well, William darling, Robert is settled in business here and doing very well. Don't you think he's better able to take care of me than you are?"

Mayfield cried a little, according to reports, and threatened and swore, but Cynthia remained adamant. Then Mayfield retired in good grace, and told Bob he could have the woman as well as everything that Mayfield had given her. But gallantly and in the best manner of a great gentleman, Cherokee Bob insisted upon paying for such properties as Cynthia's now ex-partner had lovingly showered upon her. Mayfield drifted, and Cherokee Bob went into business in a big way, by informing the proprietor of the settlement's most prosperous hurdy-gurdy that he now had a partner. The proprietor, observing that the finger on the trigger of the gun in Bob's hand was none too steady, acceded at once and placed a new sign before his place of business: "WELCOME! Under new management."

The settlement of Florence, like most gold-boom settlements, was virtually run by desperadoes. But gradually the situation changed, men tired of having their pockets picked again and again, and the desperadoes began to die under mysterious circumstances, being found in dark al-

leys and deserted diggings with large quantities of lead in
their carcasses. It was lawlessness fighting lawlessness, with
the difference that the killers of the second part were
the forerunners of civilization, establishing that civilization by the most primitive and effective means. One by one
Bob's friends left him, until at last he found himself
alone in a hostile settlement with a single companion, one
Willoughby.

New Year's Day came and the more civilized element of
Florence prepared a grand ball, elegant beyond anything
the settlement had ever seen. Cynthia said, "Robert, I
want to go." And Cherokee Bob arranged for an escort,
since he himself could not leave his gambling tables on
this, the biggest night of the year. The escort happened
to be Willoughby, and his entrance into the hall with the
settlement's most prominent scarlet lady created a sensation—such a sensation, in fact, that the feminine element
gathered its skirts and prepared to leave.

The managers of the affair conferred and took their
courage in their hands to inform Willoughby that he and
Cynthia must depart. They obeyed, and Cynthia cried on
Cherokee's chest that night, while he swore vengeance.

A few days later Cherokee Bob and Willoughby swaggered down the street, heeled with pistols and bowie
knives and inspired by red-eye. They held a conference
and decided that a certain Williams, more familiarly
known as Jakey, had been responsible for Cynthia's hu-
miliation. Therefore he must die. They ferreted out Jakey
and gave chase.

Jakey ran like a rabbit, and both Bob and Willoughby
grinned. They pursued their victim from cabin to cabin,
presently cornered him, and prepared for the polishing-off

process. But Jakey appeared suddenly with a shotgun, the surrounding building poured forth indignant citizens like a swarm of bees, and Cherokee Bob and Willoughby were forced to retreat.

Willoughby emptied his guns and turned to run, with Jakey in pursuit. He stumbled and fell, and threw his hands before his face.

"For God's sake, don't shoot!" he pleaded.

Jakey was an atheist, so the plea had little effect. Cherokee, meanwhile, encountered difficulties of his own. They picked him up, still alive, and hauled him into a saloon where they laid him on the counter in state, a whiskey bottle at head and feet.

"Tell my brother," he said, becoming oratorical the instant before he died, "that I've got my men, and now I'm goin' on a long hunt!"

Cynthia, wringing her hands and bemoaning her fate, was accorded a measure of gallantry in that the citizens of Florence offered her a guard of dishonor as far as several miles beyond the settlement. She sought out her old flame, Bill Mayfield, at once and he took her to his bosom just as if nothing had happened. There ensued an idyllic life of license, with Mayfield, inspired, rapidly becoming a prominent gambler of the gold fields. He did not, however, to his regret, remain self-effacing and modest as every successful gambler should. In a quarrel, when a knight of the green cloth of great experience might have backed down, he drew his gun and fixed it on the chest of a man named Evans.

"I'm not heeled!" said Evans, without blinking an eyelash. "But if I were—"

"Next time I see you, pack a gun!" Mayfield suggested,

and for some reason not in keeping with his temperament he sheathed his gun.

The next day Mayfield, taking the air with Cynthia, came to a muddy hollow in the street, across which a plank had been laid. Always gallant, Mayfield preceded Cynthia, testing the strength of the temporary bridge. It was his great misfortune that at this particular moment Evans should be in a cabin along which the forward end of the plank lay. Evans dragged a double-barreled shotgun from the wall, poked it out towards Bill Mayfield, and pulled the trigger.

Cynthia, wailing, dragged Mayfield from the mire, wiped him off, and sent him to the local undertaking emporium—first taking care to extract his wallet and strip him of diamond ring and stickpin.

She did not remain long in single misery, but soon attached herself to a slick-fingered gent, Fresno Ed, whose skill with what he called the "cyards" was nothing short of phenomenal—and, it followed, lucrative. Thereafter Cynthia passed out of High Border Country history.

5. Red Men Fallen

RIVER BOAT

WHERE the Continental Divide of the United States and the Canadian-American boundaries cross there rises a ridge white with snow most of the year, for it lies at an altitude exceeded only by the taller peaks of the High Border mountains. This is Triple Divide, sloping up to the frosty heights of Triple Divide Peak where a raindrop, falling on the precise point of the peak, is split into three parts, one of which slides down to the Gulf of Mexico, the other to the Pacific, the third to the Arctic. At no other place upon the face of the globe does a similar phenomenon occur.

The raindrop headed for the Gulf of Mexico dribbles across glaciers and rushes down steep streams and eventually ends up in the Milk River, so named not because, as prevaricating old-timers tell tourists, Indians upstream in the early days milked buffalo and allowed the milk to waste in the river, but because Lewis and Clark likened its waters, whitened by the clay banks between which the river ran, to milk. The Milk runs into the wild Miz-zou-rye and eventually down to the Gulf of Mexico—rather a lengthy journey. It is a trip longer than that undertaken by any other drop of water in the world, except perhaps

111

some dribble of moisture from the Andes following the Amazon into the Atlantic. It is a rough journey, for the Missouri was not idly called wild and the name Big Muddy by which it was often known also describes it adequately.

Yet upon this river, treacherous, wild, undisciplined, there existed for many years a flourishing steamboat trade, an era of romance that aided the progress of civilization and brought into the land saints and rascals, miners and wolfers, men of all walks of life following the star of western fortune. The waters of the Big Muddy were the color of coffee most of the year, yet they might have been red for all the murder and misery connected with them.

Fort Benton in north central Montana became headwaters for navigation, for here the Missouri shallowed and beyond were the great falls of the Missouri, an impassable barrier to the stern-wheel steamboats of the time. They were tall-stacked, ornate, these river boats—sons of the Mississippi, a bit soft for the wild Miz-zou-rye until their owners changed their design to allow for the treachery of a river a dozen times more erratic than the Father of Waters.

They churned and bucked and kicked, drove against snags, found themselves high and dry sometimes when the river fell swiftly—fourteen feet in one night, once— but they were riverworthy. Shallow-bottomed they had to be. So shallow-bottomed that story is woven around them.

"Y'know," said a captain, "I was plowing along in the dark, and of a sudden the river didn't sound right. So I stopped 'er and what d'you think? I was ten miles up a dry wash churning along in a heavy dew."

"I didn't tie up, come dark," said another captain, "but I kept the b'ilers full blast, bein' scared of redskins. When I figured I was safe, I tied up an' me and the crew turned in. Come morning, we found the old boat high an' dry— twenty miles up a dry branch canyon."

Steamboating began in the '50's, boomed in the '60's and '70's, and declined in the '80's when the white man's Medicine Road, making trail for the Iron Horse, pushed slender, gleaming rails westward to Puget Sound on the Pacific. But while it was in heyday, it really boomed. The mines of the Clearwater and Alder Gulch had opened, and boats headed for Fort Benton were crowded to the gunwales. St. Louis to Fort Benton—gamblers and miners, criminals and honest men, roughs and pansies, all headed for the country where gold was to be had for the picking. Most of them got there, only half or less ever returned.

A few remained, settled, brought civilization, and it is to these pioneers, rough, uncouth, dirty though they were, that the present generation of the states of Idaho, Montana, the Dakotas, and Wyoming owes a debt of gratitude.

At Fort Benton, named for the gentleman from Missouri of the middle 1800's, the steamboats tied up to discharge their cargoes of human hopes and whiskey. At Fort Benton there was a mud-walled and mud-roofed fort, remains of which were still standing in the first years of the 1940's. And at Fort Benton one Christmas Day they held a hilarious celebration, dimmed somewhat by a persistent rain that softened the clay and brought it dripping down from the ceiling into the tin cups of the revelers.

"Here's mud in your eye, pard! Drink 'er up!"

There were disasters to the steamboats. In 1861 the steamboat *Chippewa* stood off Poplar Creek, loaded with trade goods, thirty kegs of powder, and a considerable supply of whiskey. A deckhand, whom history has given one of the blackest eyes in all the annals of the High Border, sneaked below deck. He did a black, black deed —he tapped a keg. He gulped a swig. One swig led to another and presently the deckhand slumbered in bliss.

Unfortunately he had neglected to gutter his candle, taken below decks to light his evil deed. The candle presently burned down and toppled, fatefully, into a pool of whiskey. Flames ran along the floor, up into the trade goods and the powder. There was an explosion that roused the Indians twenty miles away, and presently the dust of the *Chippewa* settled on the river bank.

There was talk of hanging when the news reached Fort Benton, but since the deckhand had gone to a place beyond, the situation blew over.

Captain LeBarge, dean of the Missouri river-boat captains, said, "I could easily name a hundred points along the bank of that river where I have buried passengers or members of crews of my boats. . . . It will never be known and cannot now even be conjectured how many of these forgotten graves there are, but I can say with truth that there are enough to make the shores of the Missouri one continuous graveyard from its source to its mouth."

The *Nellie Peck,* later famed for its participation in a race to determine the speed record from Missouri to Fort Benton, lay anchored off a shifting bar in the river one day. A sudden thunderstorm, followed by a torrential downpour, broke the anchor cable and the *Nellie Peck* charged off downstream. With engines temporarily incapacitated because of repairs, she was out of hand. She struck a bar near the present settlement of Oswego, Montana, and promptly from the river bank there charged a war party of Sioux.

They were as welcome to the crew as smallpox. They boarded joyfully. They promptly took charge, locked the crew and passengers in the cabins, and held council to determine what manner of death was most appropriate— burning, flaying, or setting the palefaces out on the prairie without food or clothes.

And now another storm, vicious as the one which had set the boat adrift, struck. Some of the redskins expressed fear, thinking that their Great Spirit was dissatisfied that they had taken command of the white man's fire canoe. More hardened members of the party scoffed, and presently the timid ones, shamed, forced a show of bravery.

Not for long. The tall smokestacks of the *Nellie Peck* offered a perfect target for the lightning which flickered over the prairie, and soon a bolt crashed down that really frightened the Indians. One of the *Nellie Peck's* funnels glowed red, and the more courageous Sioux, convinced that the fears of others were valid, followed them overboard. They did not return. The *Nellie Peck's* crew repaired the engines and the journey continued.

It was the *Nellie Peck,* racing the *Far West,* that established the river record from St. Louis to Fort Benton—17 days and 20 hours.

The boilers of the river boats burned wood, and to supply this wood a new occupation, fraught with danger and hardship, sprang up along shore—that of woodcutter. At intervals in the cottonwood breaks, certain men who feared neither the devil nor, what was worse than the devil, the Blackfeet, established woodyards which became as pleasant as a rattlesnake's den; for the redskins when they found themselves pining for light amusement, raided the yards with intentions of lifting a few scalps. It took a hardened man to hold a woodyard. A certain Bill Saylor, for instance.

Bill, cutting wood industriously one day, looked up to behold several redskins. Bill ran for the river. The opposite bank was far away and Bill paused to slip off his pants. Casually ducking bullets and arrows, he swam ahead; he had almost crossed when several other Indians appeared from the brush. Bill was in the unpleasant predicament of being—in a colloquialism that has come down to the present day—"Up the crick without a paddle!"

A bit of great, good luck overtook Bill. A party of hunters appeared at his jumping-off place, and the redskins fled, taking Bill's pants with them. Bill paddled back. The rescue party pulled him out on the bank and he stood there, dripping and screaming at the vanished redskins.

"——" he said, in good frontier dialect.

"Why, Bill!" remonstrated a rescuer, "Ain't you glad to see us? Ain't you goin' to thank us inste'd of yellin' after them pesky redskins?"

"Why didn't you stop them ——?" Bill screamed. "They took my pants. I had two dollars in the pocket of them pants!"

Shifting of the river overnight sometimes inundated woodyards as well as settlements, or left them hundreds of yards from the water entirely. Water cutting under banks did other curious things, also, as when a certain party constructed an elaborate casket for one of their number. They buried him where they figured he should rest, considering his life—high on the banks of the wild Mizzou-rye. But water eating at the clay slopes undermined the burial place, and by autumn the casket had slipped down to the river to lodge on a sand bar.

"Wall, there she was!" said one river man to another. "We pried the lid off an' looked inside. The corpse was plumb peaceable-lookin'. The boys left the lid off, figurin' the party needed air, mebby—"

"What'd you do about the casket?"

"Wall, we aimed to bury it, but somehow we jest never got around to it an' the next freshet took it off down the river. . . ."

Steamboating experienced a boom, though of lesser force, on tributaries of the Missouri and other streams. West of the Rocky Mountains on the Kootenai River which descends from Canada, the *Annerly,* the *Ruth, Rustler, J. D. Farrel,* plied back and forth across the High Border line. On the Milk River, an enterprising group constructed the *Enahboah—Surprise—*for the purpose of shipping bones downstream. The boat proved a surprise indeed; it listed badly on the placid Milk, and on the Missouri it went wild. The floating bone-coffin ended beneath muddy waters, to the great grief of financial backers and the delight of redskins.

Charlie Carson, nephew of the famous Kit Carson, staked his horses and those of his party one evening in April, 1865, in the first act of what is probably the bitterest tragedy of the wild Miz-zou-rye in her steamboat days.

During the night the animals disappeared and it was assumed that the Blackfeet had stolen them. Later, near Fort Benton, Carson and several of his men went on a drunken spree, during which they encountered a small party of the Blood clan of the Blackfeet. Carson and the boys acted; they lifted a few scalps with the ease of long experience, though they knew that these Indians could not be the actual thieves.

Several Bloods managed to escape and flee south. They encountered a larger group of Bloods and went into conference, the upshot of which was a decision that white scalps, any white scalps, must be taken in return.

Where the Marias and Missouri Rivers meet the steamboat *Cutter* lay one day, discharging supplies which, it was hoped, would aid in the construction at this point of a future metropolis, to be known as Ophir. Here glaciers in ages past have denuded the country, and it was necessary to cut timber for cabins several miles upstream where the cottonwood trees grew thickly in breaks. Men and wagons set out for logs one morning in May. The timber-cutters dropped their rifles into the wagon beds while they passed the jugs around.

"Red devils!"

Someone set up the shout. The men dropped their jugs and attempted to corral their wagons for a stand. But they were outnumbered, and one by one they were killed off. The Bloods swarmed into the wagon corral and lifted scalps with wild abandon, and that night in the Blood encampment there was much rejoicing.

Somewhere the original horse thieves grinned to themselves, while Charlie Carson and his boys also enjoyed themselves with no concern for what took place on this

May day. It was a case of innocent bystanders of both sides getting the punishment.

In July of 1867 the steamboat *Trover* ran aground at a point many miles downstream from Benton, with force enough to break her back. The *Ida Stockade* took on the *Trover's* freight and passengers and later returned to salvage her machinery.

The *Ida Stockade's* crew was a motley lot, including two Negro boys in their middle teens whose ability to sidestep work and snooze when they had a task set before them was the despair of the rest of the men. These two, sent below decks on the *Trover,* promptly went to sleep, and stayed down during all the roar and confusion of lifting out engines. Nor did they awaken when the *Ida Stockade* steamed off.

They stirred some hours later, and were grievously sorrowful when they discovered that they had been left. Their sorrow increased when redskins appeared. The pair plunged into the river and swam to the opposite shore, hiding until dead of night in the thickets. Then they set out, for some reason, downstream—Fort Benton was up the river and much closer than any settlement below —and there followed a journey which ranks with the greatest in the desperate journeys of the High Border.

The Missouri is a winding river, and the boys decided they could make better time by short-cutting the curves. This did save distance, but it also prevented their discovery by such steamboats as happened to be traveling the river at that period of the year. There was constant fear of Blackfeet, of grizzly bears, and of the thousand dangers of the border land. The boys lived on bark and flower

blossoms, with an occasional frog, cricket, snake, or lizard
for Sunday dinner—anything but palatable fare, but nevertheless nourishing enough to keep them alive.

One of the boys, attempting to cross a creek which
flowed into the river, slipped on rocks and stunned himself, and before his companion could scramble to the rescue, drowned. The survivor pushed on, his eyesight almost gone because mosquitoes had bitten his cheeks until
they puffed in hard folds upward. He stumbled on for days
and days until at last he could only feel his way. Then he
reeled through the thickets on the river bank and fell
to the sand, knowing he could go no farther.

He was blessed then by what pious settlers of a latter
generation called a miracle, though river men of the time
called it pure fool luck—the steamboat *Sunset* hove into
sight, and a deckhand sighted the unconscious boy.

He had traveled a distance, it has been estimated, of five
hundred miles.

The Medicine Road and the Iron Horse doomed the
river craft. Even while trade on the river still flourished,
conductors were calling, "Minot! Minot! Next stop Minot.
End of the line. Prepare to meet your God!" The twin
rails of steel forged along, out of North Dakota into
Montana, through Montana to the Pacific. Into the Tepee
land came the "Heap Big Butte Man"—James Jerome
Hill—whose Iron Horse, said the redskins, was "strong like
mountains." Steamboating did linger into the 1900's upon
Flathead Lake, largest body of fresh water west of the
Mississippi, but the Missouri trade concluded with the
coming of the Northern Pacific and Great Northern Railroads.

DENNIS DRISCOLL

It is said that, during the '60's, Secretary of War Stanton, irritated by an officer of the 27th Infantry who pleaded for transfer from his present post, snapped to his secretary, "Where is the worst place to send a regiment, next to hell?"

"To the Powder River country, sir!"

Powder River, "a mile wide and a foot deep," flows through some of the most desolate country in all the High Border, where desolation is the rule rather than the exception. A hard country, a hard river. "Powder river, let 'er buck!" yelled the soldiers of the 91st on the Argonne, fighting with a fierceness as desperate as the land from which their slogan came.

Danger and disaster bred hard men in the Powder River country—lesser heroes and greater, many in the field of arms, fewer in the field of intellect; brightest among those in the field of arms is an Irish sailor, Dennis Driscoll, Company K, 27th U. S. Infantry, who found himself in the hell of Powder River because his commanding officer had irritated his superior.

To protect a pioneer route from southern Wyoming into the gold fields of Montana, the government in the early '60's constructed a chain of forts along the southern boundary of the territory which in 1889 became known officially as the state of Montana. Of these forts, not the least were Forts C. F. Smith and Phil Kearney—named respectively after a fallen Civil War general and an officer who became prominent in campaigns against the redskins. Fort C. F. Smith, in particular, had a spotted history, resisting constant attack by the Crows and Sioux who were beginning to resent bitterly the advance of the paleface.

If the paleface had kept himself to the eroded country along the Powder River, the canyons and cut-banks and curious, wind-carved rocks known as hoodoos, and the badlands, the Indians might possibly have expressed little resentment. But the paleface usurped the best land—the country where the buffalo roamed—and left the redskin nothing. And the redskins, turning bitterly upon the "Great White Father," fought with all the fury at their command, and all the cruelty inherent in their nature.

In this era men of the freighters, when surrounded by redskins, would first corral their wagons and then take the string from their left boots, loop it at both ends, and lay it conveniently at hand—the small loop for the trigger of their rifle, the large loop to slip over their boot. It did not pay to be taken alive by the red devils, who knew too many exquisite means of torture—methods refined by features learned from the mountain men who had earlier ranged this country.

At Fort Phil Kearney there was trouble, trouble, and more trouble. A wood train fell afoul of the redskins, and to punish the raiders the commander of the fort sent Captain William T. Fetterman, with orders to show no mercy. But the redskins trapped Fetterman's command and reversed the orders; they slaughtered Fetterman's men, down to the last soldier—an incident known historically as Fetterman's Massacre.

The bodies of the captain and his men lay stripped in the hot sun, and to bring them in the commander of the fort dispatched a number of soldiers commanded by Captain Ten Eyck, among whom was Dennis Driscoll, the ex-sailor. It is apparent that the commander considered the bodies of the dead more important than the lives of the living. Discontent broke out in Ten Eyck's command, but they sallied forth from the fort when ordered, broke through ranks of hostile Indians outnumbering them forty to one, and returned with the bodies. The supreme daring of Ten Eyck and his soldiers and their recklessness in the face of fire awed the redskins; the whites were able to come back without casualties.

Young Dennis Driscoll had received his first taste of the desperate infighting which characterized this warfare. It stood him in good stead later when he was a member of an expedition returning from Fort C. F. Smith to Fort Kearney. The trip to Smith had been uneventful, and every man kept his fingers crossed in hopes of an equally peaceful return. Halfway between the forts, Sioux warriors attacked, fifty to one. They charged from ambush and rode down on the wagon train, yelping in a manner calculated to scare any but the most hardened prairie campaigners.

The stock stampeded and left the soldiers with only a few riding animals—and, for the ex-sailor, Dennis Driscoll, a single, decrepit mule blind in one eye. The men promptly shot their horses to provide a barricade, upturned the wagons, and prepared for a desperate siege. The outcome, assuming the siege endured, could never be in doubt, they saw with grim clarity, since they lacked adequate water supply and ammunition. So they said their prayers—some of them—and held a council.

"Volunteers to reach Fort Smith!" the commander called. Silence followed. Nobody stepped forward. It was too desperate—one man against two or three thousand. No one could possibly get through.

But help must be sent for, and again the commander called. Again no response.

"I reckon I'm the best man here, considerin' my experience," remarked Canadian Jack Henshaw. "And I won't try it! I'll take my chances here with the buzzards. It's a chance at life here against sure death, tryin' to get through—"

The third time the commander called, Dennis Driscoll stepped forward. "I'll try!" he said, white-cheeked, and he crowded back against his half-blind mule which he had not had the heart to slaughter.

Canadian Jack unhooked his guns, swearing in a shout, and fastened them around Dennis Driscoll's middle. He took off his field glasses and slung them around the ex-sailor's neck. And Dennis Driscoll, riding his mule, raced out into the open, wondering why he had ever been fool enough in the first place to leave the sea for this section of western hell.

Miraculously, he eluded all guards the redskins had posted and penetrated beyond the Indian lines. Riding by night, he covered a distance great enough to convince him that he was safe. At dawn he halted on a ridge and looked back with his field glasses. The prairie lay clear, except for a small herd of buffalo that seemed to be following him. Driscoll breathed more easily, but again stared at the herd, which drifted with unusual speed—and his heart pounded when he identified each shaggy animal as an Indian rider concealed beneath a buffalo robe.

Driscoll drove his spurs into the one-eyed mule and raced away. The redskins threw off their disguises and lashed their ponies. The mule struggled valiantly, but the night's ride had been too exhausting and presently he slowed down. The Indians charged up like a herd of bloody centaurs, and Dennis Driscoll, realizing fate was against him, slipped from the saddle of his animal and did what he had hesitated to do before—he shot the mule. Then he dropped behind the protection of its body, got Canadian Jack's guns ready, and waited.

Only a few seconds. The redskins rode close to him, confident that there could be no escape for Driscoll. This confidence doomed several of them, for Driscoll was an excellent shot and Canadian Jack's guns were of the best. Driscoll dropped one warrior after another until the party drew off warily. There was a brief conference, followed by another attack. Again the guns spoke with deadly accuracy. Again the attackers withdrew.

As they huddled in council, Driscoll knew he had awed them. They debated and Driscoll began to hope for their voluntary withdrawal—an honor sometimes accorded to a man whom they recognized as brave. But they made no move to retreat; they spread out, surrounding Driscoll, and set fire to the thick, dry prairie grass. Flames ten feet high and of such heat that no human being could withstand them came leaping forward.

There was a slight dampness to some stretches of the grass, causing smoke thick as fog to billow up. Dennis Driscoll took his chance, left the protection of the dead mule, and slipped along wrapped in smoke that almost choked him to death. By trailing over freshly burned ground he evaded both the flames and the redskins, and escaped. Presently he stumbled into a creek some hundreds of yards away, downwind; Driscoll plunged into this, breaking the ice along the edges. He swam upstream and, where brush grew thickly down to the water, waded ashore among the willows. For the second time he had eluded the red devils.

Night had come. Driscoll, half dead from alternate cold and heat, boots almost burned from his feet, cheeks and fingers numbed from the cold, groped his way forward. Clouds blotted out the sky so that he could not take his direction from the North Star. He wandered on, forced to move because the frost bit into his bones, sure of but one thing—he must keep his guns dry and loaded.

In the grayness of dawn he stumbled into what he first thought was a group of sharp-tipped rocks. Then a dog barked shrilly, another and another, and he recognized his surroundings—the outskirts of an Indian encampment!

Wearily he turned and fled, hoping that the alarm of the dogs would go unnoticed, but before he had managed to cover more than a quarter of a mile, a dozen bucks appeared in pursuit. They were on foot. Dennis broke into a dog trot, forcing his body into action only with the utmost effort. Speed was not in him; the bucks, fresh from rest, raced on like a wolf pack. No chance to outrun them, Dennis knew, so he dropped behind an upthrust of rock and drew his pistols.

He had wavered with desperate fatigue but in this moment a calm took possession of him and his aim did not veer. He laid the sights of his guns dead-center on the pursuers, with such accuracy that, at each shot, one of them tumbled into the grass. Dennis killed them all. Then he dragged himself to his feet, groaning, and reeled onward. He turned his look, hazy now, to the rear, fearing that more of the village might be in pursuit, but the prairie was clear. He stumbled ahead towards where he hoped Fort C. F. Smith was.

He kept on the move all day. At dusk he dragged himself atop a rim of hills, from which he peered eagerly hoping to see the flag above the dark, sprawled mass of adobe that was the fort. But it was evening and the flag had been taken down; the fort, wherever it was, had become only a dark shadow lost in the blackness of the prairie, invisible beyond a few hundred yards. As far as concerned Dennis now, it might as well lie a million miles away.

For the first time he gave up. He reeled down the hillside, stumbled through scrub timber, and, because he hated the thought of simply lying down to die, forced himself onward. Death seemed only a matter of hours, anyway.

"And I always figured I'd die on the ocean—drowned—" Dennis began to laugh, a little out of his head.

His feet dropped into a worn rut and followed it instinctively—wheel tracks to the fort. But he never reached the fort conscious; he stumbled, his knees cracked the grass, and he lay very still. In the early dawn men headed for the fort found him and carried him in; from his ravings they learned of the siege down Kearney way. The commander sent out a relief expedition at once.

They were just in time, for heat and thirst and nervous terror had taken toll of the besieged, who raised a feeble cheer when the relief detachment appeared and then dropped off to sleep, the first they had had since the beginning of the siege.

Dennis Driscoll had got his message through, in a feat

as daring as any in the sagas of bravery of any nation. No
metal plaque or statue or story in a schoolboy's book has
ever honored him, but throughout the Indian campaigns
on the northern plains his name stood high in the esteem
of fighting men—a bright and shining star of courage, soon
forgotten after the subjugation of the red men.

As for Dennis himself, he was out of his head for one
week and lingered in a hospital bed for six. His last days,
in the 1900's, were spent in an Old Soldiers' home in
California.

How They Conquered the Blackfeet

On an early morning in January, 1870, the Blackfeet
bowed at last to the white man. Proud, cruel, honorable,
the wolves of the plains, the "pesky" Blackfeet had gradually ceased their wide-ranging activities which had taken
them beyond the Continental Divide and into Wyoming;
they had drawn further and further into the north central
section of Montana, which was their ancestral home. They
took little part in the widespread Indian wars of the '70's,
for in 1855 they had made a treaty with the white man
which their chiefs intended to honor. As for the white
man . . .

This January morning the thermometer stood at minus
forty.

Major Eugene Baker and his men rode through the
snow towards the encampment, in the scant timber along
the Marias River of northern Montana, of Mountain
Chief, leader of the ruling Piegan branch of the Blackfeet. Two men out of every three in Mountain Chief's
camp were flat on their backs from the plague, many of

the women dead, the children in misery. This was the formidable enemy Baker rode to face.

The Marias country lay north of the treaty line of 1855, in territory reserved for the Blackfeet. But white men had invaded it, first to look for gold, later to settle, at last to complain to the government that the Blackfeet refused to surrender their lands, which according to the theory of the period were the property of the government and not of the Indians. The cattlemen especially expressed violent and profane anger at the raids of the redskins upon their herds. They had thought up one simple solution to this problem of the Blackfeet—one shared by Major Baker.

Exterminate them.

A few miles from the Marias and Mountain Chief's camp the command halted. The major, though it was against rules, took a drink. He had been drinking for hours—so steadily that his men were concerned. A lieutenant asked, "What are your orders, sir? There should be no resistance. Shall we arrest Mountain Chief—"

"Ex-stherminate 'em! Don't leave one damned redskin alive!" The major reeled, almost fell from his saddle.

The lieutenant, cheeks already frostbitten, turned still whiter. "They are ill and in trouble, sir!" he protested. "We have no orders to be so merciless. If we simply arrest Mountain Chief—"

"Dammit, you young whippersnapper, didn't you hear me? Don't leave one of 'em alive!"

The lieutenant rode stiffly away, and the major took another drink. He wavered so badly that he was forced to cling to the flat horn of the saddle. His head drooped to one side. "Ride on an' massacre 'em, the red devils! We'll finish this Blackfeet outfit once and for all!"

Mountain Chief's camp lay down in a wooded hollow along the shallow Marias. The few men and women still sound of body or mind wandered here and there, caring without enthusiasm for the ill. Steam and smoke drifted through the cracks of the lodges. The sky sifted a grayness down that seemed part of the camp itself. Here was misery incarnate. But it was simple suffering compared with what took place when the cavalry charged over the rim of the river's bank and began a slaughter revolting to most of the soldiers, but which they dared not evade under their commander's order.

"Kill 'em! Every —— red hide of 'em!" Major Baker yelled.

There could be no resistance, of course. Soldiers broke into lodge after lodge, knifed or shot the dead and dying. People who were able to move ran out into the timber; some of them escaped, others went down with a saber through the back. Then the troops set fire to the lodges, and within a few hours the last of the great Blackfeet encampments was in flames and the power of the Blackfeet was broken.

General Phil Sheridan, in command of the campaigns of that period against the western Indians, was called upon by the War Department to explain Major Baker's actions, which roused widespread condemnation in the East though little criticism among the whites of the West. The only good Indian was a dead Indian. And there were those in the War Department who held the same view; after some small fuss, the influence of these officials led to the exoneration of Major Baker without official investigation.

Thus were the Blackfeet crushed. But there were other tribes—the Sioux, Crows, Cheyennes, much more troublesome to the whites, and during this period of High Border history they made their last stand against the white man —battling for the country which had been theirs from time immemorial, dying on their hunting grounds. They fought with the steadfast determination of free men who would not be shackled, and for several years they baffled the flower of the United States Army. But all things end; and the Indian wars ended, not through a crushing defeat for the redskins, but, curiously enough, through a battle the white men lost—Custer's defeat on the Little Big Horn, in the south central section of the state of Montana.

They Died Hard

On the afternoon of June 25, 1876, Lieutenant Colonel George A. Custer and his command of 203 men rode down into the valley of the Little Big Horn, to attack the village of the Sioux spiritual leader, Tatonka-e-Yotanka, better known as Sitting Bull. "Hold your horses in, boys, there are plenty of them down there for us all!" called the commander. It was generally believed that they would engage, at the most, 900 or 1000 warriors; instead, they presently found themselves trapped in a hornet's nest of between 4000 and 5000 redskinned fighting men, armed with the latest weapons and spiritually strengthened by the fact that they were defending their country.

Measured by the red man's time, they fought "as long as it takes a white man to eat his dinner"; when it was over history had written two things: the saga of a modern Thermopylae, and the last chapter in the resistance of

the red man to the onrush of the palefaces. Tatonka-e-
Yotanka, brooding in his lodge that fatal afternoon, realized for the first time that the white wave sweeping in
from the East was too great to be stopped by the small
number of bronze warriors. Here was the Indians' Water-
loo, although, ironically, it was a complete military victory for them. Thereafter, except for rare outbursts, the
Indians allowed themselves to be placed upon reservations;
they never again attempted a mass fight.

The dashing George A. Custer, whose yellow, curly
hair hung to his shoulders and was the envy of every white
girl and red scalp-hunter, had made a record for himself
during the Civil War by his devil-may-care bravery and
ruthless conduct. Subsequently, in the Indian country west
of the Mississippi, he had added to this reputation, and
when in 1876 Tatonka-e-Yotanka concentrated his Sioux
people and their Cheyenne allies in the Powder River
country for a last stand against the encroachment of the
whites, he was selected to assist in crushing it.

The Sioux, Cossacks of the northern plains, were a
thorn in the side of the government. Sherman had advised
Grant, "We must proceed with vindicative earnestness
against them, even to their extermination—men, women
and children. Nothing less will reach the root of the
case."

Under the command of Alfred H. Terry, and at the
head of the famous 7th Regiment of U. S. Cavalry, Custer
moved westward from Fort Abraham Lincoln, in Dakota;
at the same time, General George Crook marched from the
South into the upper Powder River and General John
Gibbon moved forward from Fort Ellis, Montana. On
June 21, 1876 the Terry and Gibbon columns united at

the junction of the Big Horn and Yellowstone Rivers and the commanders held a conference aboard the river steamer, *Far West.*

Out on the river bank the soldiers jested and laughed, but the Crow scouts were silent. There had been a late spring snowstorm—omen of disaster. In the cabin of the Far West, Terry and Gibbon listened to reports of an Indian encampment along the Little Big Horn, and plotted their campaign. Custer listened quietly, fingering his sword, a handsome weapon taken in a hand-to-hand encounter with a Confederate officer during the Rebellion. On the hilt was the motto: *No me sin razon: no me envaines sin honora*—Draw me not without reason: sheathe me not without honor. When, at the conclusion of the council, he was ordered to proceed with his 7th to the attack before the Sioux discovered the presence of the soldiers and fled, his fingers clenched the sword.

Thunderheads, which had gathered during the conference, now burst loose with flame, and the commanders returned to their camps through a torrential downpour.

On June 22 Custer's regiment headed up the Rosebud River along an Indian trail. That evening orders went out to silence the bugles and smother the fires. Thereafter all commands were given by signs. On the twenty-fourth the horsemen passed a number of places where the Indians had held Sun Dances, at one of which they discovered the scalp of a white man tied to a willow twig. They rode most of the night of the twenty-fourth and at break of the next day halted in a deep ravine near the divide between the Rosebud and Little Big Horn Rivers. Horses were unsaddled. Custer intended remaining here until night, but information brought him by his quartermaster indicated that the Sioux had discovered his presence.

Knowing that further attempts at concealment were useless, Custer marched his command atop the divide and gave orders to rest while he, his guide, orderly, and chief trumpeter, went on in the direction of the Indian camp. In his two hours' absence he saw enough to convince him that here, indeed, was a village worthy of his attention, though of its true extent he remained ignorant. Upon his return to camp he ordered the sounding of an officers' call.

If he had any premonitions of disaster, they were not apparent. He was as enthusiastic as a fox-hunter. To him, this campaign was in the nature of a sport. Ever since the Civil War he had collected Indian victories as a hunter collects trophies, and as a hunter gains glory in the killing, so had he gained his own—until, indeed, contemporaries spoke of him as "The Glory Hunter."

He was a product of his times—of an age when a man with red skin was fair target for any marksman's lead. Here beyond the Mississippi was a vast territory of virgin riches to be had for the taking, and the fact that it had belonged from time immemorial to someone else was of small moment. The raucous laughter of a mob greeted the statement of Curly, the Crow, at his hanging when he sought to justify Sitting Bull's call to arms: "The soil you see is not ordinary soil—it is the dust of the blood, the flesh, and the bones of our ancestors. You will have to dig down to find Nature's earth, for the upper portion is Indian, my blood and my dead. I do not want to give it up."

The red defender fought with all the craft and skill

he had, and his theory was that a man was dead only when nothing remained in his body to support life. In his language there was no such word as "maimed." Either an enemy lived, or he died. And if the enemy died slowly, so much the better. Untouched by any higher plane of civilization, he was concerned with the flesh, not the spirit. War was war.

Custer, in council, made known his decision to attack at once. He divided his command into three detachments, under Major Marcus A. Reno, under Captain F. W. Benteen, and a third, consisting of a battalion of five troops, under his personal leadership. Of his plan of battle he was sure, for it had won him a decisive victory at Washita on the southern plains, where he had forever broken the power of the Kiowas: a triple-point thrust from three directions, furious enough to scatter the red devils to Kingdom Come in the twinkling of an eye.

But here along the shallow, winding course of the Little Big Horn was no insignificant encampment to be thus casually destroyed; here was one of the greatest gatherings of Indians ever seen on the plains. A bend in the valley cut from Custer's sight the greater part of the village and kept him in ignorance of the odds until too late. The Little Big Horn flows northwesterly between low, barren bluffs, rain-washed and windswept and as desolate as some neck of hell—an appropriate setting. Benteen's orders were to advance to the left and scatter any Indians encountered, then line for the encampment; Reno's battalion was to cross the river and charge the village from its upper end while Custer himself attacked along the lower boundary.

It was noon, June 25.

With Terry's column was a special correspondent for the *Bismarck Tribune,* Mark Kellogg. His last dispatch reads: "We leave the Rosebud tomorrow and by the time this reaches you we will have met and fought the red devils, with what result remains to be seen. I go with Custer and will be at the death."

He was.

Custer and his cavalry rode swiftly down the river, about a mile away from it, with a ridge of high bluffs cutting off sight of the village that lay in the valley. They went by fours. Presently they came across a vacated Indian camp where one lodge remained, in which was a dead Indian. The men joked. Custer signaled them to continue. Then Indians appeared—dusty shapes that slunk away at sight of the horsemen. The soldiers cheered. Another Washita was imminent.

It was now two o'clock in the afternoon.

Custer ordered a full gallop down the creek bed they were following. Presently the valley of the Little Big Horn spread out before them, and all of a sudden the whole of Tatonka-e-Yotanka's village leaped into view, only a half mile away—a vast encampment two miles wide and four miles long. A cheer went up, and some of the horses, scenting Indians, became unmanageable. It was then that Custer said, "Hold your horses in, boys, there are plenty of them down there for us all!"

But a look of apprehension swept his face. He motioned to Captain Tom Custer, his brother, and said something to him. Tom Custer at once dispatched a messenger, Daniel A. Kanipe, to Captain Benteen. "Tell him to come quick—a big Indian camp."

The charge rushed on. They made a formidable and

colorful array, this 7th Regiment—bright guidons in the breeze, trumpeters at their head, horses bellying low against the ground with the force of the onslaught, hat-brims bent up by the rush of air. In the van was Custer, dressed in buckskin and long riding boots, a Remington breech-loader in his hand and two ivory-handled revolvers in his belt. His sword was not on him, nor did his men, armed like their leader, carry swords or sabers, which were considered useless in actual Indian fighting. Near Custer rode an old comrade of the Army of the Potomac, Myles W. Keogh, astride his charger Comache. The correspondent Kellogg trailed in the cloud of dust in the rear.

From his lodge opening, Tatonka-e-Yotanka watched them come. Chief Gall of the Uncapapa Sioux and Crazy Horse of the Ogallala looked at their leader. All around was confusion, for at the first news of the invaders, Sitting Bull had given orders to break camp.

"They ride so bravely!" said Tatonka-e-Yotanka.

He motioned, and Gall and Crazy Horse left him. Custer's men were pulling up now to form a line of battle. Slowly, Tatonka-e-Yotanka lifted a handful of dust and let it dribble between his fingers. He meant to keep some of it, just a little of it, in his palm, but when he turned back into his lodge, it had escaped, though he had clutched at it hard.

Custer's charge halted a short distance from the camp. The yellow-haired leader dismounted two troops, Keogh's and that of First Lieutenant James Calhoun, and placed them in position atop a knoll. A third troop, famous as the gray-horse riders, deployed as skirmishers, while the remaining companies spread out to form a line of battle about 1500 yards in length. Roughly, they held the crest of an uplift of that extent. No man knows what the orders were.

While Crazy Horse engaged one wing, using guerrilla tactics, Chief Gall massed his horsemen in a gulch below the knoll where Keogh huddled. He was in no hurry. He made sure that everything was in readiness before he charged.

"As long as it takes a white man to eat his dinner" he and his red horde swept along the rise, by sheer force of numbers overwhelming all opposition. Down in his lodge, Sitting Bull stared at his palm and wondered why the dust had run out when he had held it so tightly.

It was now three o'clock.

Reno, meanwhile, was in difficulty. Besieged by an overwhelming force, he was compelled to retreat to the bluffs along the river, where presently he was joined by Benteen's command and the messenger from Custer. The situation became so desperate that the soldiers dismounted and huddled in the sod. In shallow trenches, swiftly dug, many of them soon lay dead, while others were dying and a large number were wounded. Between the hours of three and three-thirty, most of the attackers withdrew, but shortly after they returned, to charge with renewed vigor until dark.

All during that night the Sioux camp was a bedlam of celebration, for what grim reason the men on the bluffs did not know until later. At dawn the Indians renewed their attack, but towards evening they rode down into the valley and made preparations to move the village. The next morning not a redskin was in sight. Shortly after noon General Gibbon's command appeared, and the men learned then, for the first time, of the fate of Custer's command.

In the terminology of the West two words stand out in dramatic contrast: battle—the wholesale slaughter of Indians by whites; massacre—the wholesale killing of whites by Indians. On Custer's field of massacre there was but one bit of life: the horse Comache, down with a dozen wounds. All else was lifeless. Custer's men lay where they had fallen, stripped and mutilated by the squaws. And the hot sun of two days had been as merciless as the women. Identification was, for the most part, impossible.

Except in the case of two men. One of them was Mark Kellogg, the correspondent, whose body for some reason was not touched. The other was Custer himself. His yellow hair matted around his head, he lay where he had fallen, one bullet in his left side and another in his temple. No man knows why vengeance was not wreaked upon the flesh of this most merciless of Indian hunters; some say it was due to the respect in which he was held by certain of the Sioux chiefs, others, thinking of the bullet in his temple, attribute it to the peculiar reverence of the Indian for a suicide.

No matter: he was dead, and his command was dead.

"From Where The Sun Now Stands—"

No story of the bloody days of the Indian resistance during the '70's is complete without mention of Joseph, noblest of the redskin leaders, who in 1877 made his bid for peace and rest, and failed. Thunder-Coming-over-the-Mountain was the name his father gave him—in the tongue

of his tribe, the Nez Perces, Hin-mah-too-yah-lah-kekt—
but the white men dubbed him Chief Joseph.

A man of peace in the beginning, he had war forced
upon him and the day came when he was sad-and-weary-
thunder indeed, spat upon, scorned, vilified.

In the Valley of the Wallowa—the winding waters—
in Oregon, Joseph lived, as his father and grandfather and
the grandfather's father and so on for generations had
lived. But the land was good; so the white men came along
and hovered eagerly on the rim of Joseph's land. The
father of Joseph died, saying, "You must stop your ears
whenever you are asked to sign a treaty selling your home.
A few years more and the white man will be all around
you. They have their eyes on your land. My son, never
forget my dying words. This country holds your father's
body. Never sell the bones of your father and your
mother!"

Never sell the bones of your father and your mother.
But the white men were too many, too powerful, and
though Joseph answered his father's dying plea with the
statement that a man who would not love his father's grave
was worse than a wild beast, he saw the future with a
grim clarity. The white men were wolves. Their government sent word that the Nez Perces under Joseph must
be concentrated upon a reservation far from the graves
of the fathers. There followed general rebellion and certain murders laid to the Indians but of suspicious origin.
Though Joseph, brooding over his fire, scorned the land
as the Old Woman's Country, his advisers called for a retreat to Canada, where reservations in the West were still
unknown. Weary at the start from the pain of parting
from his valley of the winding waters, Joseph gathered

his band, his horses, cattle, warriors, women and children, blind and sick, and headed eastward over the rugged Bitterroot Mountains into Montana, whence lay a clear trail north along the Tobacco Route to Canada.

The word went out that Joseph fled, that he had headed for Canada to seek freedom, that he wished to hurt no man. So the Great White Father sent an army to round him up and concentrate him on the rocky patch of land set aside as a reservation for his people.

O. O. Howard, a one-armed general, commanded the white soldiers. Howard was an average officer of the period; brave enough, tough enough, and imbued with the dead-Indian theory. Joseph's band numbered only a couple of hundred; Howard's well-equipped soldiers were overwhelmingly superior, seasoned campaigners. Yet Chief Joseph, encumbered by baggage, cattle, horses, women, children, led those soldiers over a trail 1800 miles long; he surrendered at last only when he hesitated a single day this side of safety.

Deep in the Bitterroots the soldiers overtook Joseph but, strong as they were, they were nevertheless outmaneuvered by Joseph in a manner that earned him the sobriquet of Red Napoleon. Coming down out of the Bitterroots, he found his band confronted by a stockaded fort manned by soldiers from the recently established Fort Missoula and a group of settlers. The settlers promptly collected their baggage and guns and went home, and resistance fizzled out—for all time the fort became known as Fort Fizzle.

Joseph rested at the southern end of the Tobacco trail which would take him directly north into Canada. The trail ran through barren country, and the white soldiers possessed a terrible weapon impossible to evade where there were no trees for protection—a Gatling gun. Joseph, seamed of face now, worn, weary, went into council, and after listening to his advisers decided to cross the jagged, ten-thousand-foot passes of the Continental Divide, through the present Yellowstone National Park, and join the Sioux under Sitting Bull who then were fighting to the death over on the plains—in the "country of the buffalo."

Leisurely then, Joseph's band moved along under the rim of the Rockies, seeking passes that might lead eastward. There were white settlements here, but Joseph showed no hatred to the paleface; his warriors traded at their stores, paid for goods, chatted and smoked good-naturedly with the merchants. No rumor came of the one-armed pursuer, Howard, and Joseph concluded that he had left the white soldiers back in the depths of the mountains. But General John Gibbon and his troops from Sun River had come up hard on the heels of the Nez Perces; one dawn they attacked the unguarded camp of Joseph, shot the women as they fled dazed from the lodges to huddle in terror knee-deep in a creek, whooped when a warrior fell, and spat tobacco juice into the eyes of the dying. They were upon the point of lifting scalps when Joseph rallied his men. Before the day had gone, he defeated the white men decisively.

This was the battle of the Big Hole. Two newspaper clippings of the time tell the story: "Exhibiting strategy which put to shame the best efforts of the palefaces, Chief Joseph led his 'Sioux' warriors to a glorious victory over General Gibbon's forces at the battle of the Big Hole." Free speech or not, that editor lost subscribers. The second clipping: "Howling hosts of horribly painted Indians nearly massacred General Gibbon's United States forces

at the battle of the Big Hole. . . ." This particular editor
gained subscriptions, for whites of the period did not
care to know that a redskin could also be brave. . . .

Joseph rallied his shattered band, the wounded warriors, the aged, the infirm, women, children, his horses
and his belongings, and headed into the mountains. His
own wife had fallen victim to a white man's bullet as she
huddled in the creek too frightened to move. Joseph
brooded the more, for he had loved her. His alertness of
mind, his grasp of strategy, felt none of the force of his
sorrow, and through the ensuing days, as his shattered band
with the one-armed Howard hard on their heels—for Howard had come down out of the Bitterroots—staggered on,
Joseph guided them skillfully. Across the high passes,
through the jagged mountains, and down upon the plains.

Then came word of what had happened a year ago—
the Custer battle and the end of the ambitions of Sitting
Bull. Sitting Bull had fled to Canada and Joseph decided
to follow him. He pointed north across hundreds of miles
of prairie and raced against death, disease, starvation,
against the one-armed general's dusty warriors, and though
he did not know it until too late, against the white man's
new telegraph system.

The telegraph defeated him. Word of Joseph's move-
ments flashed by wire to General Nelson A. Miles at Fort
Keogh, and the telegraph enabled Miles to short-cut
against Joseph's line of retreat. At that, Joseph almost
reached Canada and safety. At a position where sight of the
border is possible from mountains which rise abruptly
from the prairie—the Bearpaws—he went into camp for a
few days. Perhaps he felt that he had already crossed the
line. But Miles and Howard overtook him; and Chief

Joseph fought until he saw that it was no good, no good at all. Then, wearily, under the faint sun of a gray winter's day, he went up a hill towards Miles and Howard, drawing around his shoulders his gray woolen shawl with the five bullet holes through it.

"I am tired of fighting!" he said. "Our chiefs are killed. The old men are all dead. . . . It is cold and we have no blankets. The little children are freezing to death. My people, some of them have run away and have no blankets and no food. No one knows where they are, perhaps freezing to death. I want to have time to look for my children and see how many of them I can find. Maybe I shall find them among the dead. . . . Hear me, my white chiefs, my heart is sick and sad. From where the sun now stands—"

Joseph lifted his hand to the faint sun and then drew a blanket around his head. Under the bullet wound on his forehead his eyes burned like dim flames; his right hand twitched from the bullet in his wrist. He turned away, seeing perhaps his years of exile, his death in a land far from his winding waters and the graves of his ancestors. Bitterly, perhaps, he cursed himself that he had not been able to bring his people to safety.

"From where the sun now stands, I fight no more against the white man!"

In one hundred and ten days he had traveled eighteen hundred miles. He had outwitted the best brains and experience of the army.

But he failed.

6. The Last Struggle

AGENCY

THE redskins were vanquished. Only once in a while did they attempt to throw off the yoke of the white man. Towards the end of the last century some of the Dakota Indians, while dancing wildly a folk dance forbidden by the white men, fell victim to the mass hallucination that they were "messiahs" born to deliver all their people from bondage. The white man promptly put an end to this foolishness, in the course of which the great spiritual leader Sitting Bull, who after the Custer battle had fled to Canada but who had returned again, was killed. Sitting Bull, shrewdest of the High Border Indians, died hating the palefaces and desolate because he could do nothing about it.

The Indians, guarded by the United States Army, were concentrated upon reservations throughout the region; they were supervised by agents and sub-agents. Many and strange are the tales of reservation Indians—"tame" Indians.

Mrs. Johnnie Thorn, from Massachusetts, was the wife of a young Westerner acting as a sub-agent on a High Border reservation. Mrs. Johnnie found herself in a country appallingly new to her—on as bleak a section of the prairie as existed, in a small settlement consisting of dirty houses and dirty wigwams which, because of the eternal wind which whipped up eternal dust, remained eternally dingy and impossible to keep clean for more than an hour at a time.

Mrs. Johnnie refused to be daunted; she scrubbed and swept, hung lace curtains in the twin-roomed shack which out here on the prairie achieved importance as the sub-agent's "mansion," and otherwise did her best to prove a good wife to Johnnie Thorn.

Mrs. Johnnie was sometimes sorely tried. There was the day of the beef issue. . . .

The Federal government's policy, since the buffalo had vanished, was to issue live beef to the tribesmen. Sub-agent Johnnie arranged it, corralling the cattle near the settlement, and sending out word to wandering tribes-men that there was to be an issue of beef. In from the prairie trooped the tame Indians "civilized" by the United States. They set up their patched, worn wigwams and ranged through the village, pilfering such articles as they could lay grimy hands on.

This was Mrs. Johnnie's first sight of the red children of the Great White Father. She found herself a little shocked. Where were the noble red riders of the plains, the wildly beautiful women, all the romantic grandeur she had always associated with the red men? These were a beaten people; stoop-shouldered warriors rotten from disease and malnutrition, girls with pockmarked faces and greasy hair, crying children, many of them hacked al-ready by tuberculosis while the eyes of others gleamed dully horrible with trachoma.

"The Great White Father's children!" Johnnie said

when the vanguard appeared. "That's what he called them when he forced them off their land. Now that he's subdued them they're bastards as far as he's concerned."

Mrs. Johnnie felt sorry for them. Sorry for the "braves" who invaded her kitchen, who cringed when she threatened them with a broom. Mrs. Johnnie had to air out the room after they left. Sorry for the half-blind papooses and the young girls with their pockmarked faces and the young men who coughed incessantly.

"Why do you give them the steers alive?" she asked Johnnie, and he replied that it was the government's policy. When she asked to watch, he said that she would not like it, but he yielded when she insisted.

The cattle had been shifting uneasily in the corral. Outside on the open prairie Indian riders lined up, and when the corral gates swung and the herd charged forth, they darted in with bows and arrows and clubs. Few owned guns; most relied on their primitive weapons. But these were not the buffalo hunters of a decade before; they had lost the buffalo hunter's skill and they had to feather a beef full of arrows before it would fall. Even then they must beat it over the head before it died.

Squaws and children darted in with knives. Mrs. Johnnie sickened a little at the barbaric joy in faces she had found so pitiful and haunting. Women and children ripped meat from animals still alive, tore out entrails, drank blood, cut up the still-quivering heart and chewed it. Laden with meat, they trooped back to their wigwams, and all that afternoon and night there came the sounds of gluttonous feasting. Next morning Mrs. Johnnie forced herself to go among the celebrants. She fled abruptly. Men, women, and children lay stretched on the ground, their bellies distended from a beef saturnalia as unrestrained as any alcoholic debauch. And, what was worse from Mrs. Johnnie's point of view, the dead cattle on the prairie were only half- or quarter-eaten—nor were the redskins able, that day or the next, to care for the rest which might have provided food for a month. By the time they recovered the prairie heat had begun to decompose the meat. With the beef issue ended, the tribe scattered over the prairie again, to starve until next time.

Then there was the case of St. Peter. St. Peter lived around the agency and, since he could handle horses, he was named official coachman for Mrs. Johnnie. He drove for her on her round of social duties in a manner that was flawless—as far as handling the reins of the team went.

Society in the community was simple. It consisted of a Methodist sewing circle that met once a week. One meeting, however, was to be a state occasion and the women prepared for it days ahead of time. "With St. Peter driving you, and the old buckboard washed and shined, I guess you'll make a better show than any of the women at the next meeting!" Johnnie had said when he learned that this meeting was to be held in the three-room home of Mrs. Josh Jones, better known as Mrs. Snakeoil Jones, leader of the local set.

Mrs. Johnnie was pleased, for few of the women had a carriage of any sort, much less a driver. She hoped Mrs. Jones would be favorably impressed, since Mrs. Johnnie was the newest addition to the community and as such still an object of suspicion to the wives who had lived there several years.

The day arrived and St. Peter appeared. His equipage
was fine—the buckboard had been washed, and there were
only a few burrs in the manes and tails of the horses. St.
Peter himself wore a plug hat, with a feather lifting from
its crown. Only one false note spoiled the picture.

From the neck down St. Peter was stark naked.

Mrs. Johnnie blushed as St. Peter handed her into the
buckboard, but St. Peter himself was wholly at ease. It
was summer, the sun blazed down, and he had taken
efficient steps to make himself comfortable. Mrs. Johnnie
writhed in the trap: What to do! What would Mrs. Snakeoil Jones say (more, what would she *think*)? The best solution, Mrs. Johnnie concluded after some frenzied thinking, was to dismiss St. Peter and walk to the sewing circle.
So she leaned forward and tapped St. Peter on the shoulder.

She had not reckoned upon the fact that St. Peter
spoke little English and understood less. Johnnie had
given him instructions in his own tongue, and no matter
what Mrs. Johnnie said, St. Peter would carry them out.
In fairness to Johnnie, it must be added that he had had
no idea of St. Peter's informality of dress.

"Uh, God damn hot day!" St. Peter said, as Mrs. Johnnie tapped his broad back with her daintily gloved hand.
"Me getum you there! Getum you there damn quick!"

He lashed the cayuses ahead to Mrs. Snakeoil's mansion
and there he handed Mrs. Johnnie out of the buckboard
with a flourish as smart as that of any Vanderbilt footman.
Very stiff and straight, with her cheeks very red, Mrs.
Johnnie marched up to the door and went in to join the
circle.

"At least," she thought, "I—I won't have to ride back. I can walk."

But she reckoned without St. Peter, whose orders were to wait for Mrs. Johnnie. All through the afternoon the equipage and the naked coachman could be seen through the window. Towards the end of the meeting St. Peter became impatient. He paced around the buckboard, came up to the house occasionally to peer in the window, and was clearly relieved when Mrs. Johnnie, unable to delay her departure any longer, appeared.

"You have 'um God damn good time?" he inquired serenely. When Mrs. Johnnie nodded Yes, he delivered himself of a philosophic utterance, "White squaws, uh! Talk 'um too much. No have 'um papoose enough."

Mary Ronan, at sixteen, married Peter Ronan who was old enough to be her father and went to live with him upon the Jocko Indian Reservation which lay in the mountains of the western High Border Country. The Jocko, named after Jacques Finley, a fur trader, was inhabited chiefly by the peaceful Flatheads, and the chiefs and squaws and bucks took young Mary to their greasy bosoms in an enthusiastic manner which she endured since it was politically important that she should humor her husband's red children. Mani-kena, a chieftain of inferior rank, adopted her into the tribe, and at solemn council gave her his name—which, as it turned out, was a heroic sacrifice, for presently young Mary, noticing that the other redskins paid no attention to him though previously he had been a man of standing in the tribe, learned that he was now as good as dead.

"I have no name!" he said, squatting on his hams in

the sunlight, and sucking at his pipe. "I have given it willingly to the young girl with the long golden hair. No name—therefore I am the same as one dead!"

A disconcerting situation indeed. Mary contritely asked if there were any way in which he might secure a re-birth. She consulted her husband, who in turn consulted superior chiefs. A great deal of talking went on; before long Peter Ronan, in company with some of the chiefs, went down into the country of the Kootenai redskins where there had been a recent death. Here for the sum of several horses he purchased the name of the deceased, and a few days later in solemn council the Flatheads gave the erstwhile Mani-kena the name Ronan had bought for him, useless as far as concerned the deceased. Mani-kena, rechristened, came alive again, and once more the tribe gave him the attention they could not give to a dead man.

"It is well to be alive!" he said, in the sun again, with his pipe in his mouth. "It is very well! But I did not mind being of the dead. I was satisfied that my name should be that of the little girl with the long golden hair!"

One day Mary washed her long, golden hair; to let it dry, she was sitting on the porch of the agent's cabin. Several grim chiefs appeared. One of them snatched Mary's hair and stretched it out, while the others watched. Hand over hand the chief unfolded the braids, as if he were climbing a rope. Mary, too paralyzed with fright even to scream, had visions of her scalp fluttering on a stick in the camp circle. But before the fatal action took place, the chief released his grip and turned away.

"Sixteen hands long is the hair of the white squaw!" he said. "I win the wager!"

The white man, having successfully corralled the red-skins, decided during the '80's and '90's that the offspring of his wards should become educated in the paleface manner. Since the roving habits of the parents were scarcely helpful to education, the government established boarding schools, at which white teachers by hook or crook or force were supposed to teach the rudiments of reading, writing, and arithmetic.

By this time the buffalo had vanished from the scene and the red men existed on supplies issued by the agents. These supplies were invariably of the poorest, for a long distance lay between Washington, D. C., and the High Border Country, and numerous hands itched for graft—indeed, the Indian racket was the foundation of some fortunes. When the red wards ultimately received their dole, it consisted of what was left over. They endured stoically, because they were in opposition to something too powerful for them. They ate or starved, according to the supply of the moment, and cursed the white man with every invective known to them. But they were docile for they had no choice.

When word spread among them that their children must attend the white man's school, consternation broke loose. They did not understand—except that the white man was all evil. Many of them boldly refused to send their offspring to the boarding establishments. However, the white man spoke law, and each successive generation of red children found itself corralled by force into drafty, ill-lighted, and ill-heated buildings where the food, thanks to graft, was universally revolting and the instruction, which aimed at remaking the red children in the image of the white man, worse. Students fled from these schools, even in quite recent years, and the directors of some of them were forced to build high wire fences around them —prison fences; any student who attempted to escape and failed was flogged to within an inch of his life, or less.

Periodically the white man sent a wagon around to gather up the children who came of age for admission to the schools. There was great wailing within the lodges. The guardians of the wagon faced danger much of the time, for there were times when a red parent, desperately afraid of giving up his son or daughter, picked up his rifle and made things unpleasant. It was a matter of battle. The men who collected the children earned their money.

After the children had departed, the parents mourned for them as if they were dead. Sometimes they followed the children and camped near the school—to talk to their offspring as the youngsters gathered along the wire prison fences, or to pass food to them, though authorities forbade this.

Young Thunder Bull was one of the children taken from the lodges of his ancestors to learn the white man's mores, and mathematics. His parents gave him up sorrowfully and did not attempt to see him until some months later. Then they moved into the agency settlement, set up their lodges and fireside near the boarding school, and day after day huddled along the wire enclosure when the children were permitted to roam in the yard. Thunder Bull's mother slipped him a dried mess of pemmican, to the young redskin's great sorrow for when the supervisors discovered it, they took it away from him and beat him. They used a device resembling a cat-o'-nine-tails and when the last stroke was counted, Thunder Bull did not get up. Nor did he get up later, and eventually they sent his body back to his parents for burial. The officials in charge wrote in their report of the matter, simply: "Thunder Child. Aged ten. Died from gorging on pemmican."

Then there was White Calf, aged around ten or eleven, whose parents had not followed him but who, nevertheless, pressed his face against the wire and stared yearningly at the outside world—specifically at a cow grazing in an adjacent pasture. Thin and malnourished, White Calf found himself shaking with a passion for milk. And so he planned to secure it in a scientific manner—deliberately he wooed the cow and coaxed her to the fence. Eventually he succeeded in training her to stand still, pressed against the wire, while he hooked a teat through the netting and sucked his fill.

This he did so subtly that he managed to avoid the eagle eye of his supervisors. However, when he began to take on weight, they concluded that here was a phenomenon to be watched. They set a guard over White Calf, and presently surprised him at one of his impromptu lunches. They did not give him credit for cleverness; he took just as terrific a beating as the student who filched what there was in the garbage.

One Indian agent in the '80's found himself confronted with a problem of disappearing redskins. He was in charge of the Bannacks, along the Wyoming-Montana border, and while he did not particularly love his charges, superiors forced him to give an account of each person under his jurisdiction and he was justifiably perturbed when his charges began to vanish. Invariably those who disappeared were bucks and in time the agent learned that each of them had last been seen alone in a played-out mining region known as Bloody Dick Gulch where there were several ranches. The following spring the agent was climbing around an old mine shaft at the head of the gulch one day when he discovered all his charges, together, but in no condition to move about. They had been pitched into the shaft. The agent hastened to town, spread the news, and there were no further mysterious disappearances.

The explanation was simple enough, the agent found when he went into the matter. Some of the boys on one of the ranches were a little playful and, having no love for Bannacks, had decided upon a policy of extermination that at the same time gave them some small entertainment. Whenever they saw a Bannack brave riding alone they saddled and raced in pursuit. Flipping a noose around his neck, they would drag him off his cayuse and bump him along the ground for some distance—not so violently as to do away with him, and gently enough so that when they slacked up on the lariat, he would attempt a get-away. Thus the boys had their fun, as well as the satisfaction of knowing they were doing the white race an invaluable service. When the game was over, they pitched the remains into the mine at the head of Bloody Dick.

There was a considerable hue and cry raised, on the part of certain persons without a sense of humor, at this manifestation of playfulness. Someone demanded that a coroner's jury be called and that arrests be made. The coroner's jury found that the twenty-odd Bannacks had come to their deaths through their own carelessness in stumbling into the shaft, the sheriff permitted the prisoners to go free, and all declared themselves satisfied. Except the families of the deceased, and they really did not matter.

During the earlier years of the reservation system a certain Lord Jamison arrived from Scotland; he was interested in remains of redskin heroes and in buffalo hunting. Outfitted on such scale as to make the inhabitants gape, he moved along the later Wyoming-Montana border. One evening he came upon "Musselshell" Reed, a squaw man not averse to acquiring a few dollars by unethical means.

"Know of any Indian remains around here?" asked his lordship, and Reed, scenting more than ordinary curiosity, said that a Piegan burying ground lay near. He added that it was the Piegan custom to bury their dead in trees above the ground. His lordship wanted to know if the remains of any famous chiefs were to be found at the ground, explaining that he was a patron of the Edinburgh Museum and that he had been commissioned to secure, if possible, the mummy of a great redskin chief.

Reed took his lordship out to the burying ground next day and the museum patron, nose clenched by his right hand, for neither the crows, the insects, nor the weather had been able to care for the dead sufficiently to clear the atmosphere, inspected burial after burial. Presently Reed pointed out a withered body in somewhat better condition than the rest.

"Now this yere's a great chief!" he said, nudging the mummy. "Greatest in the country. He skelped thirty Crows an' a hundred Blackfeet—"

Lord Jamison bent over the mummy eagerly, but Reed restrained him.

"The Injuns are right touchy about him. They don't

want him moved. But I'll tell you what. My wife's a
squaw, an' I reckon I could fix it—fer mebby a hundred
an' fifty dollars!"

Jamison, finding the mummy in a condition to permit
removal, did not haggle over the price but left everything
in Reed's hands. He expressed, however, some wonder at
the peculiar position of the corpse's head.

" 'Twas the way they killed him in battle—" Reed explained, uneasily, and breathed more freely when his lordship accepted the explanation.

Reed put the money in his pocket and later he returned
to the burial ground where he sewed the corpse up in an
old buffalo hide. He then delivered it to his lordship—
without mentioning that the corpse was really that of his
father-in-law, who had been hanged for horse-stealing.

"Had a right hard time fixin' things with the tribe!"
he explained. "But I did it! Yes, sir, that's a big chief—"

Lord Jamison placed the mummy in a packing case and
supervised its shipment to the Edinburgh Museum where
for many years a popular attraction was the mummy of a
great North American Indian chief.

The story has a sequel. Reed's wife, who had been
away at the time of the affair, returned soon after and
became suspicious when she discovered her husband in
possession of such a large sum of loose money. Later she
discovered the absence of her father's body. Perhaps she
put two and two together; anyway, she went into mourning because of this desecration of the burial ground.

The Piegan custom of mourning was uncommon—the
bereaved simply chopped off a finger or two.

Now, Musselshell Reed's squaw was a good squaw, a
hard and faithful worker, and the loss of a finger or two

would impair her efficiency. Reed had not witnessed the
first amputation, but he caught the woman just as she
was about to go into mourning afresh. He took the ax
from her by force. A squaw minus two fingers—or even
three fingers, dependent upon the extent of her sorrow—
might be worse than no squaw at all, he decided; he
thereupon confessed, adding fervent promises of repent-
ance.

There followed a vast amount of wailing among the
other relatives, particularly in view of the unsavory life
the deceased had lived, and to silence the clan Musselshell
Reed was compelled to distribute what remained of the
mummy money. Peace was returned, the squaw desisted in
her mayhem, while Reed dwelt moodily upon what might
have been.

JOSEPHINE

In the parlance of the earlier High Border Country, a
"woman of convenience" was the Indian squaw a white
man took unto himself while he lived in the region. He
might have a family back in St. Louis or east of the
Mississippi, but out on the plains or in the mountains
he yearned for female companionship. Accordingly he
would buy a redskin squaw in the open market for a price
ranging from a few beads to several horses. The mountain
man sometimes had a squaw in every one of the tribes,
or at least in the tribes with whom he was friendly. River
men took brides from the tribes along the river. Even
army men hired squaws for the duration of their campaigns against the redskins. And, since generally the red
men got little but contempt from the whites, these women

of convenience were mistreated more often than not, sometimes with a fiendishness that is hard to believe.

On the upper Missouri there lived a man named Grinnell, who for two horses had purchased a woman from the Indians. He took her with him to the white settlement—not an unusual procedure, for the term "squaw man" as applied to a white living with an Indian had not yet become a term of contempt and white settlers thought nothing of such unions.

Grinnell treated his squaw with the utmost cruelty. Evidently a hard man in the first place, with little love for the redskins, now that he owned an Indian he expressed his dislike for the race by treating the woman in a manner which, even in this rough frontier settlement, roused indignation.

Her name was Josephine, and she seems to have been something of a beauty, and a good and faithful enough wife to Grinnell. In time, she bore him a son who one day, in the midst of a bitter blizzard, wandered forth and lost himself. Josephine rushed to the settlement, wailing, and at once a search party formed.

But then Grinnell appeared on the scene. He reached out his ham of a hand and grabbed Josephine's hair, dragging her head against him. He grinned at the search party. "That little black so-and-so!" he snarled. "I don't want him found. I ain't lettin' a man of you go out an' search for him. Understand me?"

Grinnell, big and powerful, commanded fear in the settlement. Some of the party backed down. But a buffalo hunter whose name has been lost to history defied Grinnell and went forth into the storm. He followed the winddrift and presently found the lad, half-frozen, under a cut-bank. The hunter carried him back to Grinnell's cabin and laid him on the bed. "I found 'im!" the hunter said to Grinnell, gloweringly watching him. "A while back you aimed to break the neck of any man who went after him. Wall—I'm waitin'—"

The hunter thrust his hand under his coat and pulled out his knife. Grinnell, fingers playing nervously with the slipknot in the leather thong he always wore around his neck, welshed. The buffalo hunter went out—walking backwards.

Spring came. One day a couple of men plowing sighted Josephine in flight down the road, Grinnell after her. They leaned on their plow and watched, not interfering because this was obviously none of their affair—just a family row. Grinnell seized Josephine by the hair, dragged her back and forth and slapped her face while Josephine fought back like a wildcat. They reeled together, went down into the dirt, wrestling so furiously that dust clouded up to conceal them. Then suddenly Grinnell stilled and Josephine lifted herself, staring in horror.

Grinnell lay dead. The sliding knot of the leather thong always around his neck had tangled in Josephine's hair, and her furious efforts to escape had tightened the noose. Grinnell strangled. The spectators dragged him back to town by the heels, his head thumping hard in the ruts of the roadway, and then turned Josephine over to the authorities. For murder.

They called a coroner's jury and held an inquest. That jury's report was succinct and clear: "Grinnell came to death through an act of Almighty God, by the hand of His agent, Josephine Grinnell."

7. Progress

Cowboy

MEN have been equal only three times since creation, they say along the High Border—in the Garden of Eden, in the Declaration of Independence, and in the cow country before fence. But there were times even in the cow country when a man's equality was incomplete. When a man was about to be hanged, for instance.

Towards the end of the last century a gentleman from one of the larger settlements of the High Border Country found himself in difficulty. He had cut another gentleman, not in a social way nor in the manner generally regarded as strictly honorable—he had pushed a knife into his victim's back. And now he was receiving attention from a hastily formed Vigilante group whose aim was entirely businesslike. They bound his hands behind him, balanced him on a packing box under a telegraph pole near the railroad station, and several members of the posse, who prided themselves upon their knot-tying ability, deftly fashioned a hangman's loop and dropped it over the bound man's head.

Vigilante justice had its way, and the victim danced briefly on thin and insubstantial air. The Vigilantes withdrew, and a local photographer, sensing a scoop, rushed up with his camera to take several views of the unfortunate gentleman. Whereupon he too retired, and for several days the body hung there, to the astonishment of travelers debarking from trains.

In time the photographer developed his plates and placed his photographs in the window of his establishment. Members of the posse gathered to inspect the pictures. There was a moment of complete horror, then a concerted rush into the establishment where the posse bought up all available pictures and in no uncertain manner ordered the photographer to destroy his negatives. He protested until they explained. If the pictures were allowed to circulate there would be a dark blot upon the efficiency of the Vigilantes.

The hangman's knot had been adjusted under the wrong ear.

The Vigilantes who hanged Flying Bill Cantwell, at about the same period and in another section of the High Border Country, did not worry about adjusting the knot. After catching Flying Bill for horse-stealing—the blackest crime of the frontier, save perhaps that of being a sheepherder in cow country—they simply tied his hands behind his back, looped a lariat around his neck, and knotted the loose end in a grindstone. Then they threw the grindstone into the Judith River, and Flying Bill flew after.

Justice in the cattle days—pseudo-justice or genuine justice, depending upon which side of the fence you rode —was apt to be sudden and sometimes unexpected. The High Border Country's most famous cowboy is a man whom the citizens of the United States later elected their president and about whom High Border stories are legion because he was a Dakota rancher—Theodore "Four-Eyes" Roosevelt. They say that Roosevelt, green from the East, dropped into the then settlement of Mingusville, later renamed Wibaux after a cattle king, and found himself housed in the loft of a saloon, the only respectable rooming establishment in town.

The lady Minnie and her husband Gus, after whom the settlement had been named, assured him that these were the best quarters in town, and added that they were sure he would not mind the frequent gunfights in the saloon below, bullets from which sometimes penetrated the ceiling, nor the fact that he would have to share his bed with another gentleman. Roosevelt assured them he did not mind, and climbed to rest.

His bed-partner turned out to be a tough-looking hombre who somberly kept silence and slept with his gun under his pillow. At midnight Roosevelt awoke, and saw several men with handkerchiefs around their noses and guns in their hands. They hauled his bed-partner out without ceremony and disappeared.

The next day, making inquiry, Roosevelt encountered blank stares and in one case a threat, "It ain't healthy to be stickin' yore nose into what ain't yore business, stranger. Kin yuh take thet hint?" Roosevelt could.

Roosevelt just missed a frontier gentleman, one socially known as Hell-roaring Jones. Mr. Jones, a habitual lounger around the railroad station, one day sighted a whiskey drummer whose head bore that sign of Eastern effeminacy which always annoyed Mr. Hell-roaring—a derby. Mr. Hell-roaring stirred himself, drew his gun, and took several potshots at the headgear in question, incidentally creasing the drummer's already neatly parted hair, though not fatally.

"Git back on that there train!" warned Hell-roaring. "We don't want that damn thing in town. Get outa the Dakotas—"

The drummer never again ventured into Hell-roaring Jones' territory.

Catfish Joe, from Grand Forks on the eastern edge of the High Border Country, emigrated from prison into the Roosevelt section. Catfish was a tolerably ill-natured individual whose specialty consisted of batting unsuspecting individuals over the head and then, by way of profit, inspecting for keeps the contents of their pockets. Catfish had a low forehead and very little imagination, and a skull whose capacity for punishment has become classic.

It was in the Medora country, just across the Montana-Dakota line, that our hero encountered a breed who did not respond in the usual way to Catfish's none-too-gentle massage of the back of his head with a gun butt. The breed arose in wrath, took a firm hold on a convenient rifle, and broke the stock over Catfish's skull. When Catfish dropped to the floor the breed stared both in awe at his own strength—for a rifle stock is difficult to shatter—and in horror at the fact that he had killed a white man. He fled into the unknown, and the Medora country never saw him again.

A few minutes later someone passed by the shack. There lay Catfish, stretched out. The passerby inspected him, spat casually, and opined that at last Catfish Joe had got his.

But just then Catfish roused, got to his feet, and rubbed his head. He cursed briefly. "That —— breed hit me! If

I ever get him I'll break his neck. The —— gave me a headache!"

Messrs. Catfish and Roosevelt never met, and in time Theodore Roosevelt went to the White House while Catfish Joe drifted westward into the mountains. There he got into his last trouble, for one night, waking at midnight with a consuming hunger, he ordered his partner to rouse himself and prepare a snack. When the partner drowsily refused, Catfish arose in anger and spoke in the manner to which he was accustomed.

"——" he said, and shot the man through the head.

That was the end of Catfish, for a posse tracked him down and a jury which did not like his looks sentenced him to hanging. Catfish Joe faded from the High Border without tears from anybody.

Catfish Joe, Hell-roaring Jones, Theodore Roosevelt, et al., were in the vernacular of the High Border "cowpokes," "rannies," "rannycavoos," "hombres," or in a more refined manner, simply "cowboys." For many years, roughly from the '70's to almost the end of the first decade of the present century, the prairie High Border was a cow country, lorded over for a long period by cattle barons whose kingdoms, ruled as ruthlessly as any dictatorship, comprised areas greater than many of the states east of the Mississippi River. Originally the cattle came from the South where after the Civil War and the breakup of feudal cow domains in Texas, longhorn cattle ran wild. Out on the High Border prairie there was sweetgrass and, especially up under the mountains and along the Missouri and in central Wyoming, shelter where cow critters might multiply.

And so from Texas came herds of pilgrim cattle to stock the ranges of the High Border Country. Bonanza ranching became the order of the day, and gold flowed on the prairies as in the '50's and '60's it had flowed from the gold mines of Alder Gulch and Idaho. Even mining men, who had lost their fortunes, took up ranching.

"Bunch grass is good; you can drive it to market when you can't move quartz!" the saying went, and up from Texas, along the Texas Trail, came streams of longhorn beef under the leadership of trail bosses, shoved along by trail men who had been sent north by a single order, "Keep your eye on the north star; drive straight ahead until you can wet your feet in the Yellowstone!"

The cowboy was a godless man, equal to his fellows because Mr. Colt's six-gun made him equal. He had a touch of morbidity, too, perhaps induced by the vastness of the plains and the mountains, for as he rode along in the dust of his trail herds, he sang morbid songs about the Great Divide and the Land Over Yonder and the Sweetgrass Country Where All Good Cowboys Go. He was optimistic in intimating that there was such a thing as a "good" cowboy—except in a purely technical sense.

> *There's a land that is warmer than this,*
> *Where they never have to shovel snow.*
> *Bob Ingersoll says it never did exist,*
> *But that's where good cowboys go!*

Robert Ingersoll was currently preaching that religion was futile and that any deity was powerless. He achieved considerable fame; even the cowboys of the western plains sang songs about him. Invariably he was mentioned in

the more sentimental ditties—but never in songs like this
one:

I'm an o'nery-eyed blister from the wild an' woolly west,
Where the rattlesnakes rattle an' the buzzards have nests,
Where the she-wolf hollers an' the cactus grows,
Where they don't give a damn if it rains or snows.

I'm seven-foot-five without standin' on a stool,
I'm a quarter-breed polecat an' three-quarters mule,
I've jaws like a bulldog an' I bawl like a bear. . . .

I've got hands like a goriller, I've got scales on my feet,
There's bristles on my jaws an' spurs on my teeth,
I'll wade the river and to hell with the boat. . . .
Yipee! I'm a wild she-wolf from Bitter Creek,
An' it's my night to howl!

"Mamma, do cowboys eat grass?" the small daughter of
an eastern tourist asked. When the mother replied, "No,
dear, they're part human!" the cowpoke in question looked
up and scowled. He was hawss-tradin', sometimes a lucrative but more often a devastating occupation, for the ail-
ments of horseflesh which may be concealed temporarily
are legion. This particular poke judged his animal by the
rule-of-thumb of the range: "One white foot—look him
over. Two—try him. Three—buy him. Four—no good."
This somewhat improbable verse was followed religiously
by the more superstitious of a tribe that had a fondness for
superstition.

The cow ranny in question was not, strictly speaking, a
cow ranny. He did deal in cattle, but his dealings were
of an underhand nature, consisting for the most part of

night raids upon the herds of the cattle barons. After a few minutes of work in blotting out the brands, he owned the cattle. Throughout the country they called him Rattlesnake Jake, and his reason for the horse trade was uncomplicated. He and a friend, Longhaired Owens, intended to ride into the settlement of Lewistown upon a Fourth-of-July spree and he wanted to make a handsome appearance.

He did not know that he was destined for immortality, that both he and Longhaired on into the '30's of the present century would by proxy ride into the streets of Lewistown each Fourth of July as part of an Independence Day pageant. When he and Longhaired did enter Lewistown the day after the horse trade, he was decked out in his best, hilariously happy—he yearned for a little noise. He pulled his gun and began to shoot. When someone interfered Rattlesnake Jake took another swig from his bottle, sulked, then threatened to kill the first —— who should interfere.

"Let's make this here a smoky town!" Longhaired suggested. A "smoky" town was one properly smoked, with burnt gunpowder. Whereupon Rattlesnake and Longhaired rode the length of Lewistown's main street, emptying their guns good-humoredly into the business establishments along the way and demoralizing the citizenry.

There was some grumbling but no decisive action until the boys began to ride down the street again, when various individuals got down their Winchesters with no jesting purpose in mind. Presently both Longhaired Owens and Rattlesnake Jake lay dead—right in front of the tent of an itinerant photographer, who rushed out to snap them jubilantly. It was his first bit of luck since he had drifted into the Judith Basin cow country of which Lewistown was the center.

There was much to-do about the deaths of these two knights of the saddle, for they were known to be members of an organized gang of cattle thieves that had a hangout in the cottonwood breaks along the upper Missouri River. These entrepreneurs of rustling had grown so powerful and shown such cleverness at thieving among cattle and horse herds, that the cattle barons of the country decided upon desperate action. The country was inhabited pretty exclusively by cattle barons, who did not particularly care to be reminded of former days when they had not been quite so strong—and when sometimes three and four calves, bearing their brand, trailed each of their cows while smaller outfits impotently claimed ownership of at least two of the calves. This claim the larger outfits, though all the range world knew that there never was a cow capable of bearing more than twins, squelched by pointing out that the barons' brand lay on the calves—definite proof of ownership. The little outfits went bankrupt, one by one, while the big outfits got bigger, until only barons were left—barons who cried out in wrath when organized rustlers began to make forays from the breaks of the Missouri.

Twice in the cattle history of the High Border Country has organized rustling threatened the barons: first in 1884, in the Judith Basin of Montana after the death of Longhaired Owens and Rattlesnake Jake; again, in Johnson county, Wyoming. In Montana the barons organized and sent a young army to wipe out the rustlers for once and all. The Wyoming affair was considerably prolonged and much more involved.

The location of the Montana hideout became known to the cowmen through the devious means of greasing a few palms with gold, for the rustlers were as human as the barons. One dawn the raiders crept up to the cabin and tent in which the rustlers slept their sleep. Presently a rustler, troubled by an early-morning thirst, appeared and headed for the river. A raider's nervous trigger-finger jiggled, and there began a battle which lasted all that day and ended in the rout and destruction of all but six of the outlaws.

These six, however, did not escape scot-free; they were found later hanging in a neat row under a cottonwood limb. There were other hangings, not strictly legitimate—under circumstances which are still discussed with the suspicion that certain barons seized this opportunity to rid themselves of personal enemies.

Be that as it may, the barons broke the power of the rustlers and never again did men outside the pseudo-law organize in any force. They suddenly ceased to exist. One musical gentleman, entertaining his executors with a doleful rendition of *Nearer My God to Thee* and *Rock of Ages,* almost won his freedom but someone remembered that the singer had visited his shack weeks previously, helped himself to the larder, and departed without washing the dishes—a cardinal sin of the cow country.

"Stretch his —— neck! Won't wash his dirty dishes after him, won't he?"

Thereafter the Montana cow bonanza boomed for a few years until the terrific setback of the winter of 1886-87, when hundreds of thousands of head of soft "pilgrims" from the South, unable to endure the cold of the northern plains, froze to death. When the spell of exceptionally bitter weather—sixty and sixty-five below zero—ended and the warm Chinook winds from the Southwest broke winter's grip and cleared the snow away, cattle lay as thickly over the prairie as the slaughtered buffalo of a decade before. Bonanza ranchers, counting their losses, realized they were broke. Those who had heeled themselves sufficiently to carry on developed a new and hardier breed, upon which is founded the cattle industry of the state of Montana today, while others vanished or found employment with their more fortunate and far-seeing brethren.

WYOMING

The war between the Wyoming cattlemen and rustlers affair, while less bloody than the Montana fracas, was much wider spread and of a more lawful aspect, at least as far as the rustlers were concerned. They even bought off judges of the law, thus giving to their operations an air of legality not generally associated with rustling. The large outfits, having frozen out the smaller during the year centered on 1891, found themselves unwittingly the source of the beef supply for hungry hordes of railroad workers then engaged in construction of the Burlington Road from Alliance, Nebraska, to Billings, Montana. The rustlers, most of them formerly small operators, simply cut steers out from the big herds and drove them to the railroad camps, there to receive pay from purchasing agents who did not care where the supplies came from so long as they were cheap enough to permit a few odd thousands of dollars of profit.

There was a great outcry in several counties, mainly

Johnson, but the barons were thwarted because many of the county sheriffs sympathized with the rustlers and no amount of baron gold could change that sympathy—though most of the lawmen accepted the gold willingly enough. The double cross was the only cross known in Wyoming of that day.

In Johnson County the rustlers had absolutely the upper hand. It is reported that the barons in four years brought some one hundred suits and won exactly none of them. But Johnson County was unimportant as far as the barons were concerned; their influence extended to the state capital at Cheyenne, where in 1892 a group of stockgrowers met and posted a blacklist of some one hundred and twenty-five men suspected of rustling activities and doomed to death, if caught.

The barons decided to raid Johnson County and clean it up—by hanging and shooting. They imported a number of the tougher element from Texas and forty-three men with a raiding outfit including wagons, equipment, guns, not to mention a number of ropes for California collars, set out.

Let it be made clear that the rustlers' rise to power had been gradual and painful. During the baronial imperialism of the late '80's the small stockmen, driven out of business and blacklisted so that they were not even permitted to ride for any reputable outfit, skulked in the river breaks and ventured to steal a beef or two for food. Some of them were caught and hanged without a prayer; others took heed and fled, and established themselves in a natural Wyoming fortification: the Hole-in-the-Wall, a great depression guarded by cliffs with only two entrances, one at the east and one at the west. This Hole-in-the-Wall became a favorite hangout for Kid Curry's Wild Bunch, of whom more later, and though many of the ex-ranchers were urged to join the Kid's train-robbing crew, few of them did. They were interested only in the return of cattle the barons had originally stolen from them.

The barons sent several posses to the Hole-in-the-Wall without success, for the place was too easily protected. To fortify their outlaw domain the more, the rustlers had rustled a Hotchkiss gun from a company of soldiers in Buffalo; this they planted at the east entrance. No more posses attempted the fort; by this time the rustlers had come out in the open to work with all the efficiency of a legitimate organization, and the barons were on the run. The gun rusted and disappeared altogether while the rustlers gained control of Johnson County, partial control of other counties, and harassed the barons to the point of the Johnson County raid.

The raiders started out in April. They dropped in unexpectedly at a ranch where rustlers supposedly held forth; they found two men, Nate Champion and Nick Ray, who, when they rushed to the door to see what went on, were shot down. The raiders then fired the buildings and prepared to ride on, when Jack Flagg, rustler, cantered up.

There followed a hot chase, but Flagg escaped and acted the part of a High Border Revere to warn his fellows. At once the rustlers leaped to arms, and a small guerrilla army advanced to meet the raiders. The rustlers numbered over three hundred, and though the Texas men were tough, they found themselves so outclassed that they broke in retreat. Providentially a ranch offered shelter, and here the raiders settled down for a siege.

This siege was noisy but not bloody, though had it

lasted longer than it did—three days—the result would without doubt have been massacre. At the end of three days the United States Cavalry from Fort McKinney arrived and captured the raiders, who were delivered to Cheyenne, while the barons squirmed. Public opinion was not with them, and when it became definitely known that they had sponsored the raid, they figured and rightly that there would be hell to pay, with the Federal government investigating.

The bail demanded was exorbitant—several millions of dollars. Lawyers wrangled for three months in Cheyenne, on charges arising from the death of Champion and Ray. But at last the barons triumphed, and the Texas men went free on lowered bail, collected their fees, and departed, never to be heard from again. Trial of other members of the raiding party dragged on, to fade out eventually.

OUTLAW

Every section of the United States, especially in the West, has its pet outlaw, about whom stories are legion. Most of these sagas are without foundation of truth, many of them are on the border line between fiction and fact, a few of them are authentic. The High Border's outlaw was Kid Curry, leader of a band which has become known as the Wild Bunch. Tales of his prowess, told by old-timers who claim to have known him, are varied and wonderful and reach into the supernatural; what facts exist concerning him are meager.

Associated closely with Kid Curry and his Wild Bunch is the name of Charlie Siringo, agent extraordinary, who proved to be the partial if not complete nemesis of the outlaw band. Siringo was a detective; he wrote a book of his adventures to prove that he was an extraordinary detective, and facts seem to substantiate his claims to a large extent. He broke the power of the Wild Bunch; later, in the Coeur d'Alene labor troubles of the '90's, he acted in the pay of the silver barons and found himself in less happy adventures, as we shall see; still later he dabbled in other labor and criminal activities. He died in Arizona in the present century.

Kid Curry, a brother Henry, and others, began the career of the Wild Bunch in the Little Rocky Mountains of north central Montana. This group of hills, thrusting jaggedly above the prairie several hundred miles east of the main range of the Rockies, offered a perfect hiding place for outlaws.

The Kid seems to have been honest enough to begin with, for in 1884 when he drifted with brother Hank into the Little Rocky Mountains, there was no blemish on his record save perhaps a few redskin killings which did not really rate as murder. He originally called himself Logan, but in a land where name changes were frequent, this fact had no especial significance.

Henry and the Kid became ranchers, settling near one Pike Landusky, after whom a boom gold camp had been named. Landusky was as tough a hombre as ever knocked the teeth out of an opponent, and deserving of a story himself. When in a fury—"r'iled up!" being the High Border expression for anger beyond the ordinary—or filled with whiskey, he became a dangerous man, though he seems to have been amiable enough, in a rattlesnake way, as long as he remained calm. The Kid distrusted him from first meeting, and warned Henry against him. For a time all went well. Then Pike borrowed a plow and returned it later than was reasonable, in a condition certainly not new. Henry blew up, but the Kid maintained his calm and offered no offense to Pike, partly because Pike had become an officer of the pseudo-law then in force, partly because he was apprehensive of Pike's ability with fists.

The Kid merely rolled his cigarette and stared at Pike, in the best movie tradition. He hated Pike, and Pike saw it. Thereafter Pike plotted to get the Kid. The Kid knew what Pike was up to, and Pike knew the Kid knew, and everyone understood everybody. Which, in that day, meant something had to break, sooner or later.

Meanwhile two more of the Curry clan, Johnnie and Lonnie, appeared on the scene. Lonnie presented an innocuous aspect, with a wide-open mouth and adenoids that gave him the name of Fishmouth, but Johnnie was rat-faced and rat-minded and he took to carrying a gun. He wanted to be known as bad and it was not long until he achieved his ambition to a far greater degree than he had imagined. He finished up in the place where landed most men of the High Border Country who aspired to be bad—on boothill, as a High Border graveyard was called.

The cause was a lady—"lady" is perhaps not right, since her reputation was anything but snow-white. No believer in monogamy, she had endeared herself, or at least made herself known, to several men of the community by her willingness to leave the board and bed, especially the bed, of her lawfully wedded husband for an evening. She became presently a common-law wife of most of the males in the vicinity, with emphasis on the word common. One Winters, the man to whom she had been joined according to the Book, attempted to bring her back to the path of virtue, but, failing, washed his hands of her when she moved in with Johnnie Curry.

"Wall, she was married to Winters," Johnnie Curry ruminated, inspired beyond the conventional paths of logic. "That makes everything Winters owns hers, don't it? Now that she's with me, that means everything that Winters owns is mine, don't it? He's got a damn good ranch—"

The more Johnnie thought about it, the more convinced he became of the soundness of his reasoning. Accordingly he expressed his opinion to Winters, and that individual embarrassed him by laughing like a horse. Johnnie Curry began to sulk; eventually he decided that right lay on his side, especially since he packed a pair of Colts. Armed with shooting-irons and bolstered with red-eye, he rode forth to eject Winters from the ranch by force.

Winters saw him coming and took a shotgun from the wall. Bad Johnnie Curry, liquored beyond the point of caution, reined up before the door of the ranch cabin. He hiccuped a command.

"Come out, Winters!"

Winters came, both barrels blazing, and Bad Johnnie Curry died abruptly. They lowered him into his grave, considerably heavier than when he had lived. The lady in question moved on, and before sundown found sanctuary in the cabin of a friend of Johnnie's. She had limited her period of mourning to about five minutes.

Hank Curry meanwhile had imbibed too freely one chilly night. He toppled into a creek. Pneumonia set in, and Hank went ingloriously over the Divide, unmourned except by the remaining Currys and his creditors.

All the while Pike Landusky eyed Kid Curry and the Kid in return eyed Pike—each waiting for the other to make the first move. Pike took the offensive. The Kid was accused of some minor infraction of the law and Pike Landusky, as deputy sheriff, took him into custody. Pike was a big and powerful man and when he relieved the Kid of his gun, he had Bad Johnnie's brother most certainly at his mercy, for the Kid lacked size. To make doubly sure there would be no resistance, Pike chained him with a log chain to the wall of the jail.

Then he went to work. There was little left of the Kid when he finished, except an inner conviction that Pike Landusky's days were numbered.

"Pike, you've dug your own grave!" the Kid remarked, and Pike went to work again, and knocked out a few of the Kid's teeth for good measure. The Kid became more convinced than ever that Pike had elected to die.

Fort Benton, upriver on the Missouri, called itself the seat of justice, and there they took the Kid. A jury declared him innocent, following the custom of juries of the period as concerned almost every crime except horse-thievery and sheepherding, and the Kid returned to the Little Rockies to assist fate in the early death of Pike Landusky. Christmas lay in the offing, and the Kid waited patiently. On Christmas night he stalked into the saloon of Jew Jake where Landusky bellied against the bar. His manner could mean but one thing—killing.

Pike Landusky, weighted to the gills with rattlesnake juice, toasted the Yule spirit in beer steins brimming with whiskey. He had just emptied a stein without taking breath when the door of Jew Jake's place swung back and the Kid stalked in. There was a rush for cover on the part of the saloon patrons. When the uproar subsided the field lay clear. Pike Landusky, looking huger than ever in a buffalo-hide coat, stared at the Kid who came softly across to him.

Pike tried making peace. He wiped his mouth and began, "Now see here, Kid—" Then his temper, shocked still for an instant, flared up and he roared, "Goin' to get me, are you? Take this—"

He lunged and his huge fist smacked the Kid on the mouth and loosed a few more teeth. Kid Curry's knees buckled and he went sliding through the foam-soaked sawdust on the floor. Smiling, hand on his mouth to mop up the blood, he lifted himself to his feet. Then his hand flickered to his gun.

"I told you I'd get you, Pike—"

Pike drove his hand under his buffalo coat and snatched out a gun—not the conventional, sure-fire Colt in vogue, but a pistol of the automatic kind, a new-fangled contrivance, which a drummer had persuaded him to purchase. This automatic jammed.

Mr. Colt's equalizer was, as usual, too foolproof to fail, and fate, assisted by the Kid, spelled Pike Landusky's death.

According to the frontier view of the situation, the Kid shot in self defense, and though everybody knew that he had sworn to kill Pike, any jury of the period would undoubtedly have declared him innocent. But the Kid gave no man the opportunity to judge him according to law. He went out into the Christmas night and became Kid Curry the outlaw, who with his band spread a good deal of trouble if not downright terror throughout the High

Border Country, especially where there were railroads, against whom he directed his holdup abilities.

But before he left the Little Rockies he secreted himself near the cabin of the man Winters, who had cut short the career of Bad Johnnie Curry. Winters, coming to the door to answer the Kid's hail, stood there with the light behind him and offered a perfect target. The Kid did not miss, of course.

Lonnie Curry, in the saloon the night of Pike's demise, was accused by personal enemies of assisting in the murder of Pike, and such was their influence that the authorities forced him to stand trial. A jury declared him innocent and he left the courtroom to join his brother. Under their leadership, the Wild Bunch came into being—a lawless band that ranged from the Canadian border to old Mexico, specializing in train robberies but on the lookout for any small change they might acquire by bashing in the head of a stray traveler. It was no close-knit organization such as most of the famous bandit gangs of the West, but rather a group of men outside the law bound to each other only by the fact that they rode beyond the law.

Ranging along the backbone of the Rockies, they evolved a kind of post-office system to keep their far-flung members in contact with each other. From the Hole-in-the-Wall region of northern Wyoming to Alma, in southern New Mexico, they marked certain geographic locations, at one specific point of which they would leave letters and instructions and any material they thought might be of value to members drifting along the same route. These post offices were generally cracks in the rock and hollowed tops of mounds. How many of the outlaws were literate enough to read more than the numbers on a United States banknote is open to question, but they seem to have remained in reasonably good contact through correspondence.

In time, the Wild Bunch became so obnoxious to people in general and especially to the railroads—which they robbed in spite of guards, spies, and all precautions—that murmurs began to be heard. People figured that Kid Curry and his Wild Bunch had outlived their usefulness as headline-makers for the Eastern newspapers. Railroad officials bestirred themselves and came forth with Charlie Siringo, a human bloodhound whose reputation bore no stigma of failure. They pointed him in a general western direction and told him to go and get the Wild Bunch.

This Charlie Siringo, in the High Border Country, is regarded by some as a sneak and by others as a hero. Charlie was a spy, one of the best, and in some places, especially in the mining region, a spy is considered lower than a snake. Be that as it may, Charlie Siringo was an undercover agent extraordinary, employed most frequently by private detective agencies and at other times by organizations which had need of a man whose ability to gain the confidence of unsuspecting parties was phenomenal. Charlie's talents were really unusual and when the Kid discovered that he was to be complimented by the attentions of the great Siringo, he became apprehensive, as did the more prominent members of his Wild Bunch —Butch Cassidy, Henry Smith, Flat Nose George Curry (no relative of the Kid's), Harry Longabough, known as the Sundance Kid, Bob Lee, and Big Nose George. The gang was not worried to the point of calling a halt to their activities, however. They figured the country, a thousand miles wide and a thousand miles long, offered them enough space to avoid Charlie Siringo.

A man of God, riding on the Northern Pacific, stirred uneasily when the train squealed to a stop and several masked and armed men appeared. The passengers needed no second admonition to empty their pockets. The foremost of the bandits revealed himself as Kid Curry.

"All right, everybody!" he called. "We're takin' up a donation, an' if you don't want trouble, don't hold anythin' back!"

The passengers contributed liberally—to the limit of their resources, in fact. All except the preacher, who had nothing in his pockets. When the Kid came to him, he meekly removed his hat.

"I have nothing, nothing at all," he said, and emphasized the point, as in his sermons. "Nothing at all!"

"Wall, ain't that a hell of a note!" the Kid returned. "Who're you, anyway?"

"I am a reverend."

"Wall! Wall!" the Kid burst out. "You don't say. What kind of a reverend?"

"I'm a Methodist."

The Kid reached into the donations and poured a handful into the reverend's hat. "Yuh need that," he said, backing away. "Y'see, I'm kind of a Methodist myself!"

In 1901 the Kid held up a Great Northern passenger train near Malta, at that time a shoot-'em-up cow metropolis of Montana. He got $80,000, which is a sizable haul in any language, but unfortunately the loot was in bills which, disastrously for the Kid, were unsigned.

The robbery is perhaps the most famous of the Wild

Bunch's exploits. It was consummated with effectiveness and precision and gave evidence of the Kid's organizing ability. That the swag proved difficult to handle did not blemish the Kid's record, that he failed to recognize unsigned bills when he saw them does not detract from his glory as a notorious and superior guerrilla.

Charlie Siringo, disguised as a horse buyer, drifted into Great Falls and later, in a blinding blizzard, headed across country to the Little Rockies, the Kid's original stamping ground where it was reported that even now, during the height of his career, nostalgic memories tempted him to return at intervals. Charlie, posing as an outlaw from Arizona one jump ahead of the law, discovered the Kid held title to a ranch in the mountains where he had a partner, a hard-faced gent of uncertain disposition who did not, apparently, run with the Wild Bunch but furnished the Kid with horses. Fortuitously by intent, Charlie's horse bucked him off near this ranch and he limped in to meet the Kid's partner, moaning loudly about his injuries.

"My name's Charles Carter," he said, in a shifty manner which he hoped would indicate fear of the law. "Need any help here?"

The Kid's partner was bluffed, and thereafter Charlie Siringo became a ranch hand. Charlie cultivated the acquaintance of a young lady of slightly dim mentality, one Julia, daughter of Pike Landusky. Curiously enough, Julia was the sweetheart of Lonnie Curry, and between them there flowered a romance not infrequently marred by Lonnie's habit of blacking Julia's eyes. But Julia loved him, or had no better chance; she knitted patiently while awaiting his infrequent visits, and told Charles Carter all about her romantic outlaw lover.

Most of her information was harmless prattle, but one day she confided that Lonnie had been to see her the night before—and would come again after he had done a small job. A bit of questioning brought out information that gladdened Charlie Siringo's heart; some days later when Lonnie Curry and Bob Lee, the latter a killer and all-around bad man, attempted a small holdup, it backfired on them. The victims turned out to be lawmen, and both Lonnie and Bob were killed.

At the same time, though strictly by chance, the mighty of mighties, Kid Curry himself, fell afoul of the law. He tried some target practice upon the persons of two police officers in Knoxville, Tennessee, and the law treated him to a 130-year penitentiary sentence. This disconcerted the Kid, for he was in the prime of life, filled with the urge to action, and still determined to pass some thousands of dollars in unsigned bills which he had cached in northern Montana. But the Knoxville police had not liked the Kid's treatment of two of the force, and for the time being things looked dark indeed.

But the Kid held an ace in the hole, and this time the bills were signed and thoroughly negotiable. At the trial a certain cowman from the Little Rockies attracted attention both for his interest in a man generally regarded as a romantic but nevertheless dirty killer and for the roll of bills which he flashed at every opportunity. Frequently the eyes of the jury rested on those bills; but it resisted temptation and nobly did its sworn duty. There were other law officials, however, not so conscientious. The penitentiary never swallowed Kid Curry. Someone left a door open for him and he walked out. As easy as that.

Meanwhile, others of the Wild Bunch, mainly through

the undercover efforts of Charlie Siringo, passed on: Big
Nose George, in particular, ceased earthly existence in
a manner to make him remembered. Thrown into jail in
Rawlins, Wyoming, he made eyes at the jailer's beautiful
daughter, recently converted by an itinerant sky-pilot.
The lady saw in George fresh material for conversion, and
he listened long and patiently to her lectures concerning
the evil of his ways and the joys of the hereafter, listened
and assented and then began to cry a little over his past
sins.

The jailer, as well as his daughter, was touched. He un-
locked the cell door one day while George hunched over
his knees, moaning that life had been cruel. He placed a
comforting hand on George's shoulder—whereupon Big
Nose George hauled a metal rod out from under his shirt
and slapped the other man down, with such force that
even the victim's daughter realized interference was useless. So she slammed the door shut before George could
escape, notified the townspeople of George's ungracious
act, and forgot her newfound theories in her eagerness
to return to the jail before the mob reached it.

They placed Big Nose George on a kerosene barrel,
looped a rope around his neck, and cinched the loose
end around a telegraph arm. Then someone kicked the
barrel out. The rope broke, and Big Nose George claimed
that entitled him to freedom; the mob failed to agree
with him, however, and their second rope did not break.

A doctor, who had been eyeing Big Nose's torso with
considerable interest, now came forward and claimed the
body. A body next to useless, the mob agreed, and the
medical man lugged the earthly remains of the outlaw to
his office, where he stripped most of Big Nose's hide

away from back, shoulders and chest, tanned it, and from the best of it made himself a pair of boots.

This last is possibly without foundation; nevertheless, there are those old-timers who claim Big Nose made the best pair of boots in Wyoming.

The roll of bills that freed Kid Curry has a story—not a long one. Curry's sweetheart, they say, owned a horse ranch, stocked by the Kid himself. The Kid loved horse-flesh. The ranch lay in the Little Rockies, and often the Kid, weary of robbery, would return to live with his sweet-heart and his horses, apparently caressing each with equal favor. Indeed, such was his consideration for his animals that he forced the girl to promise that she would never under any circumstances sell them. But when news of his capture in the East came to her, she broke her prom-ise, disposed of the horses, and entrusted the roll of bills to a rancher friend. When the rancher returned, the bills were gone—and so was the Kid.

The Kid never came to light again, or even ran afoul of the law. Persistent rumor had it that he emigrated to South America. Be that as it may, he never troubled the railroads, the law, or the High Border Country again.

PIKE LANDUSKY

Pike Landusky was a rough-necked individual with the strength and build of a bull and the same sort of mentality. "I'm from Pike County, Missouri!" he would bellow at you by way of introduction, loading his pipe out of a tobacco pouch made from the bladder of a dead redskin. "And by God, I can lick any —— —— —— who says I ain't!"

Few challenged him, for Pike did not fool when he fought; he battled in earnest and the least his victim could expect was an eye gouged out or an ear torn off. So men permitted him to go his merry way, shooting Indians, raping squaws, and otherwise amusing himself according to his conceptions. Eventually he struck gold in the Little Rocky Mountain region and settled down to a relatively calm and peaceful life, broken by only one decisive event —his death.

He died with his boots on, and he lived most of the time with them on. It was a damned nuisance, this effeminate habit of removing footwear—he would explain when companions raised hairy eyebrows at bedtime. A man could sleep just as well with 'em on as with 'em off. "I don't aim ever to have 'em off!" he boasted, and after his death they respected his wishes to the extent that they dumped him into his grave without ceremony, though a certain soft-hearted preacher remonstrated that, unwashed and unshaven, Pike Landusky was no fit object to kneel before the throne of his Lord.

"It don't matter," someone said, spatting casually over Pike's body, "He ain't goin' to do any kneelin'—not where he's goin', parson!"

Pike's gold discovery had originally been within the confines of the Fort Belknap Indian reservation, upon which white men were theoretically not allowed to set foot. Pike and his partner, respecting Federal law, worked their claim by night and carted off their quartz surreptitiously. It was not long, however, before other white men learned of the gold, and there was a minor stampede which resulted in the establishment of several small boom settlements. After the United States government obligingly declared this land outside reservation boundaries, these settlements became typical High Border smoky towns. The amount of lead flung promiscuously about was enough to fill a mine, according to the old-timers who have been known to exaggerate. In some settlements, after a general shooting affray, one could go out in the street and pick up a quart of bullets in a pint cup; and one enterprising saloonkeeper paved a street in front of his dispensary with cartridge shells.

Before he discovered gold, Pike had followed various lines of endeavor, none of them too ethical. In his younger days, he became noted for his temper. One afternoon he squatted beside his campfire, frying a steak, when he looked up to behold a party of redskins around him. Pike grunted and went on with his activities. The chief of the band stepped forward and contemptuously kicked ashes and sand into the frying pan—to his regret, for at once Pike lifted himself upright, with a demoralizing yell of anger, and attacked the redskin with his frying pan.

Such was his fury that the chief's followers dropped back in awe, nor did they attempt to interfere when Pike, having beaten the skillet flat, tore the chief's breechclout off and proceeded to lash him with it. Only when the redskin lay half dead did Pike desist; then he stepped back, still howling curses and frothing at the mouth in a manner that made the redskins think him crazy.

They withdrew, carrying their chief. And they left Pike Landusky five of their best horses, to propitiate him.

In his next encounter with the redskins Pike's luck failed. A glancing bullet shattered his jaw and loosened his teeth. His mouth a mass of bloody froth, he rushed into camp after the affray ended and shouted inarticulately.

"Looks like Pike is in a plumb bad way," one of his companions remarked without interest. "Give him a shot of whiskey!"

Pike drained the bottle at one gulp and, feeling better, gingerly massaged his jaw. Then and there he performed a feat of self-dentistry—he wrenched half a dozen loose teeth from his jaw and flung them out into the sage. Then fortified with bottles, he retired to some secluded spot where he alternately cursed and drank until the bottles were empty and he slept.

No doctors lived within hundreds of miles, and Pike, his jaw tied up with a strip of red flannel, suffered until the party finished its trading and reached a military post. The surgeon at the post examined the jaw and found it partly healed, so misshapenly that Pike could scarcely speak with coherence. The medical man suggested that the only method of remedying the difficulty was to break the jaw again. He made the suggestion hesitantly, because his instruments were of the crudest and anesthetic was lacking.

Pike, however, made a simple and direct answer. "Sure, break 'er!" he roared, as best he could. "The —— —— thing!"

A couple of soldiers held Pike while the surgeon tore the jaw loose and reset it. The surgery was simple and not too skillful, but Pike's mouth straightened so perfectly that in later years only those who were told of it knew about the adventure with the redskins.

Pike himself did not forget. Some months later, in the company of a pair of traders, he sighted a lone redskin loping over the prairie. That this particular redskin belonged to a friendly tribe, as evidenced by the fact that he continued to lope along instead of fleeing when he sighted Pike's party, did not trouble Pike at all. "There's one of them —— —— —— —— as made my jaw sore!" he growled, unslinging his rifle. "Here's where I do a little shootin'!"

"Aw, Pike, he ain't goin' to hurt us," a companion protested.

"Hurt my jaw, will yuh?" Pike howled, and fired. The redskin tumbled off his horse and Pike ran forward, dragging out his knife. His aim had not been good, and the Indian crawled frantically away. But Pike overtook him, cut his throat, detached his ears—and then, to finish the thing, ran his knife down the corpse's belly.

Even Pike's companions demurred at this, but Pike did not hesitate. He explored the redskin's interior, cut out the bladder and carried it triumphantly with him. Later he tanned it and for the rest of his days carried it as a tobacco pouch.

Pike's death, described elsewhere, took place in the establishment of Jew Jake, a gentleman himself deserving of a few words. Jake had the most important liquor emporium of the then smokiest town in the Little Rockies, named after Pike Landusky—Landusky. Landusky today, a moldering almost-ghost town, squats in an outworked, eroded gulch, but at the time of Pike's death it was booming, especially upon the night of Pike's demise, for Pike passed on during a Christmas celebration. Jew Jake, formerly of Wyoming, had drifted in with the discovery of gold, and Pike had staked him to the wherewithal to establish a saloon—not a large amount, for all that was needed to start a saloon was a tent, a bar, and enough kegs and bottles, filled, to quench the thirsts which made such a dispensary by far the most important business venture of any boom camp.

Jew Jake prospered to the point where he threw together a clapboard and log building of which the downstairs was the booze hall and the upstairs a region inhabited by charming, though somewhat overly decorated, young ladies in charge of a Mrs. Dwight, better known as Wattles because of her goiter.

Jew Jake had only one leg, the other having been removed as a result of an encounter with peace officers sometime in his past. He scorned such aids for the handicapped as crutches, and hobbled around his saloon and presided over the bar supported by a Winchester rifle. This novel crutch made him an object of interest to patrons and Jake was quick to capitalize on it. He packed his place night after night with men who wanted to see Jew Jake.

It was his misfortune that a drunken cowboy one day challenged him to use the rifle. Jake attempted to pacify the drunk, but the cowboy roared insistently. And when Jake did shift the Winchester, to brace himself rather than to bring the weapon into action, the cowboy drew a Colt and perforated Jew Jake as neatly as if he had drilled through him with brace and bit.

LADY SMOKING A CIGAR

One time Miss Martha Jane Canary, better known as Calamity Jane, and Miss Kitty O'Leary, more commonly called Madam Bulldog, had a falling out. They ran what was euphemistically known as a dance hall, and while the cause of their disagreement has been lost to history, it is understood that they differed on some minor point of policy.

"You —— —— —— ——!" said Calamity Jane, squashing out her eternal cigar. "You —— —— —— —— —— ——!"

"You —— —— —— —— ——!" returned Madam Bulldog, with like spirit. "You're a —— —— —— ——! I'll tear your eyes out, you —— —— —— ——!"

Livingston, Montana, scene of this little interplay, was a bang-bang, shoot-'em-up frontier town, a roaring hell-hole supporting more prostitutes per square foot than any boom settlement before or since in all the High Border land. The establishment of Mesdames Canary and O'Leary was regarded as a relatively decent joint, thanks to the uplift spirit of the latter who had announced at the grand opening that she would stand for no damfoolishness. Bouncers, she had found, were not too trustworthy, and she took upon herself all bouncing duties. She was thoroughly capable. She weighed in at one hundred ninety pounds—stripped. Which was frequent.

Incidentally, she saved a bouncer's wages by thus policing the establishment herself.

The altercation with Calamity Jane aroused considerable interest. The original Bucket of Blood Saloon across the way sent a delegation to pass judgment on the merits of the antagonists. From a gambling house down the street came Tex Rickard, Kid Brown, and Soapy Smith, whose next destination was Alaska where Soapy dabbled in lead and Rickard in gold, and Soapy achieved the more lasting fame of having his skull whitewashed for tourists to gape at.

The fray was a disappointment. The delegation from the

Bucket of Blood returned and the barkeep raised his eyes questioningly.

"Calamity fight back?" he asked.

"Calamity's tougher'n hell!" one of the committee remarked. "But she ain't plumb crazy!"

Lest it be concluded from this incident that Miss Canary was a powderpuff, consider: During her heyday a convivial congregation was whooping it up in the old Brewery Saloon in Deer Lodge, Montana, when who should enter but Calamity Jane herself. She was doing a bit of entertaining at her shack some hundreds of yards behind the saloon, and the bucket in her hand explained her presence at the bar. Strictly minding her own business she shoved her container towards the barkeep, when one of the boys who had imbibed Valley Tan neither wisely nor well gave birth to a practical joke. He palmed a lemon, drew back, and let fly.

Calamity took it on the right ear. She promptly made known her displeasure by bouncing her bucket through the mirror and demanding of the assemblage, by now shocked silent at this discourtesy to a lady, the name of the dirty —— —— —— —— who had no better manners than to slam one of the fairer sex on the ear with a lemon. When no reply was forthcoming, she backed to the pool table and racked up the balls.

"You ain't talkin', eh?" she snapped, and began hurling pool balls.

Though it was in the 1880's and ladies were supposed to swoon upon the slightest provocation, Miss Canary was no Victorian heroine eternally upon the verge of a faint. She could flick a fly from a mule's ear with a bullwhacker's sixteen-foot lash—which took a blacksmith's muscle, in quality if not in quantity. When she threw a pool ball, it became a missile to be avoided. There was a mob rush through the front door that cleared the room promptly, except for a single unfortunate, Bud Brown, who subsequently spent several hours waking up and several weeks recuperating. Calamity scorned him later as soft-headed. Though a pool-ball, bouncing from his skull, had almost torn a hole through the side of the saloon.

Calamity Jane, the West's most famous woman, was born to the name of Martha Jane Canary, in Princeton, Missouri, on May 1, 1852. She drifted with her father to Virginia City, Montana, which in the '60's was the scene of the wildest gold rush of all time. Miss Canary, a young lady of some perspicacity, carefully considered the situation from all angles after a combination of circumstances forced her to earn her own living, and concluded that menial labor was not for her; neither was home life, except in its loosest sense. Before she was eighteen she had established herself in a small but cozy cabin down Alder Gulch where the miners, weary after a day's work and in the mood for a bit of relaxation, were inclined to play and pay.

Jane was youthful, not bad-looking, and enthusiastic; in addition, she possessed a natural vitality conducive to mass output, and before she left Alder Gulch to join the army she was well on the road to becoming one of the best-known women on the frontier.

Meanwhile she had not scorned the acquisition of arts other than those related to efficiency. She learned to ride, to shoot accurately enough to make a sieve out of a can tossed into the air, and she gained a working knowledge of the bullwhacker's lash—this last accomplishment becoming responsible for a widely related adventure of her later years when she tarried briefly in Deadwood, South Dakota.

Jane had a weakness for animals, and one day encountering a whacker who belabored his oxen mercilessly, she protested. The whacker's response was swift and curt, to the point, and not in the least polite: No so-and-so was telling him how to drive his bulls. Jane, lighting a fresh cigar, demurred further, whereupon the whacker did a very unwise thing. He flicked his whip at her and knocked her hat off into the dust.

Jane rolled her cigar into the corner of her mouth and ducked her hand down to the Colt forty-four in her belt. The driver wilted under the menace of a blued muzzle.

"That ain't no-ways to treat a lady!" Calamity protested, the cigar muffling her unhurried voice. "Now, if you'll jest pick that hat up, dust it off, an' hand it to me polite-like, I'll feel mighty obliged!"

She added, "An' if you don't, I'll fill you so full of holes thet carcass of your'n won't even shed rain!"

The whacker complied and continued to shed rain, and Calamity Jane went her way. She had adopted the garb of a man, and it was her boast that she could outcuss, out-smoke, outdrink, outride, and outshoot the best of them. She did everything a man did. And more. In the early 1870's she joined the command of General George A. Custer, when that glory-hunter was conducting his campaign against the Indians. The troopers found the expedition without interest. The marches were long and arduous, the redskins persisted in vanishing over the horizon before a bullet could get them, and evenings around the camp-fire were lonely. The presence of Miss Canary was regarded with enthusiasm, though there was a bit of grumbling at the lady's insistence that credit was merely a word in the dictionary. Miss Canary seems to have been an astute business woman, at least in her younger days.

Martha Jane's transition to Calamity Jane is accounted for in three ways: (*a*) Bill Nye gave her that name in his newspaper, the Laramie (Wyoming) *Boomerang,* in the early 1870's. (*b*) She was an active participant in almost every calamity that befell the frontier Black Hills country of South Dakota. (*c*) In lower Dakota, during an Indian raid, she rescued a certain Captain Eagan, who said, "A man is mighty lucky to have a woman like you around in times of calamity!"

Whatever the truth may be, Calamity Jane was known throughout the West by the time she was twenty-one. And because emulation is the price of fame, the West was plagued with a variety of spurious Janes during her heyday, the most famous of whom died in Denver, Colorado, in 1878, at her death signing a confession that upset several gentlemen who, unknown to each other, had taken upon themselves the task of caring for the little heroine.

Traveling with Custer's command, Calamity was the first white woman to penetrate the Black Hills. Her official capacity was that of scout—at least, during daylight hours. Here we have evidence that Jane was no nitwit, for by riding with the army she avoided the competition she was bound to encounter in the settlements. She had, in effect, a monopoly. But even a monopoly may prove trying, and presently Jane pulled stakes and left Custer's command to get along as best it could—a wise move, for she might easily have been one of the two-hundred-odd troopers who rode into the trap which Sitting Bull had baited for them along the Little Big Horn.

A few vital statistics concerning our heroine: She was five feet eight inches in height, weighed between 135 and 140 pounds when in condition, and in youth, according to reports, had a lithe form and auburn hair. Like most prairie flowers, she faded fast and in age was anything but lovely. She is known to have been married, legitimately, three times; to have borne several children, all of whom either died or were pawned off on orphanages.

She was not always coldly professional. During her life she had one great love—Wild Bill Hickok, the G-man of the frontier, whom she first met at Fort Laramie, Wyoming, when she was in her early twenties. Their meeting was brief but subsequently they came across each other at Deadwood, in the Black Hills country. Jane fell in love with Wild Bill with all the ardor of a schoolgirl. He was surrounded by glory; before his appearance at Fort Laramie he had cleaned out the McCandles gang in Kansas— a notable feat, with the odds at exactly ten to one. There were forty notches on his gun, and Jane felt he was the man for her. Wild Bill was not one to resist; the ensuing affair, while hardly of the romantic variety, was nevertheless memorable enough to inspire a moving picture of recent years and a host of tearful tales.

Tragedy culminated the affair, for Wild Bill died with his boots on. The gunman's code of the day forbade shooting a man in the back, though killing an unarmed individual was permitted—on the assumption, evidently, that the victim's after-life was made more cheerful by knowledge of his killer's identity. Jack McCall, rated by some a dirty dog and by others a savior—for Wild Bill was no angel—overlooked this point of border etiquette long enough to place the muzzle of his six-gun against the back of Bill's head while the latter was playing poker—holding, incidentally, a pair of aces and a pair of eights. McCall pulled the trigger. They buried Wild Bill on boothill, and Jane wept; but she soon wiped her bleary eyes and vowed vengeance on her lover's killer.

One day when she was unarmed she met McCall by accident in a butcher shop. Calamity acted promptly; she snatched up a meat cleaver and made for McCall. Only the opportune arrival of the law prevented her from "spillin' that skunk's guts all over Hades!" Her gift for colorful speech is looked upon with awe even to the present day.

Bill was the big flame of her life, but there were minor sparks. While she was in Deadwood a Mr. Swarringer, a business man of sorts, noted that his stock needed replenishing and sent Jane to Nebraska for a fresh cargo. On her return trip, chaperoning ten young ladies, she was delayed by the outlaw Jim Wall, whose chief lieutenant was a handsome dog named Blackburn. Blackburn made eyes at Jane, and Jane abandoned her charges to ride along with the gang. Later, in Laramie, the desperadoes were rounded up and hanged—all except Jane, whose elemental appeal to the judge and jury won her freedom.

Her later years were in contrast to her swashbuckling youth. She picked up a living wherever she could. Temporarily, she established herself in Highland City, today a decayed ghost town near Butte but once a metropolis of the Northwest, and here she chummed around with Shotgun Liz, a lady of uncertain virtue but definite ability at sharpshooting. Shotgun Liz passed out of the picture, and Jane followed a trail that was rapidly becoming lonelier. She found herself shunned by both men and women. She heard of Bronco Maggie, who dressed as a man and drove freight wagons between the Coeur d'Alene mining region of Idaho and Thompson Falls, Montana, and in a fit of desire for the company of her own sex, had a letter written to her. But Bronco Maggie was young, lusty, and absorbed by her own life; she had no time for an old woman. Jane returned to haunt the scenes of her younger days.

She became a saloon ghost, begging liquor at every bar. Drunkenness was her habitual state. She enjoyed a burst of fame when an Eastern author published the story of her life. Calamity hawked copies of the book from door to door, with indifferent success. At last she gave up. She, who had been the most famous woman on the frontier, was now greeted with nothing but contempt. A sloppy slattern, she went her lonely way, happy only when alcohol was singing through her veins.

During one winter she holed up in a shanty between the shacks of a pair of horsethieves, the lowest caste in the Western social scale. She chopped down pine trees, split them, and sold the slabs for fence posts. The few pennies she earned went for red-eye.

Her last days were spent in the poorhouse. She died August 2, 1903, twenty-seven years to the day after the killing of Wild Bill Hickok. Kind citizens, recalling her former grandeur, chipped in to bury her beside Wild Bill.

Jane's philosophy was simple. One day in middle age, when she reeled before a bar, a man asked, "Calamity, why don't you reform and get civilized?"

"You —— —— ——! All I want people to do is let me alone so I can go to hell in my own way!"

JOHNNY HEALY

The Great White Father banned the whiskey trade among the Indians in the early stages of High Border history. This ban was something of a joke until the '60's when authorities clamped down and made the breaking of that law dangerous. Whereupon traders, exchanging whiskey for furs (other than beaver, trade for which had practically come to an end), moved over the High Border line into Alberta, whence they continued to furnish liquor to the redskins in Montana. Of these traders the most notorious was Johnny Healy.

In the early '70's Johnny began his career as a whiskey-runner by buying the liquor of a sunken Missouri steam-boat, the *Amelia Poe*. He salvaged kegs and bottles intended originally for white men and with several wagon-loads headed straight north to Canada. Government authorities, getting news of the train, raced to overtake him but Johnny beat them to the line. He corralled his wagons and went out to meet his pursuers, laughing heartily in their faces. Later surveys revealed that Johnny's wagon corral lay several hundred yards within the United States, but by then he was firmly entrenched in his stockaded trading post on the Belly River—a fort which he had built to protect himself and his men from Indians made drunk by his liquor.

"Wall, how's things at Johnny's fort?" one freighter at Fort Benton, from whence supplies were freighted to Johnny's post with increasing frequency, asked another who had just returned from the high country up under the Canadian Rockies.

"They're whoopin' it up!" was the reply, and thereafter Johnny's fort became known as Fort Whoop-up, and the trail between Benton on the upper Missouri and the fort was called the Whoop-up Trail. This trail, fifty and sixty yards broad in some places, was still visible a few years ago—faint wheel tracks overgrown by buffalo and needle grass.

Johnny prospered but he encountered difficulties. The traders to the north, the free traders and those in employ of the Hudson's Bay Company, refused to exchange liquor for furs, and became annoyed when all the redskins began to patronize Fort Whoop-up. To meet Johnny's competition they organized several rival trading posts close by, of which the most successful were Forts High River and Stand-Off.

By high-pressure means—which involved dragging redskins with furs into their forts by force—they attempted to wean trade away from Johnny. But they found they could not compete with Johnny's rattlesnake juice. Whereupon they consulted among themselves and formed the Spitzee Cavalry—so named by the Blackfeet, who called the high country at the foot of the Canadian Rockies the Spitzee country—and descended upon Fort Whoop-up for the purpose of wiping Johnny off the map.

Johnny saw them coming, but he said no prayers for he was not a praying man. Instead he ran into a back room, lugged out a keg of gunpowder, and planted it under the counter. He laid a trail of powder from this potential bomb to his accustomed place at the end of the counter in the trading room; he then lighted a cigar and waited.

The Spitzee men came to the point at once. "We're closing down on you!" they informed Johnny. "We've had enough of you here in Canada. The redskins ain't trading with us any more!"

"So—?" said Johnny, and they went on, "So you're closing down! You're high-tailing out of this country. As long as you're reasonable you can take all your stuff except the liquor. We're destroying that!"

"Looks like you boys hold four aces and a joker!" Johnny admitted, puffing furiously on his cigar. He dropped his chin close to the trail of gunpowder. "But I got a better idea, an' that is, I'm staying right here! Be reasonable, boys—if you get tough, I'll just drop this here cigar right into this here powder, and we'll all go to Kingdom Come! Some of you ain't ready to die. Think it over!"

Bluff or not, the maneuver worked, and the Spitzee Cavalry withdrew in disorder. But Johnny Healy's days were numbered, for into the country came certain red-coated lawmen who were known officially as the Royal Northwest Mounted Police, but unofficially as the Queen's War Dogs. They were not to be trifled with, as Johnny discovered when they established Fort MacLeod and moved against him, armed with a cannon.

Johnny did not resist. He packed and pulled out, later to meet his fate in the Yukon days of '98. Fort Whoop-up passed on, the Queen's War Dogs got the liquor situation under control, and never again was there a wholesale running of liquor to the Indians of the High Border Country. Johnny Healy represents a certain phase of an era

—a transportation era, to be exact, when goods were carried, not on steel rails which then had hesitated just beyond the eastern border of the land, but in coupled wagons dragged by oxen. Bull-teams cared for by bull-skinners or whackers—rough and tough men who had to be rough and tough.

Nowhere, probably, has the bull-team been better described than in the somewhat unpolished (and unpublished) poem by one Stoutenburg, bull-whacker, who took time off from the back-breaking labor of freighting to woo the muse in the following somewhat exaggerated, but nevertheless basically sound, tribute to the chief mode of transportation throughout the region just before the coming of the railroad:

What we call a bull-team are twenty Texas steers,
Armed with horns upon their heads like mules are armed
> *with ears,*
Their hind ends are protected with heels instead of horns
And woe unto a fellow when he steps upon their corns.

I've watched them through a field glass, their bodies are
> *long and lank,*
And minus of their dinners they're no thicker than a
> *plank.*
They stand on legs like beanpoles of spider-shape and
> *queer.*
Their horns, I swon, would shame an elk, they're eight
> *feet in the clear.*

Times are kind of lively when these critters take a run.
There is no use in trying to ketch them for the thing can-
> *not be done.*

Our fleetest white-eyed cayuses are left far in the rear,
And lightning can't run crooked enough to catch a Texas
steer.

Had the South a thousand of these steers at the Battle of
Bull Run,
They never would have given up the chase 'til they'd taken
Washington,
And when they'd placed their banners o'er the ruins and
the dead,
Would have painted there a Texas steer beside a Copper-
head.

You cannot use a blacksnake in driving of these steers,
For the lash will tangle 'mong their horns and lap around
their ears.
It's sure to work into a knot you never can untie,
And if a fellow ain't a fool he'll surely never try.

They drive them with a goad-stick like the handle of a
broom,
And the main points in driving them is to give them
plenty room.
But as to minor items I never stop to see,
For fear the critter would break loose and then take after
me.

I always get on top the house when a bull-team is in sight,
Armed with a Winchester rifle when they turn them loose
at night.
Then you bet that I feel tickled to think how safe I be,
For a steer cannot climb a house though he can climb a
tree.

A driver that is married and has a pretty wife,
She will generally convince him that he'd best insure his
    life,
For when a steer once takes a notion to kindly lay him by,
She'll first thing draw the money, then she'll have a little
    cry.

I wouldn't drive a bull-team on the Belly River road
For all the bullion from the Last Chance Lode.
And take the desperate chances when the drought is at
    its wust,
Enveloped ever in a cloud of alkali and dust.

'Tis hard on Christian drivers who believe in church and
    prayer,
For you cannot drive a bull-team unless you curse and
    swear.
And after it's all figured out, they will all of them agree,
That you cannot work a bull-team by the double rule of
    three.

Now you may think I'm joking and my veracity may
    doubt,
But if it's not certain fact, my name's not Johnny Stout.
And if you think it's somewhat mixed, 'twill still all your
    fears
When you have seen a bull-team of full blood Texas steers.

Prods were not generally used, and the long, wicked whip—blacksnake or bullwhip—served almost universally to prod a bull-team onward, the author of the above to the contrary. By night the bulls ate and slept; the drivers caroused until late. In the dawn the heavy yokes were

thrown on the necks of the oxen and the wagons, a dozen
of them coupled one after the other, rolled into action.
Then across the prairie or along the canyon road the bull-
team would toil, drivers wielding their blacksnakes gen-
erously, cursing furiously—"For you cannot drive a bull-
team unless you curse and swear"—and sometimes in a
lull of easy grade where the animals went easily, singing
the universal song of the whackers, a somewhat sentimental ditty entitled *Joe Bowers:*

My name is Joe Bowers—I have a brother Ike;
I came from old Missoury—And all the way from Pike;
I'll tell you why I left them—And started for to roam;
And left my dear old mammy—So far away from home.

There I loved a pretty girl—Her name was Sally Black;
I ask her fur to marry me—She said it was a whack;
Said she to me, "Joe Bowers, before you're hitched for life,
You'd better get a little home, to keep a little wife."

Said I to her, "Dear Sally gal, if only you will wait,
I'll go to California and I'll try to make a stake."
Said she to me, "Joe Bowers, you are the man to win!"
And she sealed the bargain with a kiss—And threw a dozen
    in.

There were more verses, of a somewhat more intimate
nature. If a bull-skinner were versatile, he would im-
provise. There were innumerable variations, some bad
and some good, but all unprintable.

STAGECOACH

Back in the middle of the last century, Ben Holliday formed the Overland Stage Company, operating from Atchison, Kansas, to the Pacific. Passengers were transported over vast amounts of territory but they took a terrific jolting; moreover there existed gentry known as "road agents," who made a more or less regular living from the passengers of these stages. If the road agents were polite, they would offer the travelers a drink to prepare them for the sight of the murdered driver's blood, and then would sing out genially, "Ladies may remain seated, gents form a line to the right. We're takin' up a collection!" The rougher element simply delved into the passengers' pockets.

Courts, such as there were, inclined to be lenient. Hence it was the custom to hang road agents by the neck until dead without benefit of a court. A certain Judge O'Malley released a pair of eighteen-year-olds who had shot the driver of a stage and the guard who rode beside him. Said the judge, "Them younkers is too young to hang; it'd be a danged shame to put 'em on the wrong track!" His sentiments were perhaps laudable, but the younkers in question raced out to shoot another driver and another guard for the sake of the lone passenger's ten dollars, whereupon a Vigilante committee disposed of them. The pair did not live to join the gang that held up, one spring day, the Overland Stage when it was carrying the mighty of mighties, Ben Holliday himself.

Sputtering, Holliday climbed out, hands reaching skyward. A road agent, silk neckerchief over face, thrust a big gun into his face and said, "An' keep them hands up, partner! Drop 'em an inch an' I'll drill you!"

Holliday sputtered some more, but kept his voice down, for the muzzle of the gun wavered too close for comfort. Presently he became aware of a twitching at the tip of his nose—an irritation not to be overlooked. Tears came to his eyes and he gasped, "My—my nose itches! I've got to scratch it!"

"Keep yore hands up!" thundered the road agent, but he showed sympathy. Clearly he, too, at some time or another had been troubled by just such an affliction. Ben Holliday made a futile effort to drop his hands, but the outlaw was adamant. "Keep 'em up!" Then when tears came to Holliday's eyes he muttered, "Keep 'em up, I say! But—here, scratch it!"

He stiffened his wrist while Ben Holliday leaned forward and relieved the itch by friction against the muzzle of the gun.

Holliday's passengers were sometimes treated to accommodations less than luxurious. There was, for instance, the stage depot known as Dirty Woman's Ranch. Here a slattern named Maggie held forth, and annoyed by passengers who expressed distaste for the messes she placed before them, saw that her meals were relished by the simple expedient of twirling a gun in either hand—a "sass," as the riders of the period put it, "mightier fine that hunger. An', partner, hunger is a mighty fine sass!"

Holliday's stages carried mail as well as passengers. The day of the Pony Express rider passed—though, in the late '60's and '70's various companies made attempts to establish routes into the Montana and Idaho regions not yet penetrated by stage lines. The Pony Express rider has been pictured as a paragon of virtue, virility, and vigor; these riders were far from that. Some of them had the habit of opening the mail—reading what they could of it, which was little—and then throwing it away to lighten their loads. Or, in a great majority of instances when they carried mail by winter, they built fires with it while they paused in a gulch for a snort of rattlesnake juice.

STEEL RAILS

The stages passed on, and steel rails, the real trails of civilization, drove into the setting sun. A settlement of one of the Dakotas, later the capital, named itself Bismarck, courting the favor of the Iron Chancellor in an effort to secure from him the wherewithal to finance the Northern Pacific Railroad. Out in Wallowa on the western edge of the High Border Country settlers became too impatient to await the coming of steel rails; they built their own railroad, experimenting with wooden rails surfaced with rawhide. The track was not a success, for during a long and hungry winter, the coyotes gnawed away the hides. Later efforts to reinforce the rails with steel strips failed also, for they persisted in springing loose at one end and curling up, to the disgust of the engineers who had to stop their train to flatten them. It was faster to go by bull-team.

The great transcontinental systems, James Jerome Hill's Great Northern, the Northern Pacific, the Union Pacific, the Milwaukee system, forged steadily ahead to link East and West. Local railroad building began—branches intended to join the main lines, luck and finance permitting. On the upper Missouri the Jawbone Railroad thrust a

steel trail across the prairie—"jawbone" because it was
financed mainly on verbal promises. The Turkey Track
crossed the boundary into Alberta—a weaving, unsteady
parallel of rails on an uncertain roadbed that gave passengers seasickness. "She rolls like a turkey making tracks,"
they said.

The transcontinental lines gave birth, at intervals along
their surveyed routes to boom camps that roared hell-for-
leather for a few brief months and then faded into memory. These were tough settlements, appropriately dubbed
Hells on Wheels, rivaling the gold camps of a former day.
Toughest perhaps but no more than representative of the
camps was McCarthyville, on the Great Northern where
that line today parallels Glacier National Park on its
southern edge.

For eighteen months, most of them winter, McCarthyville boomed as a frozen mudhole of death and free
money. Men at the railhead, fifty miles away, hiked across
the prairie in blizzards for work. Most of them reeled into
McCarthyville half frozen. Here the railroad company established its hospital, which accidents and freezing kept
well filled. The hospital was not overly staffed—one doctor, who received so much per head for his patients, and
a male nurse, a Swede, who usually came forth from the
hospital each morning with a corpse which he lugged up
the gulch and interred there in a snow bank.

By spring the Swede had made himself highly unpopular. One day there was a gathering of men who did not
like his task, and presently the Swede, barefoot, found
himself headed out over the prairie. The doctor, too, was
ordered without formality to hike. Later, warm Chinook
winds poured out of the Southwest to melt the snow from

the corpses up the gulch, but by then the railroad had passed and McCarthyville remained as nothing but a few shacks and a memory.

The railroads pressed forward, sensing in the country a source of untold wealth—though only a few decades before Daniel Webster had thundered in opposition to attempts to open this territory, "To what use could we put those great deserts of endless mountain ranges, impenetrable and covered to their base with eternal snow?" Deep into the peaks of the western High Border, aiming at the Spokane River and the great desert in the big bend of the Columbia beyond, the Northern Pacific plunged in the '80's, through a region mapped at the beginning of the century by David Thompson, greatest of the region's cartographers.

Thompson—first in the employ of the Hudson's Bay and then of the Northwest Fur Companies, was an indefatigable traveler who covered over fifty thousand miles of wilderness trails throughout the High Border Country, Canada, and the Oregon Northwest.

The redskins named him Koo-Koo-Sint—"The Man Who Looks at Stars"—and feared him because they believed that the glass of his transit was also his eye, an omniscient eye that could see stitches in a squaw's moccasin ten miles away. He made maps, miracles of accuracy considering his indifferent instruments. He died in poverty, yet he was the greatest map-maker of the region. He traversed roughly the route followed by railroads into the panhandle of Idaho, and the Northern Pacific engineers found nothing better than the water grade he had followed almost a century before.

Here, along Thompson's route, occurred the real rail-

road building of the mountains. Out on the prairie the
laying of steel rails, except for coulees and certain minor
obstructions, was a relatively simple procedure; here where
cliffs lifted precipitously both the engineering and labor
problems became acute. Especially the labor problem, for
among granitic formations there was work to be done
such as no white men would do. The omnipresent Chinese,
however, obliged, at lower wages, incidentally, than white
men called for.

At Weeksville, a camp near the present settlement of
Thompson Falls, Montana, building operations were
halted by a rocky upthrust against which blasting crews
labored all winter. The Chinese labor, imported coolies
for the most part, established their camp within blasting distance of the barrier—and day by day, as huge
boulders exploded into their camp to destroy and kill,
they stoically carried their dead away. The authorities took
no steps to insure their safety. Coolie labor was cheap.

Presently they broke camp and scattered into groups,
some groups persisting still in settling on dangerous
ground. In one instance a blast set off near such a camp
without warning thundered murderously, hurling boulders, stumps, debris down on the flimsy tents, so that the
coolie toll of dead that day counted more than half a
hundred.

Weeksville, like McCarthyville, was during its brief
career as hell-roaringly representative of railroad camps
as any. It was crowded with those who followed the money.
Saloons comprised practically one hundred per cent of
the buildings. Railroad boomtown characters are for the
most part forgotten, but the stories of Weeksville recall
certain persons: A Buzz Sweeney regulated, or attempted

to regulate, the town's saloon social life. He bumped into competition from Curly Campbell, whose wet-goods emporium was the hangout for various individuals of a more or less unwholesome character—Ohio Dan, Dick the Diver, the Barber, and Broncho Liz.

The clash between Campbell and Sweeney, sure to happen, came swiftly and ended in sudden death. Since innocent passersby were also involved, respectable citizens roused in wrath. There was a Vigilante meeting, and Ohio Dan, Dick the Diver, and the Barber died at the end of a rope. The Barber, with a recently broken leg, hobbled on crutches; they accorded him the honor of burial under the ground, and they thrust his crutches into the mound where they bleached in sun and snow for many years. Other persons whose reputations were not spotless headed out of the settlement with the Vigilantes after them. Some evenings later the law-enforcers gathered for a formal disbanding and a shot of whiskey, well satisfied with themselves.

"Law has come to Weeksville!" they said, hoisting a series of potent drinks. "Yuh can sleep now without barricadin' yore bed behind a bale of hay!"

At the same time railroad officials conducted an investigation and a general clean-up, and the Vigilantes offered a further toast to "no more corpses on the payroll."

In the spring the powder crews blasted the last of the granite upthrust away and the railroad went on. Whereupon an ancient redskin, who had declared that the mountain would not bow down even to the white man, lost faith in all creation and, saying, "The white man is too powerful. Even the mountains make way for him!" he threw himself into the river.

Other camps boomed. Some prospector discovered gold in the Coeur d'Alenes and there was a rush, through high mountain passes and over terrain so rough that even pack animals hesitated. The railroad brought supplies to the foot of the mountains and from there delivery was made precariously by mule- and burro-back, or most often by man-back. Sometimes men packed as much as a hundred pounds, and a big Norwegian is said to have wrestled a weight of two hundred pounds regularly. One freighter carried in a sheet-iron stove, taking no more than a week for the trip, and such were the rates asked—and paid—that his fee for that week's work was over $300.

Large as the profits of the railroads were, they never equaled this. But while human packers encountered natural obstacles on their trips, they never confronted some of the problems which beset the railroads.

There was Hominy Thompson, for instance, who did not like railroads; he considered them "too crowdin'," as he said when he rode thirty miles to warn away a family that had just settled in his territory. The family moved and left him to his solitude, but at a later date a railroad, also warned, failed to heed his order. Hominy tore out several lengths of rails, moved his legal domicile—a two-by-four shack—into the gap, and challenged all and sundry to remove him from his castle. To enforce his right further, he hoisted an American flag, and with a rifle in the crook of his arm was thumbing through an old text-book Constitution to find a passage descriptive of his situation when a sheriff and United States marshal arrived to arrest him. The railroad pushed on, and whistles and puffs shattered Hominy's peace for the rest of his days.

The Utah and Northern, in the '80's, encountered the

same difficulty when it attempted to cross a certain rancher's land without legal proceedings. This rancher was
not only adamant, but he knew his law, and for a time
it seemed that the road would be halted. Then neighbors,
not in sympathy with their stubborn friend, banded together to buy him out. The railroad continued on its way
and the buyers, taking what was left over of the land,
formed the settlement of Dillon, Montana.

In general the railroads crossed unclaimed land or land
given them by the government, but when they found their
progress balked by squatters or ranchers, their methods of
securing a right-of-way were apt to be direct. But their
attitude to their own employees seems to have achieved the
epitome of the paternal, at least to judge from a set of
rules released in 1913 by the Milwaukee Road: "Treat
your wife as you did when she was a sweetheart or bride.
You can't jaw your wife and make good on this job at the
same time. The man who leaves his wife in anger is the
man who broods over the quarrel and turns the switch
the wrong way. . . ."

CHANCE

High Border people have always been gamblers of one
sort or another; first with their lives against the redskins
and hardships, later gamblers for fortunes in the mountains and on the prairies. Everywhere you go you hear
stories of the great gamblers of the past; hear their names
spoken with reverence and awe; hear the tales, possibly
to a large extent apocryphal, of the mighty games and
mighty stakes. It is impossible to sift fancy from fact,

for there are certain elements about the High Border Country that pass credibility. But as they tell it . . .

The first gamblers were the redskins, and just as the white man's standard game was faro, and then poker and roulette, their standard game was a primitive kind of "Eeny, meeny, miny, mo," played with sticks. It is still played on the reservations, and its form is elementary: Ten sticks (and this is the fundamental form which may be changed extemporaneously according to certain rules) are placed between a pair of players, each stick representing a certain value. This is what in white man's poker parlance would be the pot. Then one of the red players takes two smaller sticks, one longer than the other, and doubles his fists over them, meanwhile holding his hands behind his back, and, usually, chanting. It is then the duty of his opponent to guess which hand holds the shorter stick. If he guesses right he takes one token from the pot; if he guesses wrong, the other player takes a token.

The game is played to the accompaniment of much chanting and screeching upon the part of the kibitzers. This is the equivalent perhaps of the so-called music which accompanied the dancing in the old-time hurdy-gurdy houses where the white man's jousts with chance took place—combination gambling dens and dance halls, where hurdy-gurdy girls, imported from the East, made clean-ups every season—and gamblers made larger clean-ups than the prospectors and miners who swarmed around their roulette tables and faro layouts.

The professional gamblers, sometimes known politely and poetically as Knights of the Green Cloth, plied their trade everywhere, by hook or crook, too often in the latter way; many a Knight, caught with an ace up his sleeve, went to his eternal sleep on boothill. They swarmed wherever there was money—down to Miles City, Montana, for instance, where the cattle barons stayed after they had sent their crack trail bosses and trail riders south to Texas to bring in pilgrim cattle. It might be spring before the herd arrived, and during the winter, when time hung heavy, mighty games of poker flourished—$20,000, $30,000, $50,000 on the table during a single night.

This consisted in the main of backroom playing, however, for while the barons did not hesitate to bet with friend or competitor in the cattle business, they shied away from professional card sharpers. The institutions for professional gambling flourished in the larger settlements —in Butte, the richest hill on earth; in Helena, city of gold; Cheyenne, on the golden trail; Bismarck, where steel rails brought a flood of money. Some of these gilded establishments were large—the Morehouse and Dutch Henry gambling house in Butte was large enough to permit 2000 persons to play at once.

High stakes, in which hundreds were counted as tinhorn and only thousands excited more than casual comment, passed over the green cloth, for in the '70's and '80's and in the '90's the High Border was a country of wealth. Even in the '60's, at the first gold strikes, money flowed freely. In the sluice boxes of Alder Gulch the miners allowed the children of the settlements to scrape gold from the riffles, with which to buy candy. Each little pool yielded around fifty cents. A quarter was the smallest monetary unit in circulation.

Sixty years later, in the 1930's, a placer miner considered himself lucky if his take of gold dust, after a fifteen-hour day, was fifty cents.

Swede Sam Wallin, in a Butte hotel, laid down three aces against an opponent's two pair and raked in a pot worth $25,000. In Helena several of the boys held a stud-poker session that ran five days; biggest pot was $86,000, and there were some five hundred packs of cards used. In a gilded Butte establishment at the turn of the century Freddie Heinze, arch-foe of the copper barons, played at roulette one evening and casually dropped $60,000. At one time he stood ahead almost $200,000. A certain girl named Gladys wriggled alluringly by his side and Heinze handed her $5000 worth of chips, with the comment "Buy yourself a fur coat!" to get rid of her.

Dick Schenkells, with four bits' worth of crackers, drifted into a settlement and bummed a dollar. Munching crackers, he bucked a small-time roulette wheel, and progressively went up the scale to the more gilded and expensive games. By dawn he stood $30,000 to the good.

His crackers not finished yet, he drifted on. By evening his crackers were gone and so was his roll. Contentedly, he threw his pack across his back and headed out of town, without even crackers.

In Fargo a dirty, ragged miner invaded the gilded precincts of one of the higher-class establishments and went directly to the roulette wheel. The croupier regarded him with a contemptuous eye as he drew a dirty roll of bills from a dirtier pocket and threw it on a number. "All?" asked the croupier. "All!" said the miner, fiddling nervously. The croupier looked at the bet, noted the twenty-dollar bill on the outside, and guessed there was perhaps a hundred dollars in the roll. Small-time stuff, he thought, and not bothering to pick it up, spun the wheel. The miner won. The croupier said, "Pretty lucky, pop!" and opened the roll. There was $5000 inside. The gilded establishment went out of business. . . .

Bill Graves, stagecoach driver between Virginia City and Salt Lake, hunched on the seat and wondered how the game down in the concord progressed. Four notorious gamblers of the '70's, Joe Goddard, Mike Conoley, Bill Ayers, and Gaspard LeCoeur, the sole passengers, wheeled the cards around to kill time. Bill Graves slowed his two-team vehicle and peered down at the men who were so intent on their cards that no word at all passed among them. Graves sighed, speeded his horses, and wished he could watch. Certainly, when four experts got together, there should be a wheeling of cards of a quality second to none.

There was. The four amused themselves very pleasantly until almost within the outskirts of Virginia City. Then Mr. Joe Goddard, who should have known better considering his years of experience, was so unwise as to question the validity of the cards in Mr. Mike Conoley's fist. There appeared, he insisted, to be a slight mistake somewhere, and if Mr. Conoley didn't have an ace up his sleeve, Joe was a ring-tailed wampus from Kokomo. Mr. Conoley countered abruptly by drawing his derringer pistol, while Mr. Goddard parried by drawing his; not to be outdone the Messrs. LeCoeur and Ayers drew theirs. Up on the seat Bill Graves flinched and decided the game could not be going so well. When silence descended he peered into the concord, to see Goddard, Conoley, and Ayers slumped lifeless on the floor, and LeCoeur gasping feebly. Of the four, LeCoeur alone lived. The game was over.

Betting was, and is, a universal pastime in the High

Border Country. As a pastime it is not confined to mechanical means; you can secure odds on practically anything, though the days are mostly over when the length of
a frog's jump, or the spot where a fly would alight, the
length of a sermon in church, or the number of peas in an
unopened pod, will draw money in the thousands of dollars. Gone are the days when Lucky Dan, successful miner,
and his drinking companion, both considerably under the
effects of liquor, bet on reciting the Lord's Prayer.

"You—hic! You don't know the Lord's Prayer!" the
companion said, and Lucky Dan replied, "I do—too!
Wanna bet?"

The companion did, and several hundred dollars were
placed on the table between them. Lucky Dan took a good,
long pull at the bottle, folded his hands, and recited,
"Now I lay me down to shleep—I pray the Lord my shoul
to keep—If I should—die before I wake—I pray the Lord
my shoul to take!"

Disappointed, the companion slammed his bottle down.
"Damned if I thought you could do it!" he cried. "But
you know it, word fer word!"

Gallopin' Dick Corbin, Butte itinerant and small-time
gambler, arranged one afternoon that the driver of a
wagon loaded with cordwood should park his team casually by the door of a saloon. Then Gallopin' Dick, just
as casually, sauntered among the loungers before the
place, and remarked that he bet the number of sticks on
the wagon was so and so. Instantly someone took him
up; various sports contributed a pot of some hundreds of
dollars. A count of the load proved Gallopin' Dick's estimate correct. He pocketed the money, paid the driver on
the quiet, and disappeared.

Gallopin' Dick had taken no chances—he had counted the blocks beforehand.

Most dramatic of the gambling games in all the High Border Country, past or present, took place on a night of June, 1876, aboard the steamboat *Far West* which lay off the mouth of the Big Horn River in the Yellowstone country. Custer's famed cavalrymen were aboard that boat. Early in the evening the officers assembled for a round of cards before the campaign they were to begin next day. Heaviest players, the plungers, were Captain Tom Custer, brother of the leader, and Lieutenant Calhoun and Captain Cromwell of the Sixth, and Captain Marsh of the Far West.

Custer himself did not join in the game, but remained in his stateroom, writing letters. He retired early, but could not sleep well because of the noise of the game—which did not break up until dawn, when the players adjourned, with Captain Marsh the heaviest winner. That day Custer's command headed up the river, and Captain Marsh never saw his poker companions again.

Most of the organized gambling took place in hurdy-gurdy houses. The hurdy-gurdy was a combination gambling den and dance hall with, of course, a bar along one side or end of the hall. Hurdy-gurdy girls came generally from the East; they were the equivalent of the dime-a-dance girls of today, though they cost their partners considerably more than that—the minimum for a dance usually being a dollar and a drink, on which the girls might receive a tip of another dollar.

These hurdy-gurdy houses were not, strictly, bawdy, though a large percentage of the girls would, for a price (not too high) comply without hesitation. They were more general, all-around entertainment, and their owners attempted to make this entertainment as inclusive as possible. In later years traveling troupes played in them, and miners toasted can-can dancers with mugfuls of what passed for champagne—or, if they were on the rocks but had a prospect, with shots of red-eye bought on the cuff.

Billy and Kitty Nuttall specialized in hurdy-gurdys throughout the High Border and it was in one of their places, the Bella Union at Deadwood in the Dakotas, that Jack McCall killed Wild Bill Hickok. Kitty Nuttall became known far and wide for her houses which offered the best—including killings.

Far more notorious, however, was Josephine Hensley, a native of Ireland grown to womanhood in Chicago. Her husband Jack, commonly known as Black Hawk because he hailed from the mining camp of that name in Colorado, added to the family treasury by gambling in a manner that tripped him up at intervals. Josephine, or Chicago Joe, was forced to settle his scrapes. She scattered much gold, well able to afford it after she had become one of the most successful hurdy-gurdy proprietors in the mining region. Her establishment in Helena, Montana, had an outgo of more than a thousand dollars a month and an income of sufficient volume above that to make her a rich woman.

In the '8o's the territorial legislature of Montana passed a law making hurdy-gurdy houses illegal. Chicago Joe continued blithely on her way. When an ambitious young attorney threatened her with an enforcement of the ruling and demanded that her hurdy-gurdy house close up at once, Chicago Joe merely sniffed, had the young attorney thrown out of her place, and continued to furnish high-class entertainment of any sort—*any* sort—for those who had the price.

But the attorney could not be bluffed. He brought suit and made things uncomfortable for her. Josephine was not to be downed, however, for she hired the best lawyers in the territory and by the simple trick of producing a copy of Webster's Dictionary cleared herself of the accusations of the attorney.

According to Webster, a hurdy-gurdy was a musical instrument. Joe's lawyers argued that a hurdy-gurdy house therefore would be a place where hurdy-gurdys were made, sold, or played. They challenged the jury to find a single hurdy-gurdy in Chicago Joe's place. They even took the jury there and turned the place inside out in their eagerness to prove the non-existence of hurdy-gurdys. The jury reeled back to the courtroom, one of the gayer blades clutching a lady's garter, and found Chicago Joe absolutely guiltless of the charge of running a hurdy-gurdy house.

But Chicago had had her scare. She changed her house into a variety theater, where women entertainers received a commission on all drinks they could persuade the customers to order. Vaudeville was presented on a stage at one end of the hall. Over all, Chicago Joe presided grandly, becoming greater of girth as the years passed until at last she could scarcely walk. Her dresses, invariably the same, of heavy velvet, dark green or purple, with a pink-lined Elizabethan collar and wide, golden, jewel-studded girdle around her waist, never changed. She passed on just before the new century and they buried her in a special oversized casket.

8. Metal Empire

Capital Feud

MARCUS DALY, Butte copper baron, in the '80's selected a site for a new smelter city. He gazed reflectively at a cow. "Main Street," he said, "will run straight north and south through that critter!"

The town was platted, the smelter constructed, and the name of Copperopolis selected, then discarded. It was replaced by Anaconda, after the Anaconda mine in Butte. Ben Hickey, the discoverer of this mine, read in a newspaper a decade and a half before Marcus Daly—"Grant encircled Lee like a giant anaconda." Ben Hickey could not identify an anaconda, but he was a northern sympathizer; he christened his mine, and years later the new smelter settlement of Marcus Daly's was given the same name.

Daly dreamed great dreams for his child. Scorning expense, he founded a newspaper, the *Standard*, which he staffed with the best of New York newspapermen. The only sheet in a little settlement then of less than 3000 population, the *Standard* outbid the New York *Herald* for artists to provide one of the first colored comic-strip sections in the United States. It boosted Anaconda as capital of Montana, and this soon became one of Daly's burning ambitions; there ensued a hard-fought campaign which was echoed in other capital feuds of other of the High Border states.

This was the year before Daly began to oppose the ambitions of a certain Dutch engineer, Freddie Heinze, and he had a great deal of time to devote to his scheme of changing the capital of Montana from Helena to Anaconda. Furthermore a fortune backed his move, such a fortune, indeed, that the citizens of Helena, temporary capital and political center since early territorial days, became alarmed, and dipped freely into their own gold-lined pockets, to the profit of voters throughout the state.

Helena, squatting in grimy splendor along narrow, crooked Last Chance Gulch, had been one of the focal points of Montana and northern Idaho since the days of gold discovery in the '6o's. Center of the hard-rock gold-mining region, during the '8o's and '9o's it boasted more millionaires per capita than any other city of the United States. The settlement's history, from the founding days to the turn of the century, had been turbulent, marked especially by fire after fire that swept through it because of the way in which buildings were crowded together. Helena had a large Chinese population which was, periodically, threatened with extinction; the Orientals were exceedingly careless when it came to building chimneys. But there were invariably too many of them to be evicted casually, and the white men failed to enforce any ordinances about chimney construction, with the result that fires continued, too many to be recorded—except the "great" fire of the '7o's, which blazed through the town right up to the local brewery. Volunteers, who had been fighting the flames half-heartedly, now became desperate, and made a gallant last stand until the water supply failed. Cries of grief rose above the roar of the holocaust. All was not lost, however, for just then the owners of the brewery began hoisting kegs of beer to the roof of the building, and the volunteers, gaining heart again, knocked in the kegs and poured beer at the advancing wall of fire, successfully halting it.

After the fire an enterprising citizen discovered eight chickens trapped under charred timbers, and assuming that because the birds were still alive they must possess a certain immunity to heat, he began to work on a new Helena breed which would withstand fires. His efforts were in vain.

Helena mining barons had quite recently graduated from shirtsleeves; business magnates had gained their positions against the sternest competition—and were sometimes of a type exemplified by the hero of a success story printed in a magazine of the period. This gentleman came from east of the Mississippi, and on his journey west halted on the prosperous Nebraska farm of a man about to die. He had some schooling in law, and the farmer welcomed him, asking him to draw up a last will and testament. The lawyer inspected the property with a careful eye, listed the assets, and then proceeded to pen the will. Heirs designated by the dying farmer were a pair of sisters and several sons, absent at the moment. Grasping his opportunity, our hero cut down the portion allotted to the others and added to the will a provision giving himself almost half the farm, thus, as the article put it, "showing the independence of character for which he has since been noted."

The Helena mining barons and business men and other

citizens, including the Chinese, did not want Marcus Daly to take the capital away from them and plant it in his new smelter city. They scattered publicity to voters throughout the state who would shortly be called upon to decide the issue. These broadsides aimed to tell Montanans in the hinterland about the superiority of Helena as a cultural center. "Helena—Socially Supreme—Montana's Center of Fashion" one such bulletin read, to which Anaconda rebutted in print: "—Montana's center of fashion, refinement, gentility, etiquet, kettle drums, high fives, progressive euchre and mixed drinks."

Helena, rich in gold and during that period the nearest thing to New York west of the Mississippi and north of San Francisco, made discreet reply: "The capital committee is aware that it lays itself open, in a sense, to the debauched hirelings, the obscure boors and buffoons of the Anaconda press, who upon the slightest pretext bring with coarse and ribald jest the preposterous charge that Helena is casting invidious reflections upon the society of other Montana towns. . . . Always excepting Anaconda, a poor, remote camp which seems to be buried hopelessly in barbarism, . . ." the citizens of Helena continued, hedging for votes, "The city of Helena is prepared to admit and that willingly, cheerfully, manfully, that there are many towns in Montana that have attained a high degree of civilization. . . ."

"We hesitate to use so coarse and vulgar an expression, but the fact is that Helena has always grubstaked the entire state of Montana, and it is Helena's duty and privilege to oversee all that is going on. . . ."

Arguments were summarized by the Anaconda opposition and in a pamphlet, jeeringly written, the following statements were presented to the voters of Montana: "Why Anaconda is unfit to be capital: (1) Anaconda is lamentably lacking in tallyhoes, four-in-hands, drags, waxed floors, dress suits, Browning clubs, theosophical societies, ceramics, art, coteries, eight-course dinners, button gloves, skirt dancing, and other social facilities. (2) It is impossible to walk the streets of Anaconda without seeing workingmen and their children. . . . (3) The workingmen and their families are addicted to large quantities of solid food, and the thick, nauseous fumes of corned-beef and cabbage settles over the town like a pall. . . . (4) The whistles that blow at seven o'clock, so soon after society people have retired, are an intolerable nuisance. (5) Anaconda allows no Chinamen in her limits, and all laundry work must be sent to higher-priced establishments. . . . (6) The heavy ore trains cause such a jarring of the earth for miles that it is impossible to elevate and hold a glass of liquor to the lips. . . ."

And, it was added: "(7) Anaconda tolerates social gatherings of all kinds within her corporate limits, with no requirements in the way of evening dress. It is said that people have been married there without gloves. . . ."

Other startling reasons for the continued supremacy of Helena were put forward—though it must be pointed out that most of the satirically-worded pamphlets had their origin in Anaconda.

"Reasons why Helena should remain capital: (1) Helena is the most aristocratic city in Montana. She leads in fashion, culture, and thought. In professional as well as social life, Helena is peerless." Anaconda warmed up after this preliminary innocuous statement. "Helena is an authority on all matters of etiquette and refinement and some of her society people are always ready to impart needed information to visitors of limited advantage and inferior breeding! (2) Helena's criminal classes are uniformly courteous and gentlemanly. (3) Helena possesses one of the largest, best-planned, most luxurious and heaviest mortgaged club houses in the country."

This last was a reference to the Montana Club building, designed by Cass Gilbert, which was the center of Helena's social life. The anonymous genius from Anaconda who wrote this particular bulletin now delivered his last and most destructively effective blast against Helena: "(4) In proportion to population, Helena has more balls, parties, hops, routs, toots, soirees, receptions, musicales, drive whists, pink teas, conversaziones, high fives and low dresses, drinks more champagne, runs bigger bar bills, keeps later hours, dances longer, kicks higher, and practices a larger number and greater variety of bows, scrapes, courtesies, obeisances, genuflections, salams, salutes, and squirms than any other city, east or west."

The battle went merrily on, but Helena laughed last and in the election retained her position as capital of the Treasure State of Montana. Her supremacy was never again seriously questioned until the middle 1930's when one night the earth shook, doing some millions of dollars' worth of damage and loosing the statue of Justice atop the capitol so that she swung and turned her back on Helena. This was the High Border's only disastrous earthquake, though redskin legends tell of the earth's terrific upheaval in years before the coming of the white man.

City of Copper

Butte—gaunt gallow's frames against a smoky sky, a grimy settlement huddled along an upsweep of barren rock. The "richest hill on earth," they call it, and rightly, for beneath the city run mile upon mile of timbered tunnels out of which comes the metal indispensable to modern civilization and modern war—copper. In the late '80's and '90's and during the first decade of the present century copper barons held sway in Butte, just as out on the prairie the cattle barons ruled their ranges and lumber barons ruled the timberlands.

There were many cattle barons and lumber barons, but there were only two copper barons—Marcus Daly and W. A. Clark. And perhaps a third—a little Dutch engineer, Freddie Heinze.

Clark and Daly, rough miners themselves in the beginning, foresaw the potential wealth in copper at a time when gold was still god. They built Butte—once the toughest town on earth. Echoes of that doubtful fame can still be feebly heard; police dockets of modern Butte give evidence of frequent one-man crusades to revive the past glory.

Clark, a farmer from Pennsylvania, built his copper holdings into a financial empire second only to that of J. P. Morgan and Company. Marcus Daly developed his interest in copper to a point of feudal supremacy until he and Clark, in a little city of 80,000 but still the most important settlement in the High Border Country, clashed in a war that shook the financial structure of the United States. And each of them was harassed by a certain Fred

Heinze, a $100-a-month surveyor who found a way to beat the Law of the Apex.

In the '90's Butte was a wide-open town. A reporter for a Denver paper—and Denver was a fairly rough spot—came to Butte and secured work on a newspaper. Assigned to his round, he returned several hours later, cleaned out his desk, and departed with the remark, "I'm going back to Denver where it's nice and tame!"

In the gilded mansions there was much drinking of champagne and a playing of poker for stakes not equaled in New York or London. On the streets and in the mine-honeycomb beneath existed such men as Callahan the Bum (who knew fifty-seven ways of bumming a drink), the Duke of Kakiak, the Gambler's Ghost (an original kibitzer who watched the gambling games), Dandy Jim, Fred the Rattler, Three-fingered Jack, Curly Dick, Froggy, Bail Land Charlie, Fourth-of-July, Spokane John, Pin Pool Pete, Old Poison, Red-wagon Jim, and others more respectably named, John Smith, Paddy Ryan, and Kelly.

The Irish were everywhere—and from every portion of the old country: Stonethrowers from Tipperary; Fardowns from south of Ireland; Cleathmores also from the South but differentiated in that they were somewhat less profane of tongue; Skuckman from Mayo; Bearhaven Swedes from County Cork; Big Wheelers from Waterford; Catmen from Kilkenny. Everywhere, too, were the Welsh—Cousin Jacks and Cousin Jennies, they called them, in a respectable corruption of the word "Cussin'."

By day miners risked life and limb in dark tunnels; by night the red-light districts, not yet emasculated and transformed into the section known as Venus Alley but out-and-out, raw, old red-light districts, boomed with a

noise that reached to the Atlantic coast. In the dawn, when
the hands of the clock reached six, an engineer named
Bigelow played *Annie Laurie* on the whistle of the smelter
where he worked; over the city, ceaselessly, the smelters
belched forth smoke and noxious gases that made the already barren lands surrounding more barren.

Butte—the unbelievable. In the palaces of men who
only a few years before had been starving miners the finest
of French wines flowed, while down the street, in shacks,
the Salvation Army cared for other men who chanted:

> *In the days when I was hard up,*
> *For want of food and fire*
> *I used to tie my shoes up*
> *With little bits of wire.*
> *The times were hard and troublesome,*
> *Oft hungry I did feel,*
> *And it was a great temptation*
> *That I didn't turn to steal.*

In the district court cases included the City of Butte,
respondent, *vs.* Mon Chow; City of Butte, respondent, *vs.*
Ah On; City of Butte, respondent, *vs.* Ah Ching; City of
Butte, *vs.* En Lung; City of Butte *vs.* Ah Ping, Lovey
Chung, and Tam Fray. A prominent business man bought
a typewriter and then beat up the salesman because the
purchase had been made under the impression that the
machine would help the purchaser with his spelling. In
court a man, charged with stealing wood, was given his
freedom with the following remark: "But some of us figure
he stole the wood, the dirty crook!"

There were Irish picnics, not only in the sense that the
celebrants were Irish, but also because the picnics invari-

ably ended in a tremendous throwing of beer bottles. A carload of grindstones was dumped on the sidewalk in front of the establishment of the merchant who had ordered them. No harm in leaving them there overnight, he decided; who would want to steal several tons of grindstones? Yet during the night a thief did make off with them.

Spratt, gentleman lawyer, dandy of dandies, represented many persons accused of the lowest crimes in criminal code. Entering the court day after day and called upon to defend some one of a soiled group huddled in the room, Spratt would sniff slightly and demand of his honor, "Will the court please designate which one of those damn —— I am to represent?"

There was the unnamed gentleman of the bar, who chanted an eternal, pet expression, *"Falso in uno. Falso in umnibus,"* in a manner to cower the most hardened of self-taught lawyers. He was the barrister who, representing a defendant in some particularly important case, launched into a lengthy oration which he concluded with *"E pluribus unum, falso in umnibus."* He won his case because the jury figured he must be good.

In this era the type of entertainment known in future years as the walkathon, dancethon, and what not, came into being. George Wilcox, the Great Pedestrian, challenged any two men to a six-day walk. A pair of hardhoofed miners, Adams and Waid, accepted after rustling up a wager of $1500. They walked the shoes off Mr. Wilcox, who trained on beer and celebrated too liberally before the starting gun.

It was a period in which Tom Coughlin shot at a rat and hit a case of dynamite, to his great pain. There were

labor troubles; the mine owners demanded more and
more work. There is the story of Paddy Hardy, working
on an ore dump, who got mixed up with a blast; he was
shot so skyhigh that he was gone for minutes. When he
slammed back, his clothes torn from him but body whole,
except for numerous lacerations and bruises, his anger
raged because the foreman docked him fifteen minutes'
pay for his absence.

Butte. Pat Crowe, famous criminal, lectured here on
temperance. Kidnapper of Edward Cudahy, he had
planned the snatch of John D. Rockefeller, and went to
Butte to turn himself over to the law. Later he came back
to lambast John Barleycorn: "You folks see before you
a man who has sinned. I know the hard path of the
drunkard! Shun wines and whiskies and beers as you
would the plague! I—I know whereof I speak! I have suffered— My brethren and sistern, I implore you to give
up drink!"

Butte. Where a shopkeeper one day drew a prominent
citizen into his place of business and pointed at five shelves
of books. "I was leary of books at first," he confided,
"but I figured somebody in the fifty thousand people
here might want to read a book. And look how big my
library is now! Maybe fifty books there!"

A priest wrote back to the old country, "Living in
Butte is like being in Ireland." A representative of the
government, on a special mission, counted forty-seven different nationalities, and later found he had overlooked
five.

Mary MacLain, later to disturb the early-twentieth-cen-
tury moral standards of the nation with her writings, stood
on Broadway with a basket of cold boiled potatoes on one

arm and a bottle of olives under the other; she watched with detached curiosity the way in which Callahan the Bum committed suicide by hanging himself to the awning in front of a jewelry store. Life in the street went on as usual, and few looked either at Mary or Callahan the Bum.

A woman owned a rooming house next to the jail grounds and one day she issued an invitation possible only in Butte: "I'm going to give a little hanging party in the morning and would like to have you join us. It'll be quiet, just a congenial few. The view from my window is better than standing in the jail yard."

The recipient of the invitation declined, remarking that he was already dated up. For a wedding, he explained. A friend whose daughter was about to be married had come to him, saying, "I think my girl will be happier if Papa and Mamma are married first. I've arranged to be married just before my daughter's ceremony—"

In Montana's historical library at Helena can be found evidence of the correctness of hangings—engraved invitations with R. S. V. P. in the lower left-hand corner.

A bride, native to the country, married a rising copper baron. Among the wedding presents she found a Rembrandt. Visitors expressed admiration for the picture, at which the bride beamed. But one day she turned to a girl friend, known as Mike, just after a guest had departed. "Mike!" she implored. "Tell me! Who in hell is this Rembrandt?"

One of the city's prominent citizens turned health expert. "The thing to do," he advised, and he practiced what he preached, "is never to bathe from the first frost of fall to the last frost of spring. The oil—" he would explain, flipping his swallowtails open and draining a glass of champagne at a gulp—"of the body forms a coating and is like an extra skin. It helps to keep out the chill."

Down at the racetracks men and women crowded against the fence for a glimpse of horses good or better than anything the East could offer. Madams brought their charges in fancy carriages, airing them and their imported silks —a type of preview for the male public. Money flowed high, wide, and handsome—hard money, silver, for paper was looked upon with suspicion. It was a saying of Butte that no man was dressed unless his pockets were weighted down with silver. Betting hit the skies; the horses came in amid a thunder of applause. Men strained forward eagerly, and women clutched their rosaries.

BATTLING MEN OF BUTTE

There are mighty fighters and mighty fights in High Border history, but the mightiest fight of all took place at the old Crystal Springs Roadhouse near Butte in the last years of the '80's. It was no championship brawl— though Butte in later years looked upon championship fights a-plenty: During one week, centering upon the Fourth of July, 1903, the sporting citizens sponsored no less than three fistic encounters of major importance— Tommy Ryan, former welterweight champion of the world, vs. John Willie, won by a knockout by Ryan in the fourth round; Joe Wolcott, welterweight champion of the world, vs. Mose LaFontise, for the championship of the world, won by a knockout by Wolcott in the third; and Joe Gans, Negro lightweight champion of the world, vs.

Buddy King, for the championship of the world, won by a knockout by Gans in the fifth round.

But the battle of John Gallagher vs. G. H. Ward, by profession a miner and a carpenter respectively, is the world's longest recorded bout. It ran for 105 rounds, and was fought, under London prize-ring rules, with bare fists.

Mr. Ward had made some slighting remark to Mr. Gallagher. Through the agency of friends who yearned to see a good, old-fashioned free-for-all, arrangements for the bout were made. It was decided that the two men would fight it out, bare knuckles, observing the gentlemanly code then prevalent, under which tearing off an ear was legal but gouging out an eye was not—unless the victim happened to be unpopular with the audience. Several sporting clubs of Butte took an interest in the affair and attended to the details, including one that had to do with fair play: The audience, strictly hand-picked and including an equal number of Ward and Gallagher supporters—in case of a general battle—was required to check guns and knives at the door.

The roadhouse owner dressed up his place for the occasion with an extra bar. It is not known if Messrs. Ward and Gallagher imbibed, but at the appointed hour of 8:00 P.M. they stepped into the ring and, under flaring oil lamps, squared off, on the face of each a scowl calculated to freeze the other into inaction. This maneuver proving unsuccessful, they pranced around, showing their muscular development.

"Gentlemen!" implored the referee, frockcoated and correct, while the police department, sent out to stop the fight, cheered from its complimentary ringside section. "Mix it!"

There followed a bit of sparring and then the fight was on in earnest. Presently gore spilled on the sawdust in the ring and both Messrs. Ward and Gallagher mouthed curses frightful enough to break the morale of an Easterner but merely irritating to these bellicose citizens of Butte. The hours passed, pleasantly enough, and cheers began to thicken as the patrons renewed their visits to the bar. Gallagher's supporters hoisted drinks in friendly fashion with Ward's supporters, and declared that the boys ought to mix it up more—though by now both men reeled, covered with blood and so battered above the waist that they might have been working on each other with bludgeons. The Butte citizens of the period liked their ring work rough.

Ward forged ahead, to drive Gallagher back. In the 48th round there was a momentary flurry of excitement, with gloom on the part of Gallagher's backers—their champion, knocked head over heels, landed so hard in the sawdust on one arm and snapped it so violently that the sound of crackling bone was audible to ringsiders. But instantly Gallagher came back with fresh fury, and his backers felt a little more comfortable about their bets. They hastened to the bar for another drink.

They were not out of the woods yet, for some hours later, in the 97th round, Gallagher went flat on his back and lay there. Someone brought him back to consciousness with a liberal application of wildcat juice, and hoisted him to his feet. He caught his opponent off guard then, leveled a haymaker with his good fist, and landed a blow on Ward's face of sufficient force to lay that gentleman low and completely unconscious, so that a dozen or more applications of wildcat juice scarcely revived him.

The blow injured Ward, and he never came back. He fumbled around for several more minutes, and in the 105th Gallagher got him again, on the side of his head. Ward's knees buckled; he collapsed, and no applications of alcohol, cursing, or pleading could rouse him. The judges decided that he had been defeated, and proclaimed Gallagher winner.

They left Ward in the sawdust and adjourned to the bar. They toasted the champion until dawn, though dawn was imminent considering the length of the match. Then someone remembered Ward, and thought perhaps he should be cared for; when they picked him up he was almost no longer of this earth. There was a universal rush to quit the roadhouse. There were citizens in Butte of a somewhat influential sort who considered this sort of thing undignified, not to mention downright unlawful, and they had enough power to stir up trouble. So the Crystal Springs Roadhouse emptied itself in a very short space of time, and the longest fight in the history of the world faded to memory.

Ward died entirely the next day and the police, expressing great surprise that such an unfortunate affair had taken place, took up a search for Gallagher. But their heart was not in the task, and besides, Gallagher's friends had spirited him away. So they marked the case closed.

COPPER BATTLE

The two great copper barons wrangled and fought and, in between times, amused themselves according to their tastes—W. A. Clark by collecting great works of art, Marcus Daly—thereby cementing his popularity with his miners—by horse racing. Daly imported the best blood of Kentucky and on a magnificent ranch in the Bitterroot Valley bred horses to rank with the immortals—such as his Ogden, Montana, Bathhampton, Scottish Chieftain, Tammany. He bet heavily on his own animals; bet, too, on a certain Fourth-of-July celebration of the early '90's when a bull and a bear, both untamed, met in the Columbia Gardens of Butte for the entertainment of the citizens of Butte. There was considerable disappointment, for the bull chased the bear back into his pen, from which no amount of prodding could budge him.

Continued the next day, the fight changed. The bear did not retreat; instead, he charged, and there ensued a life-and-death struggle which the citizens of Butte cheered loudly. They suspected but did not care at the moment that in the offing was a battle of bulls and bears destined to rock the foundations of the copper nation which Butte represented—a battle of courts and wits and force and skullduggery, in which the bears and bulls were not the relatively innocuous creatures of the Columbia Gardens of Butte, but traders on the New York Stock Exchange. The battleground was Butte and Wall Street, and the cause of all this was a hitherto unknown surveyor named Freddie Heinze.

The Amalgamated Company, colossus of copper,

sprawled insolently powerful over Butte Hill. Marcus Daly was at the head of it, king of an empire that touched, indirectly, Standard Oil. Freddie Heinze, or as his fortunes soared F. Augustus Heinze, worked for him as a $100-a-month surveyor, but yearned for bigger and better things.

He was clever, this Freddie Heinze who had come to Butte from the Columbia School of Mines in the last years of the 1880's—far cleverer than any other man in the history of Butte. As he peered through his transit, he dreamed dreams, and made plans that had to do with what was known as the Law of the Apex. When in the middle years of the 1890's he inherited a small fortune, he played about in Germany for a while, then returned to New York to form an ore-purchasing company, having decided to put his plans into action.

The Law of the Apex provided that any miner who located a vein surfacing on his property—apexing—could legally follow that vein through and under the property of another man, to hell if necessary. This was all quite clear while the vein remained intact, but Butte Hill is a mass of rock, of twisted and broken veins, and it is too often anybody's guess where a vein begins again after it has broken. Freddie Heinze located an unstaked space of ground, seventy-five feet long and ten feet wide atop Butte Hill—and claimed that the best of the Amalgamated mines apexed there and were his property.

A district judge of the period named Clancy issued an injunction stopping all production in the Amalgamated mines affected by Heinze's claim. Thousands of men found themselves out of work. There were mutterings, oaths, grumbling, for in spite of the big money in Butte, the miners themselves saw relatively little of it and even a shutdown of a few days affected them. The chorus swelled, and before long, such being the volatile temperament of Butte, a mob gathered, to charge down upon Judge Clancy with a singleness of purpose that was appalling: "Hang Clancy!"

The police, not in sympathy with Heinze's ambitions, kept carefully aloof. They regarded him, as did most of the people of Butte, as an upstart, a fresh youngster who must in time be slapped down. So the mob charged after Clancy, unhindered by forces of law. The judge managed to avoid it by hiding out for several hours; and then, at midnight of the day on which he had issued the injunction, he found himself forced to dissolve it. The miners went back to work, and Heinze's claims went to higher courts. Several years later they ruled that Heinze had no right of possession to the Amalgamated ore.

But while the case went through the courts the little man of Butte, Freddie Heinze, had no intention of sitting idly by. He cast his eye on a barren mine, the Minnie Healy, originally worked by Marcus Daly but thrown aside when it failed to present traces of copper ore. Heinze got possession of the mine and began to explore the workings, not in any hope of ore discovery but rather to find some vein which he might offer as proof of the contention he intended to make, that the vein apexing on Minnie Healy property ran off into the rich Leonard mine of the Amalgamated, just a few yards away from the shafts of the Minnie Healy. And here Freddie Heinze's lucky star brightened; his miners broke into a huge body of copper. The Minnie Healy developed into the richest ore-producer on Butte Hill.

Daly, in a fury, brought suit against Heinze, but the

case dragged on for several years, with charges and counter-
charges, through court after court, with decisions constantly reversed because of accusations—some of them sub-
stantiated—of bribery. Through it all Heinze retained possession of the mine and worked it furiously. He kept his
smelter in ore and provided himself with funds to continue the legal actions against the Amalgamated.

Freddie Heinze was still not content and, evidently on
the theory that a good offense could be the best defense,
he next secured a certain Rarus claim, adjoining the
Amalgamated's Michael Davitt. He was no longer now a
little fellow tackling the giants; he had hamstrung the
giants and the Amalgamated limped increasingly. On the
Stock Exchange the masters of finance grew anxious, and
pooled their resources to break Heinze.

Forbidden to enter the Rarus, Heinze formed a new
company, not bound, he claimed, by court orders and
began to work the mine. In the Berkeley Mine, an Amalgamated property, they could hear the blasts in the Rarus,
but were powerless to interfere. There had once been a
connecting drift between the Berkeley and the Rarus,
bulkheaded some years back with concrete. A Berkeley
foreman broke through the bulkhead one night and found
an empty chair evidently intended for a watchman at that
moment off duty. The foreman made his way slowly forward, through many hundreds of feet of workings—to discover eventually a shaft leading into the Amalgamated's
Michael Davitt which district court orders had sealed due
to Heinze's legal action and which Amalgamated had
abandoned absolutely, unaware that it could be entered
beneath the ground. But Heinze had broken in, and out
of the Michael Davitt's richest deposit Heinze's men had

carved an enormous stope and stolen from it thousands of dollars' worth of ore.

With evidence of trespass the foreman hastened back to his own mine. But Heinze managed to secure legal delay. Fined a small sum for evading the court's order to cease work in the Rarus, Heinze merely laughed, and when Amalgamated engineers measured the ore he had stolen from the Michael Davitt via the Rarus, they discovered he had almost exhausted the metallic body—several millions of dollars' worth.

The Amalgamated now ceased to be polite, and neglected to obey court orders. They began a battle underground, and underground, miner against miner, there raged presently an unparalleled war. The Amalgamated men, armed with picks and shovels, stormed into the Rarus to drive the miners out. But a flow of air from the Rarus down the narrow shaft which gave them entrance to Heinze's mine stopped them; Heinze's miners burned old clothes and boots, and the stench halted the charge. When the air had cleared, the Amalgamated men prepared to charge again, and the Rarus crew put dry slaked lime in the high-pressure compressed-air lines and blew it down on the invaders. They retreated, choking, but came back for more, and the Rarus miners grew desperate. They resorted to that ultimate weapon of mining wars—dynamite.

They set off a big blast, killing nobody though poisonous fumes knocked out two men. The shift then on duty for the Amalgamated was now through, and the men made way for a fresh crew. The foreman of the newcomers realized that his men would probably get the short end of the deal, so he ordered the attack abandoned. But first, he decided, he would build a bulkhead to close the shaft.

This structure was almost completed when a heavier blast of dynamite went off, killing several men. The Amalgamated miners retreated with their casualties, and the war shifted above ground.

There was a coroner's investigation of the deaths, but no charges ever came to light. The battle went on, verbally. Courts were swamped with suits. Heinze was growing bigger and stronger; he slashed at his mastodon adversaries until they limped from their wounds.

But they were big, these adversaries; money, more money than Heinze could ever hope to secure, backed them, and though they limped now they nevertheless forced Heinze to fight desperately. To raise the tremendous sums needed he had to mine thousands of tons of ore—ore staked long ago by the Amalgamated, and Heinze's only by right of the apex law.

He brought suit to gain possession of one of the richest veins on Butte Hill—nearly a thousand feet long. Judge Clancy awarded him the property and the Amalgamated carried the suit to higher courts. But before they could secure a reversal, they knew Heinze would have the ore all mined out. So just before Clancy's decision was made they placed tons of dynamite in the stope, and when word of Clancy's award to Heinze came, they detonated it. The stope caved in, wrecked completely, and Heinze realized with fateful clarity that before he could clear it, Amalgamated, backed by bigger money than he could hope to raise, would beat him in the higher courts.

Heinze's star began to dim; his hold loosed. He realized he was defeated underground. There was, however, still a chance above ground—he could turn the miners of Butte against Amalgamated. With his own hands Heinze blew long blasts on the Minnie Healy's whistle—the signal of disaster, which in the mines means death of the most horrible sort. Miners off shift and wives and children of miners raced to the Minnie Healy, and while they stood around wondering, Heinze spread the word that Amalgamated had flooded the shaft of the Minnie Healy, drowning the miners. Instant mob action followed; two thousand Heinze sympathizers marched towards the Amalgamated office with intentions of a wholesale hanging.

Wallace Corbett, superintendent for the Leonard Mine, saw the mob and took action. A loaded rifle in hand, and an earnest desire to use it, he raced to Heinze's office, menaced the foreman and supervisors there, and told them quite flatly that if they failed to stop the mob in time, he would blow their heads off. Heinze's men had no choice; they overtook the mob, convinced the leaders that while the Minnie Healy had been flooded (by Heinze's orders) the miners were all safe. The mob grumbled but presently dispersed. Men, cursing, wanted to know what Freddie Heinze meant. Their faith in him, beginning to waver, took another downward turn. Freddie Heinze, who had lifted himself to a point where he could speak casually of millions, was through.

Through he was, but still the Amalgamated men were forced to buy him out. They paid handsomely—$14,-000,000. "We'll drive Fred Heinze out of Montana if it takes $10,000,000!" Henry H. Rogers of the Amalgamated is reported to have threatened at the beginning of the fight. He had been optimistic. Litigation cost Amalgamated a million dollars a year. And $14,000,000 for Heinze was a fair amount of money.

With the withdrawal of Heinze the Montana courts

could attend to their regular business for the first time in six years. They dismissed eighty lawsuits, involving over $100,000,000. Butte, all of Montana for that matter, settled down to a more-or-less humdrum existence.

Heinze, $14,000,000 in his pocket, sought new worlds to conquer. In New York he founded a copper trust to rival the Amalgamated, calling it the United Copper Company, and a string of banks. But his copper star had tarnished. His mines proved worthless, his banks folded, Standard Oil opposition wrecked his copper trust. Broken, health shattered, drinking cheap whiskey now—sometimes bummed from acquaintances—instead of imported champagne, dealing in dollars where he had once dealt in millions, then dealing in cents, he wandered from city to city, a promoter of doubtful reputation. Clark and Daly passed on in the grandeur of great wealth, but the end of Freddie Heinze came under conditions he would have laughed at only a few years before.

When they lifted up his dead body they noticed that his right hand was clenched. They pried it open and found there a single coin, emblematic of the glory that had been his for just a little while.

A penny. Made, like all pennies, of copper.

Heart of an Awl

The Coeur d'Alenes, rugged mountains of the panhandle of Idaho, were christened in the early 1800's after a characteristic of the French fur traders from whose language the name was taken. During the '80's and '90's these mountains poured wealth in the form of silver and lead and gold into the pockets of certain barons who, as far as their employees were concerned, had like the French fur traders the "heart of an awl." These owners, tycoons of America's westward expansion, pocketed vast profits and damned their miners to an underground existence compared with which hell was comfortable.

The wealth of the Coeur d'Alenes, so story has it, was discovered by a jackass. The prospector-owner of the pack animal—who immortalized the event by displaying a life-size portrait of his animal in the lobby of a hotel he built in Spokane—had been tethered beside a lightning-shattered tree. The jackass pawed the ground around the tree and broke open a rock. The owner examined the rock idly—and went whooping out to civilization to record his claim.

During the last years of the '80's, there was discontent in the Coeur d'Alenes, much grumbling against the silver barons, and in 1890 and 1891 open and bloody war flared between the mine owners and their employees. The Four-Million-Dollar-Burro had uncovered great wealth, but he also caused a vast amount of trouble. "Strike" became the watchword, and it was not the polite bargaining of the present day. It was war—miner against baron—with no holds barred. The land was primitive, though its wealth compared with that of some of the richest spots on earth. The miners were primitive. It followed that battle, too, was primitive.

It can best be told, perhaps, from the viewpoint of one man—Charlie Siringo. To oppose an organization of miners known as the Miners' Union, which included the largest percentage of the workers in the Coeur d'Alenes, the owners organized the Mine Owners Association and retained Charlie Siringo as their personal contact man.

Siringo was thrown into adventures that included a near-lynching and a siege in which he had to hold thirty or forty men at bay while he backed across a street to escape.

Charlie started out in the town of Wallace—then, as today, a big-scale producer of lead and silver. He immediately hired out as a miner. Union rules being much less strict then—unions of the period were designed more to blackmail the owners than to improve the status and skill of the workers—Charlie secured work without trouble. He went to work at Gem, a mining camp some four miles back in a gulch from Wallace. Gem, built around several mines, lay deep in the hills surrounded by grim cliffs.

In time Charlie joined the Gem Miners' Union; he even became its secretary. Not without some opposition, however, for there were those who looked upon Charlie as an outsider—especially one gentleman of anarchistic leanings who, in his spare time, played with the hobby of making dynamite bombs. He had never had an opportunity to use his hobby, but as he brooded over Charlie. . . .

Winter lay upon the land, and snow crackled under the intense cold at night and gleamed by day in the brief sunshine that fell at noon down the slender length of the canyon. All through the Coeur d'Alenes—at the mines of Wallace, Kellogg, Gem, and in lesser diggings—unrest stirred and the ugliness of strike, which is unlike any other human activity, was in the air. Men walked out of the mines, refusing their pittance, rebelling against the danger and damp and lack of safety devices. Want, almost to the point of actual famine, rode high. The company authorities imported men to take the place of workers on strike, and the cry which to a striker is like a red flag to a bull rang out: "Scab!"

The strikers at Gem, miners in desperate need, did not treat the scabs in a gentlemanly manner. There were impromptu Vigilante courts, with men marching by night. Scabs were rolled out of bed, dragged to the end of the main street, and told succinctly and forcibly to "Git!" The scabs left. But many more of them, recruited in Spokane and Seattle and Frisco, unaware of the actual working conditions, came as replacements. Many brought their families.

The presence of women did not deter the strikers— wives of strikers had been driven from their houses along with their husbands, their shoes taken away just as the boots were taken from their husbands, and they were forced as relentlessly as men down the trail to Wallace. Over snow, the miles were long, long miles. Blood lay on the trail to Wallace. At last the strikers were roused.

There were some men who clung to their jobs; these the strikers dragged into the mountains, stripped, and left to escape in any manner possible. Wolves roamed the mountains, and that winter they became so fat that they appeared as strange, bloated creatures, for a wolf with even a pound of extra fat on his belly is a curious sight.

Siringo sickened of it and decided to throw up his job. But open war, in place of guerrilla battling, seemed imminent and he stayed, though the anarchist with the dynamite bombs had roused enough suspicion against him to make Siringo's position precarious. Charlie knew that if it were ever discovered that he was reporting the union's activities to the mine owners, his life would be worth less than a plugged nickle. The word "spy" stirred up even more intense feeling among the miners than the word "scab."

Open war did flare up. It was the real thing; war to the death, with men hating each other to the point where the veneer of civilization cracked. The mine owners attempted too late to arbitrate; their representative met the members of the union in the miners' hall. He stood up to speak. A roar drowned him out. "Lynch him!"

The owners settled back to fight with bullets and gunpowder and dynamite. Scabs, under armed guards, poured into the mine workings. They toiled under the protection of sentinels, breastworks of timber, and sharpshooters —who were some of the toughest thugs on the Pacific coast. Miners climbed up along the hills, to do their own sharpshooting; the thugs sometimes set out in pursuit, and the snipers knew they were through if they were captured. This war left few wounded, and those only by accident.

Through it all, the union newspaper, *The Barbarian*, screamed headlines of bloody murder. It carried neither Household Hints nor Advice to the Lovelorn, and could not be recommended for a quiet hour's reading.

Suspicion about Siringo had been growing; he decided to retire to his room in a boarding house and lie low for a few days. There he overheard a conversation between two men in a room next to his—a plot to kill two scabs, fired by the company and now apparently of the miners' group, who frequented a certain saloon. Once a scab always a scab was the slogan of the miners. Siringo learned that a Vigilante group had decided to do away with the pair after a dance in the miners' hall.

Charlie left his boarding house, sought the saloon

where the men generally lingered, and managed to drop a word of warning to them. He was on his way out when a shout halted him.

"There's the dirty spy! Sure, he's a spy! Let's string him up!"

Thirty or more men glared at Charlie; they started forward. The detective carried a rifle, and he did the only thing within his power to save his neck. He threw the gun up and menaced the mob.

"Stay back!" he warned. "Lead is mighty hot—an' some of you will be feeling it if you get too close."

The sight of a Winchester muzzle, as always, had a sobering effect, and Charlie managed to back across the street to his boarding house. He slammed the door and raced down a hall to his room, where he kept extra guns and ammunition. He intended to escape through the back way. But a look out the window halted him—the back way swarmed with men.

Siringo, hopelessly surrounded, made a movie escape. His room was on the first floor of the boarding house; the structure was built, like most of the semi-permanent establishments in the canyon, on stilts a foot or two above the swamp which formed the floor of the canyon. Charlie had prepared, some days before, an emergency exit—by prying boards loose from the floor. He lifted the boards and slipped down. On hands and knees, dragging his guns, he weaseled under the buildings until he reached safety.

There were signs of renewed warfare and riot. Charlie decided to warn the scabs and guards at the largest mine. After relating the story of his escape from Gem, he found himself, to his disgust, impressed into service at the mine —as a guard, the owners undoubtedly thinking that he might as well earn his salary. Conditions for several weeks had been quiet, and the owners had a minimum number of guards. Charlie went on sentry duty with a partner—a long, cadaverous individual known by the formidable title of Death-on-the-Trail—a suggestive title which was not borne out when the bullets began to fly. Or the dynamite to explode, as it soon did when the leader of the strikers loaded an ore car with explosives, set a short fuse, and shot it down an ore track into the shaft of the mine.

Death-on-the-Trail saw it coming and unwound his long limbs with amazing speed to disappear in panic into the mine—though under the circumstances that was the wrong place to go. Charlie sounded an alarm and sought shelter behind a pile of mine timbers. Hell was about to break loose, shutting the mouth of the mine and entombing the men in the lower levels.

But Providence stepped in. The dynamiter, whose name was Pettibone, had misjudged and the tremendous bomb exploded before it reached the mine. Charlie and some scores of miners, not to mention Death-on-the-Trail, took a breath. But worse followed.

Pettibone took counsel and one day he climbed the hill behind the workings to a wooden flume, intended originally to lead water down to the mine. At the moment, the flume was dry. Its steeply-sloped channel offered no resistance to any rolling object, and Pettibone, bundling together several sticks of dynamite, attached a fuse which he made sure was of the right length. He touched a match to the split end of it, spat on the dynamite bomb for luck, and let 'er roll. Then, in order to hear the sweet sound of the explosion, he settled himself beside the flume, his ear hard against its timbered sides.

The dynamite blew up shortly before it bounced into the mine. There was only one casualty.

That was Mr. Pettibone himself. He had not allowed for the vibration of an explosion traveling along the flume. At the instant of the blow-up the timber kicked with a force that knocked Mr. Pettibone flat. He reeled off, his ear practically torn away and the side of his face, to all appearances, massaged with a sledgehammer.

The mine had become too hot for Charlie, and he fled into the hills. He wandered down towards Wallace and, from the protection of a timbered slope above town, he watched the scabs being driven out of the settlement by the strikers.

It was unfashionable to speak well, or even think well, of the mine owners. Many of the business men of Wallace, who depended upon the mine owners rather than upon the miners themselves for their livelihood, were in a quandary. Neither expressions of sympathy nor discreet silences were possible. There was a general round-up one day of persons suspected of criticizing the Miners' Union, and shortly afterwards a vast group of men was herded towards a train in the railroad yards. They had orders to leave town. Members of the mob that was doing the herding got out of hand, and in terror the exiles stampeded toward the cars.

Bellwether of the herd was one long-legged man with a valise and stovepipe hat. The hat was a problem; as soon as he gained speed he lost it and his speed was checked while he paused to recapture it. The result was that he was in the rearguard as the train pulled out; indeed, he was last. He reached the tail coach of the train, grabbed a rail, and just as his valise split open, vaulted on board.

He threw the bag at the mob, made an eloquent motion with his thumb and fingers, and removed his stovepipe hat to bow. Bullets made a sieve out of his hat, but did not touch him.

At this point the United States government stepped in; it would have interfered earlier had not the strikers blasted railway trestles to the east, preventing the arrival of Federal troops from Fort Missoula, Montana. With troops in command of the Coeur d'Alenes, the mine owners had their inning. The gentleman in the ventilated stovepipe hat returned and took up his vocation—which was gambling—and the ordained law, once more in force, took up the task of rounding up the strikers for their appearance in law courts.

The strikers, generally called bulls, were hunted down. Upon their arrest they were placed in a circular palisade which became known as the Bull Pen. Fame of the Coeur d'Alene Bull Pen has come down to us and any mention of it is sure to make members of the miners' unions of the High Border Country see red.

Charlie Siringo, dropping his disguise as soon as the troops arrived, collected his bonus and departed. The men in the Bull Pen cursed him when he looked in on them briefly before his departure. "Spy!" they yelled. Charlie, however, called himself a secret agent.

9. Soil and People

DRY AND DUSTY LAND

THEY say Paul Bunyan logged off the great plains and left them flat and barren. That was just before his fight with the Bull of the Woods, on top of the Mountain That Stood on Its Head. Bunyan also dredged out Flathead Lake and one night drunkenly wandered towards Puget Sound, with Blue Ox after him, dragging a chain around its neck. The chain left a lightning-jagged indentation in the ground—the canyon of the Snake River.

After the era of bonanza ranchers—except in Butte and the Coeur d'Alenes where the metal barons fought each other—there came the drylanders who sought, most of them, a permanent home. They became known variously not only as drylanders, but also as homesteaders, benchland grangers, woodbillies, woodticks, squatters, and Honijockers, especially if they lived in eastern Montana and the Dakotas. They swarmed in during the first part of the present century—and their breed was wonderful to behold. A certain Honijocker identified his neighbors as follows: a Greek from a university, a Minneapolis barber who gambled on the fact that he would one day be president; a schoolteacher from Kickapoo; a second cousin of Jesse James; and an Arkansas Negro with big feet.

These men, one and all, saw in the broad plains rolling up to the Rockies cheap land capable of pouring forth golden harvests. The possibility that it would pour forth anything else, dust and poverty, for instance, never occurred to them. Most of them did not know what land really was; to possess a single square yard of it made them, according to their lights, landed gentry. Here in the High Border, land was to be had for the asking—and some small amount of work—and wealth beyond dreams would flow from it.

They expressed their optimism in the names they gave this land, such as Golden Valley Country; the number of Fairviews and Pleasantdales out on the God-forsaken prairie is hard to believe. They expressed their optimism in jokes about the man chained in heaven who cried out piteously; when the Lord was asked why He had chained the unfortunate, He replied, "This man comes from Alma (or any Dakota or Montana settlement) and if he weren't chained he's go right back!"

Land was cheap; land companies boomed like mushrooms. The standard joke on the prairies was that of the land agent who told a companion of a deal he had just made. "And d'you know, when we wrote the deed to that land, I slipped two sections off on him and the dum fool didn't know the difference!"

The prairie would grow anything, they said. In Bismarck someone tied oranges to an anaemic tree in the front yard to impress visiting dignitaries. In Montana the sharp, tall spires of the Sweetgrass Hills grew (so they maintained) from piles of earth in front of gopher holes.

There was optimism. Towns sprang up on the dry and dusty prairie wherever there was water to drink. The founders of these settlements named them sometimes strangely: Hogum, because a neighboring collection of huts attempted to secure the county seat; Cumings (Cummings), because the name of the founder was so consistently misspelled; Piniele, because postal authorities were unable to decipher the handwriting on the petition pleading for the establishment of a post office, which was to have been Pineville; Rudyard, after Rudyard Kipling.

Westward from the great plains into the mountains the land-seekers streamed. In the mountains, steep-sided peaks took the place of the plate-flat sweep of the prairies. The grades were so steep that the following story became current: Two men were talking one day, when suddenly, out of the sky it seemed, another man came tumbling. He picked himself up, dusted off his Levis, and remarked, "That's the sixth time today I've fallen off my danged homestead up there on the sidehill."

Optimism persisted as long as the squatters possessed a surplus upon which to draw. Some of the wheat ranchers in the Dakotas and Montana made vast fortunes just after the first World War; more went broke, mainly because they plunged their plows too eagerly into the virgin prairie sod, forgetting that the eternal southwest and west winds had teeth sharp enough to carry that soil away in black blizzards.

The wind did begin lifting the soil during the 1920's and kept it up in the 1930's—ripping out seedling crops until the point was reached that, on every windy day in eastern Montana, they said, "Big movement in real estate today. Our land's going down into Dakota!" And in North Dakota they said, "Minnesota ought to pay our taxes. They're getting our land!"

The squatters in the mountains did not fare much better. To the tune of *Beulah Land* they began to sing:

> *I've reached the land of wind and heat*
> *Where nothing grows for man to eat.*
> *This awful dust and scorching heat*
> *In all the world is hard to beat.*

> CHORUS
> *Oh, Idaho land,*
> *Oh, Idaho land.*

> *As on the alkali beds I stand,*
> *I look across the sage-brush plain,*
> *And wonder why it never rains,*
> *Till Gabriel blows his trumpet sound*
> *And says the rain has all gone round.*

> *The farmer goes out to his corn,*
> *I never saw him look so lorn.*
> *He is amazed, he's almost shocked,*
> *To find a corn amid the stalk.*

> *The people here are all one race,*
> *Starvation stares us in the face,*
> *We do not live, we only stay.*
> *We are too poor to move away.*

One of the squatters was Peanut Parsons, whose sole
utensil for eating was a knife, ground razor-sharp on the
edge. One day an Easterner dropped in for dinner. As
the code of the West prescribed, Peanut offered him his
best—not much, but enough.

With considerable misgiving, if not downright alarm,

the Easterner watched Parsons' maneuverings with the knife. Presently he leaned forward, constrained to utter some word of warning. But at this point Peanut Parsons laid down his knife and reached out a hairy, soiled finger to waver in the Easterner's direction.

"Y'know, partner!" he confided, "them forks makes me nervous. Every time I watch you put that danged thing in your mouth I'm scared you're going to punch a hole clean through your tongue!"

At Big Timber the local minion of the law found himself up against a situation requiring tact. A six-foot-four Scandinavian had run amok and there was no jail in which to put him. The culprit in question was not unpopular, and local opinion demanded that he be not chained to a tree, though this was known to happen on the frontier.

The marshal yielded to the demand for more humane treatment; after deep thought he lowered the lawbreaker, on one end of a rope, into a deserted mine shaft outside the settlement. Then he drew the rope up and peered at the cursing prisoner. "That'll learn you a lesson!" he said. "Law's coming to this neck of the country an' we aim to be civilized, jest like the big cities!"

For several days he lowered food and drink to the culprit; at the end of the prisoner's sentence the marshal threw a rope end to him. The Scandinavian climbed out and walked away, a man who had paid his debt to dryland society.

At that, this hole-in-the-ground jail was perhaps better than many of the frontier prisons. Too often they were of the kind exemplified in the story of the two diners in a hashhouse who met after a spell. The first said, "I thought you were in jail!" The second replied, "I am, but I got hungry an' came over to get a bite to eat."

The homesteaders on the Dakota and Montana prairies had to battle another obstacle, in addition to drought, grasshoppers, Mormon crickets, blizzard, and wind, and that was mud. Long stretches of the prairie in that day, and today, were and are gumbo. Under the touch of the least moisture this soil dissolves into a fluid as greasy as lubricating oil and as clinging. Roads turn to a mess over which vehicles slip crazily; automobiles have a worse time than wagons and carriages used to have. And gumbo drying is like concrete: Two enterprising men trailed a circus from prairie settlement to prairie settlement during a certain rainy season, and after the show had moved on each time were able to harvest a crop of overshoes and rubbers from the mud.

The erratic weather of the plains gave rise to many tall tales. A drylander sighted an ominous cloud coming up behind him and whipped his horses to avoid being caught in a shower. He heard the roar of falling rain come closer and closer, and he lashed his horses to greater speed. At last the roar subsided, and the drylander breathed more easily. He congratulated himself on having escaped, but, turning around, he discovered that the bed of his wagon was full of water.

The majority of the drylanders was made up of single men. They needed wives and they took drastic steps to remedy their not-so-blessed singleness. The following item appeared in the Anaconda (Montana) *Standard* of July 20, 1915:

"James Sullivan of Williams, Teton county, Montana, came to Butte yesterday looking for wives. He wants only one for himself, but he was commissioned by his neighbor ranchers—ranch owners, they are—to represent them in the matrimonial market. His ad appears in the want columns of the *Standard* and there is no foolishness about it.

"Up in Teton county the ranchers find themselves in the position in which the early colonists were placed— plenty of room, plenty of land, opportunity unequaled for getting ahead, plenty of everything but women. They have no tobacco to exchange, but they have homes in a land of sunshine and promise. They are a desirable class of young men who went into Teton county and acquired land a few years ago, and their farms are now in a high state of cultivation. They can furnish references as to character, financial standing and ability to make good homes for good women, and any good woman seeking a home is requested to correspond with James Sullivan, Williams, Teton county. References will be exchanged and all letters will be answered."

THE CORPSE WORE WHITE

Everywhere in the High Border Country you will hear tales of death; most of them are founded upon fact but exaggerated. They are bitter tales and humorous tales. Of the dozens of these stories, the following have been selected because, bizarre as they are, they are founded upon fact and express the High Border feeling towards death: Death is a cessation, a rest after life, a necessity, something that must come to you and which you do not fight against. . . .

A man who rode the range by summer and amused himself in the winter with cards was stricken with a malady generally fatal, and passed beyond. His companions, shedding tears into their cups, looked the town over, discovered a single casket, and prepared to give their brother a Christian burial. But a problem presented itself—the body was much longer than the casket. A perplexing problem.

The companions had another drink and pondered. They did not want to have their old partner lying around all winter, to haunt them with memories of the money he owed them; they had to get him under the ground as quickly as possible. They had another round of drinks, remarked how natur'l Ol' Rattlesnake looked, the old —— ——, and crammed him into the casket by main force. Then they dropped the casket into a hole in the frozen ground and shoveled icy clods upon it.

The winter was long and cold, and the boys had plenty of time to talk about the brave virtues of the dead man. As the months rolled by, the thought began to assail them that they had not done right in cramming Ol' Rattlesnake into his grave. Their consciences took a turn for the worse, and when the Chinook came warmly in from the southwest to announce that spring was there, they took action.

They dug up Ol' Rattlesnake, knocked out the ends of the coffin, straightened the body, and reinterred him—with his feet sticking out. Then they rode out for the range.

During gold rushes and war, bodies are a necessary nuisance. In some of the boom towns of western Montana and

Idaho, cold weather, blizzards, and accidents took a toll greater than average because of the large percentage of greenhorns who had stampeded in. At Saltese, where winter inaction brought boredom, burial became something of a rite and was looked forward to eagerly by a select group that dubbed itself officially the Mourners. The coffins they provided—usually at the expense of the corpse —were rough affairs, made of pine boards nailed about a frame, with the boards not too close together.

There was considerable ceremony involved in the excavation of a grave in the local cemetery, with frequent crookings of the right arm—especially on thirty-below mornings. The Mourners, after getting the grave ready, would foregather in a shack, place the casket and corpse in a convenient position in the center of the room, and pitch pennies from various distances and angles—the object being to hit the cracks between the boards, loser to furnish the drinks. The fun was general and was only concluded with the final slow (and unsteady) march to the grave.

One time, however, the Mourners were disconcerted. Either out of compassion or, more likely, because there was a chance of sharing the corpse's possessions, someone had picked up a frozen man on the trail and lugged him into camp. The Mourners straightened him out and put him in the conventional casket. Later they pitched pennies at him in their usual way; they were on the point of sending a loser out for another round of drinks when with an eerie skreeking of nails the lid of the coffin began slowly to rise and the corpse's knees appeared above the wooden rim.

"He's comin' to life!" someone gasped, and took a quick pull at the bottle.

There was more screeching of nails as the corpse lifted up, driving the lid off the coffin. In fascination or horror the Mourners watched; only when there was no further action did they break and run.

Suddenly sober, they returned at last to find that the frozen corpse, which had been straightened out by force and then laid out in the warmth of the room, had contracted violently. Hastily the Mourners marched to boot-hill to rid themselves of this disturber of the peace.

Death was always accompanied by a vast amount of drinking. In the Powder River country a notorious character, Sweet-oil Joe, noted for his unctuous ways, died of lead poisoning. His friends gathered to give him a send-off. They loaded him into a ruined wagon-bed and dug a hole. Then they dumped the improvised coffin into the grave. Dirt went cascading into the excavation. Tears began to flow freely as the bottles emptied, and dead soldiers were stacked up like cordwood. When the supply of bottles was exhausted, jugs appeared. In the midst of these ceremonies, however, a specter stalked. One of the boys remembered something.

"We buried Sweet-oil on his face!"

An appalled silence fell.

That was, they agreed as one man, no way to bury a departed pal. A man ought to lie on his back with his face upward, just as you lay on the prairie at night with your face into the stars. It was not even *decent* that a man should take his last rest on his face. It doomed him to perdition. Sweet-oil was probably headed that-a-way anyway, but what use were pals if they did not at least make a last attempt to save him?

After another round to give themselves courage, they dug him up, turned him over, and then once again buried him.

A bunch of the boys in a settlement later called Minot buried an individual universally known as the Spider. They began to lay him away in a relatively civilized manner, but just before they dropped him to his final rest in a grave, they upped the lid of the coffin for a last inspection. One citizen, unable to withstand the impact of the rattlesnake juice, slumped across the coffin, with his head on the edge of it.

The moment of burial came and the mourners began to close the lid. They wrestled with it mightily, unable to make it fit.

"Hell!" cried someone, "We can't stand here all day! Dump him in!"

So they dumped the box into the grave, mourner and all. They got to work with their shovels and desisted only when the mourner came to life and let out a yell. Someone remarked that the corpse had come to life—never could keep good Ol' Spider down anyway. But others spied the mourner's legs. They hauled him out by the heels, dusted him off, and allowed him to assist in the formality of filling in the grave.

10. Twentieth Century

CHAMPIONSHIP OF THE WORLD

"YOU'VE managed ham-and-eggers so long that you're a cross between a porker and a hen!" said a redheaded lady one night in February, 1923, and because of that remark Jack Dempsey fought Tommy Gibbons for the championship of the world in Shelby, Montana.

The man whom the lady abused in this fashion, Sammy Sampson, was the owner of an Army & Navy Store in Shelby and a promoter of local fights. He rose to defend his honor. He hastened across the frosty prairie to the telegraph station, where he dispatched a message to Jack Kearns in which he proposed a fight between Dempsey, champion of the world, and Tommy Gibbons, on July 4th at Shelby. Money being of little concern at the moment, he offered $200,000. The red-headed lady chipped in to pay for the telegram.

This was the beginning of as strange a tale as any in the annals of sport, one of the strangest in the High Border Country. Shelby was a cow-town of some five hundred inhabitants; an oil boom had stampeded the big money into it. The preceding summer a horde of strangers had descended upon Shelby's dusty huddle of buildings sprawled in the bottom of a dusty. coulee. Promoters, gamblers, drillers, tool-dressers, roustabouts, business men of every kind, riffraff, and the usual female contingent— all established themselves within convenient reach. Winter in Shelby, however, which often means forty-five degrees below zero, dampened their ardor and the migration at the advent of blizzards was almost total.

In February, 1923, the oil fields were congealed and the few remaining citizens of Shelby had plenty of time on their hands, plenty to drink (though the stuff was then illegal), and great dreams of millions to be made during the summer to come; moreover, they were bored. Sammy Sampson's decisive action met with instant approval. The inhabitants backed Sammy to a man and thus encouraged he dispatched a wire to Mike Collins, editor of the Minneapolis *Boxing Blade,* requesting his services as matchmaker.

Collins decided naturally that the whole thing was a publicity stunt. And there was basis for this belief—Shelby had sought and made news ever since the settlement had been a boxcar sidetracked from the main line of the Great Northern. They still tell of a drummer who, asleep in his berth at a station stop at some point down the line, was roused by a bullet brushing his nose. The shot had been fired by one of two men outside who were settling a slight difference. The drummer sat up, yawned, and groaned, "Good God, are we in Shelby already?"

Shelby was qualified to chew off quite a hunk. Collins, still suspicious but lured on by a flock of follow-up telegrams, headed for the prairie settlement. He stepped from the train into the arms of the assembled populace; such was the enthusiasm of the citizenry that he was not only convinced but became as enthusiastic as any of the rest.

Optimism ran really high. One man predicted that Missoula, Montana (pop. 20,000) would send 30,000 fans to the fight; another matched him with the claim that just as many would come from Calgary, over the line in Canada. All this enthusiasm was dampened when the subject of money received was mentioned. Collins decided he needed $110,000 to promote the fight, and was greeted by a deep silence. But the people of Shelby were no pikers; after a preliminary moaning at the speakeasy bar, they jumped in and scratched gravel. Since there wasn't enough money in Shelby, the rest of Montana was called upon. Great Falls gave $25,000; various posts of the American Legion contributed $10,000; another $25,000 came from Great Falls for Dempsey's training camp. After that there was a lull.

Then occurred a minor miracle. Up stepped a big, blond gent, six feet in height, two hundred and fifty pounds on the boot—Big Jim Johnson, oilfield figure and, by his own statement, a sport to the limits of the sky. He handed in a check for $5000, and other Shelbyites, not to be outdone, shelled out. The drive went over the top.

About this time someone decided that Gibbons ought to be notified that he was going to fight. His information had been solely what he read in the papers; official confirmation must have been somewhat of a shock to him. He said nothing, but Kane, his manager,, demanded a $100,000 guarantee, which upset the promoters who had set his share at half that figure. Mr. Kane's unwillingness to compromise might have been fatal to the whole affair, but somehow the manager got the impression that Dempsey was trying to duck the match. After that, as far as Kane was concerned, neither hell nor high water could keep his man out of the ring.

What followed in Shelby was no boom—it was a paroxysm. The population jumped to 1500, to 4000. An arena capable of seating 45,000 spectators was erected, hideous with its green lumber and yards of encircling wire. The Great Northern built a new depot, with miles of side tracks. Land values skyrocketed 3000, 4000, 5000 per cent. Dance halls and gambling joints boomed. One cattleman dropped $55,000 in a night. To a lesser degree, speakeasies joined in, though Prohibition at times reared its ugly head. One woman filled the post-office basement with cots and rented them—at $3 a night. Church pews were filled with sleepers. A meal cost $3; ham and eggs were $1, with bread, butter and coffee extra. Coffee cost 20 cents.

The Chamber of Commerce constructed, at a cost of some $10,000 a tourist park which they boasted was the largest in the world—big enough to care for 2864 cars. A band of Blackfeet Indians was imported to add color to an already colorful atmosphere; they adopted Tommy Gibbons into the tribe.

There were more financial difficulties. Shelby and northern Montana put forth until there was nothing more to put. The management of the fight changed hands five times. Rumors were everywhere: Fight's on—Fight's off—Fight's on—Fight's off—

And the rains fell. Rain on the High Border prairie has a peculiarly wet quality, probably because there is so little of it. The gumbo underfoot had all the clinging consistency of glue. Chambermaids threw away their brooms and used shovels.

Final payment came due—and no money talked. Fight's off, the rumors said. Trains from the East were canceled; the big arena, washed by dismal rain, sat forlornly in the mud. Gloom settled on the people of Shelby. Their only consolation was that they had Tommy Gibbons in their midst. They idolized him as only Americans can—sometimes—idolize an underdog. Dempsey became the villain of the piece, and councils of war were held to devise ways to aid Gibbons if ever the fight should begin. Even psychology was to be used. "When he climbs in that-there ring," old Ed Reamer, ex-sheepherder, said, "we-all will jest set still an' look at him. All our eyes will be like an accusin's conscience an' he won't be able to duck them haymakers Tommy is a-goin' to throw at him!"

Meanwhile in Great Falls, Dempsey trained; took long walks; played with Mary, his camp kitten, and Gertrude, the camp cow, and, according to newspaper advertisements of the period, ate a local brand of bread. Reports of his unpopularity in Shelby worried him; the special train which took him to Shelby carried a strong bodyguard, while just outside his corner of the ring during the fight hovered a pair of gents whose faces left little doubt as to their calling.

Fight's off, the chant ran. But the promoters prayed long and earnestly and their optimism was justified. At the last, financial arrangements struck a snag when Jack Kearns refused to let Dempsey fight. But the champion vetoed his manager's orders and entrained.

Independence Day dawned dry and hot. There was not a cloud in the blue overhead—whose emptiness was matched only by that of the acres of tracks for the special trains. Seven thousand people were deployed in the arena for 45,000 when, at 3:30 P.M., Dempsey appeared. The two fighters quickly took their positions and the champ's handlers hoisted a large umbrella over him, which provoked the Gibbons supporters (ninety-nine per cent of the crowd) into insinuating that Jack was afraid of freckling—as if a man could freckle through a quarter-inch of unshaven burr. Five minutes after Dempsey appeared, Gibbons came on deck. There was the usual prologue, and then the fight got under way.

Gibbons lasted the full fifteen rounds but Dempsey won the decision. The challenger started out to beat the champion at his own game of slugging, which was a mistake, for in the third he reeled groggily. Then, according to ringsiders, a woman's voice cut through the roar of the crowd: "Remember the kiddies at home, Tommy!", and Gibbons began to display remarkable adeptness at clinching and waltzing.

From the first, it was evident that the Mauler was not in his usual form. Perhaps he had run into a fighter who was his match; perhaps the psychology of old Ed Reamer had something to do with it. He may even have been wondering about the possibility of a bullet smashing between his ribs; there were spectators in the crowd, hard-bitten prairie men, who were capable of that, capable and willing. They hated Dempsey, not in the ordinary manner of the prejudiced fan but in a way more deadly —through their pocketbooks. The people of Shelby were flat broke and in a dangerous mood.

The fight proved Gibbons' merit as a boxer, but he lost in more ways than one. He did not get a cent of cash. His share of the proceeds was bruises and contusions. For fifteen rounds he ducked, danced, and dodged, closely watched by One-Eye Connolly, who was there; by the ninety-six-year-old Blackfeet chief Selavis, some of whose 168 legitimate descendants flanked him; and by the actress Mae Murray. Nobody in the crowd went to sleep, but there were those who yawned. It was that kind of a fight.

Shelby's boom population disappeared at once, and the settlement which had backed Sammy Sampson found itself with one of the biggest financial headaches on High Border Country record, a headache which lasted at least fifteen years. For many years after that Fourth of July a dime was big money. Several days after the fight workmen entered the arena and began ripping up boards. The executive committee of the Arizona state department of the American Legion passed a resolution regretting "that Gibbons did not knock Dempsey's block off." The Montana conference of the Methodist church denied, with some heat, that a committee had been instructed to view the battle.

WHEAT LAND BASEBALL

In the autumn of 1919, just before the World's Series in which the Chicago White Sox were to play Cincinnati, a certain White Sox player, Eddie Cicotte, turned back the cover on his bed before climbing in and found $10,000 in bills. Charlie Risberg and Happy Felsch, both ball-handlers of the first string, also found their beds lined with money. Temptation was irresistible and Cincinnati won the series, though experts had rated the White Sox one of the best clubs ever to chew tobacco.

The upshot was that on September 28, 1920, a Cook County jury indicted Cicotte, Risberg, Felsch, and four others for conspiracy to commit an illegal act. In plain words, they had sold out to the gamblers. They were condemned and kicked out of organized baseball for all time.

Cicotte, Risberg, and Felsch disappeared into limbo as far as the civilized world was concerned. But west of the Mississippi, on the upper Missouri, lay a world which, if not exactly civilized in the eyes of Easterners and Middle Westerners, at least had money to match any that Risberg and Felsch received as players in the big leagues.

On the prairies of eastern Montana and North Dakota, and north in adjacent Canada, money was flowing freely —more money than that section of the country had ever seen before and more than it may ever see again.

Wheat.

Skyrocket prices followed the first World War, and the prairie clouds opened regularly month after month to pour down rains that meant boom crops. The prairie soil was thick and fertile; virgin sod had been broken only a few years before; and the west wind had not yet begun its black work. From 1919 to 1928 the land gave forth and there was great good fellowship.

Wheat farming is not a heavy task, even when horses are used in place of machinery. The Scandinavians who inhabited this region during those big-money years found much spare time on their hands. The younger generation put it to good use—they married and began to raise families. The middle-aged and older generations discovered baseball. They took it up with a vim which will not soon be forgotten. . . .

Scobey was capital of the wheat land; it boomed in the '20's in the manner of the gold camps of the '60's and '70's or the railroad camps of the '80's. A sister settlement,

Plentywood (where there was no wood), which lay not too far away across the prairie, vied with Scobey for supremacy. When Scobey established a baseball club and hired Charlie Risberg, late of the White Sox, for $800 a month and found, Plentywood hastened to secure Happy Felsch at a comparable salary, and big-league baseball came into a small-time circuit that had big money.

The Swedes went after more talent. They corralled a goodly number of players with undeniable ability for handling a ball. The first game of the series, Plentywood vs. Scobey, saw an array of formidable talent on a diamond in which the outfield was rendered hazardous by sagebrush and rattlesnakes. A ball hit into the cars on the railroad tracks near by was to be counted, according to ground rules, as a two-base hit. The Swedes, three thousand strong, some from a hundred miles away, did not hesitate to place a bet or two, and wagers reached the point where one man bet $10,000 on Scobey. He found takers.

Scobey won the initial game: 3-2. The ball went banging into the wheat cars on the side tracks, outfielders tripped over the sage, the Swedes shouted themselves hoarse, money changed hands, the prairie wind whipped up a screen of dust through which runners sneaked from base to base, and there were 432 recorded fights before the night was over.

The second game of the series brought another wildly applauding audience, with betting just as high. But officials were about to call the game because the Scobey club had failed to make an appearance. Eventually they wandered in, suffering from a misadventure of the night before. The previous day they had played in Moose Jaw, over the line in Canada, and on their way back, attempting a short-

cut, they had become lost on the prairie. They had no
sense of direction, a limited supply of gasoline, and there
was a shortage of moonshine. At midnight they had decided to halt and wait for dawn.

With sunup they followed the road tracks and rolled
into town just in time to see their rival Plentywood club
on the diamond. Betting ran too high to permit them a
rest; they had a good drink, rushed out upon the field,
and got set. They proved their sterling worth by taking
the Plentywood club—and the Plentywood betters—without too much trouble. Then they rolled into bed and slept
the sleep of men who have done well—as indeed they had,
from the standpoint of the Scobey business men who were
putting up around $5000 a month to support them.

In other games that followed the Scobey club not only
decisively defeated Plentywood but also teams of many
other surrounding settlements so that they were forced
to move far afield for fresh opponents—up into Canada,
down into the Dakotas, and even into Minnesota. But it
was worth it, or so thought the Scobey business men.

In 1926 Hap Felsch guided the star of the Scobey club.
There were dark rumors that, inasmuch as it had happened before, the great Felsch might lose again. He
quelled suspicion, however, and continued to play ball
for Scobey the following year. In 1928 Scobey abruptly
fired him. He moved to Plentywood. Scobey scouted
around, found an Indian named Seeley from Oklahoma
who showed great playing ability if little experience. They
brought him by fast train for the first game of the season;
when the train schedule indicated he would be late for
the first inning, they sent a plane down to Minot, North
Dakota, and fetched him by air.

Baseball was on the wane, however. The big-money days were going. Two-dollar-a-bushel wheat was down to under a dollar, and the sod that had produced the golden grain was spending itself. The wind had begun to dig into the soil and lay waste vast fields. The Swedes, head over heels in debt to the big machinery companies for tractors and combine harvesters and other machinery, retrenched; baseball players were the first to suffer.

The game continued to be popular, though, and today all along the "high-line" of the Great Northern from Glacier National Park to the Dakota-Minnesota border, baseball is a major summer sport. Its boom days, like the boom days of wheat, are gone. It experienced a brief revival in the early '30's when Billy Sunday, chasing the devil, umpired many games played on prairie diamonds. The players usually were local boys whose idea of big money was a dollar with which to buy a micky of moonshine whiskey. The bad and boom days had definitely vanished.

GREAT CHIEF

Coming Day, an ancient, half-blind redskin, still alive in the 1930's, will be remembered with Wijujon, who died for truth.

Coming Day, born many decades ago to an Assiniboine mother along the upper Missouri, fell heir to the prophecy that he would become a great chief—greater than any of his tribe. But he grew to manhood without displaying any particular skill or bravery in feats of arms or hunting and his tribe branded the prophecy false. The years drifted on and Coming Day passed through youth and manhood.

One day the remnants of the tribe were camped beside

a white man's highway. In the hot afternoon sun warriors slumped lazily beside their lodges, watching the horse-drawn vehicles of the white man pass by. In the East the horseless carriage was just beginning its career; only the vaguest rumors about this Eastern mechanical marvel had penetrated the High Border. The tribe certainly knew nothing about it. So when a man from a nearby settlement came rushing along the road in a cloud of dust on the seat of a buckboard propelled by no visible means—but crashing like doom—Coming Day's tribe displayed an activity which even hunger had been unable to inspire. They leaped to their feet and fled out over the prairie or dove into their lodges.

All except Coming Day. He, and he alone, walked bravely out to the white man and, when that individual pulled a lever and the buckboard came to a stop, he alone stood bravely and stared at this strange Medicine buckboard.

"Want a ride, dark boy?" the white man asked. Without hesitation Coming Day climbed into the Medicine buckboard. The tribesmen who had fled into the prairie came creeping back, and the braver ones peered at Coming Day. Their eyes opened with awe when the Medicine buckboard moved away, spitting fire and thunder, while Coming Day, alive and unafraid, sat there beside the white man.

The prophecy that Coming Day would be a chief greater than any leader of his tribe had come true. They gave him the honor long overdue—the best of their poor meat, the best of the poor clothes they wore, and a great reverence such as a redskin can give to one who has proved that he is braver than those around him.

But fame is perishable; a new generation grew up and Coming Day's influence waned. The tribe was concerned with other things. A decade passed, and another, and again Coming Day, the unafraid, went down the scale. He was just an old, wrinkled redskin who hobbled along on a cane and scolded in a strange tongue when the children of the tribe plagued him.

The children had even forgotten that Coming Day was once a hero. They attended the white man's school, learned to play basketball and football, studied mathematics and English, and strayed far from the paths of their fathers.

One day the tribe convened in powwow, a redskin convention which was more a white man's fair than anything else. It was a gala day this, and the tribesmen celebrated. In the midst of it all the sky thundered and down dropped a huge bird, pulsating and steel-beaked, unlike any bird the tribe had ever seen.

The younger ones knew about airplanes, but to the elders this was magic medicine. They fled and hid themselves.

All except Coming Day. He hobbled up to the Medicine bird and touched it. The aviator grinned at him and, probably in hopes that with the aid of this old man he might find paying passengers among the tribe, he said, "Want to go up in the air, Pop?"

Coming Day did not hesitate. He climbed into the cockpit and huddled there while the metal beak of the Medicine bird sang louder and louder—until at last it lifted its red wings into the air. The tribesmen came from cover to gather in excited groups, their heads back and mouths open.

"Coming Day's in that Medicine bird. He rides it without fear. He is indeed Coming Day, the unafraid!" whispered the elders, while the youngsters said in good colloquial English: "Applesauce! That's just an airplane. Any fool can ride in it!"

But the word of the elders prevailed. When the Medicine bird dropped down, and Coming Day reeled from the cockpit, they rushed forward. No longer was he an old, forgotten man. Instead, he was the bravest of the tribe! Wavering minds recalled the prophecy at his birth. Others, middle-aged, recalled that he had been first to ride an automobile. In the space of a few minutes old Coming Day was again transformed. Once more he was Coming Day, the unafraid.

THE LAST OUTLAW

"Mount my head and hang it on the courthouse as a warning to all who break the law!" wrote Earl Durand, widely known at the moment as the Wyoming Tarzan, to a sheriff. Posses everywhere were seeking him, both for the reward and for the glory of seeing their names in headlines and photographs. This was in early 1939 and the High Border's last tough man had gone on a rampage.

Earl Durand was pretty small stuff compared to the outlaws of the last century, but the nation had very little violence to talk about, Hitler being still a large voice over the radio. Time was ripe for the last outlaw; Earl Durand played the part.

Earl Durand, aged twenty-one, dwelt beyond the civilized channels which spread for a few miles, more or less, on both sides of the highways and around modern cities.

Living in the wilderness, he felt himself free, unimpeded by the laws of the state, and it seemed to him absurd that there should be rules against the slaughter of wild game. He lived, it is reported, exclusively upon wild game. When he was troubled by wardens who attempted to curb his activities, he rebelled. Arrested and taken to the Cody, Wyoming, jail, he made a desperate break for freedom—killing, in the process, a pair of lawmen. He headed out on the desperate trail of outlawry—the "owlhoot" of fiction.

Twenty years earlier he might have had a chance. But this was the 1930's, and he was up against telegraphs, airplanes, sub-machine guns, automobiles, and radio. At that, a lone man against many, he managed to throw off trailing posses. Surrounded, he killed two more lawmen; his pursuers even corralled him in a den among the rocks and battered at him with trench mortars and howitzers.

He managed to make his escape once more. With hundreds of men on his trail, he began to wander in a bewildered fashion. What he did then, what he thought, is only guesswork—he ate what he could lay hands on and huddled under bushes when pursuers came near.

Some spirit of the past must have aided him; but even ghosts are helpless against steel, and the time came when Earl Durand, beaten and desperate, made a bid for that ally which has become indispensable with the twentieth century—money. He raided a bank in Powell, Wyoming; he entered, scooped up the cash, shot the teller, and holding another man before him as hostage, came into the open. But by now the spirit of the past abandoned him. A seventeen-year-old boy, from a filling station across the way, put a bullet into the last of the outlaws. Earl Durand reeled back into the bank. He stood at the end of his trail, and he knew it. He put his pistol to his head and pulled the trigger. They found him slumped on the floor —last of the High Border outlaws, dead with his boots on.

EARTHFILL

In 1934 a former Federal judge, campaigning against Burton K. Wheeler for the right to represent the State of Montana in the Senate of the United States, said: "You take this Fort Peck. It is nothing more than a duck pond. . . ."

This was a very unwise statement, for to almost all the half-million inhabitants of the State of Montana the Fort Peck Dam, greatest earthfill structure ever made by man, is known affectionately and possessively as "Our Dam." Burton K. Wheeler, sponsor if not the true father of the dam, rode to victory in November of 1934, and thereafter did his best for what is generally regarded as the greatest step in conservation and reclamation since the High Border Country became conscious of the wild destruction of its natural resources. "Our Dam" is big, which is appropriate; it is located in the midst of a big prairie in a big state, and has been built by big appropriations. It backs a big river—none other than the wild Miz-zou-rye, just above the junction of the Missouri and the Milk Rivers deep in the northeastern part of Montana. It is 250 feet high, 20,000 feet long, 4900 feet thick at the base, and across the top will support an asphalt road 100 feet wide. Five times as much dirt as went into the Gatun Dam in Panama, the world's largest earthfill next to Fort Peck— or 1,250,000,000 cubic yards of dirt and gravel—hold back a lake which will eventually reach a length of 180 miles, a width of 16 miles, with a shoreline of 1600 miles and a capacity of 19,412,000 acre-feet of water.

In the valley of the Missouri below the dam the old men of the Assiniboine tribe look upstream with distrust. They have seen a vast reservation taken from them. They have seen more and more of the land around them devoted to the growing of sugar beets—an industry controlled by the Mormons. The Great White Father in Washington does not have any good plans for his red charges, say the old men; when the dam is completed and the lake filled to capacity, he will blast out the barrier and sweep all the Assiniboines down into the Gulf of Mexico. Then he will give their land to the Mormons.

In the first week of November, 1939, a floating dredge sent the last few cubic yards of hydraulic fill surging through a five-mile pipeline to complete the dam except for "polishing"—a somewhat lengthy task. Mars was making headlines at the moment, but the people of Montana ignored him and rejoiced in headlines over the fact that at last the greatest structure had been completed. There were some who asked what all the shouting was about and still others who, in the midst of rejoicing, worried about paying a debt to which the construction of Fort Peck had contributed, but these were so definitely in the minority that they were not heard.

Fort Peck lies in a region which during three seasons of the year—depending upon the season—is a dusty or dreary or frosty cross section of hell. But in the spring, for a few weeks when the prairie is a softer, deeper green than any a painter can mix and when marching clouds cross the sky in slow motion and when by night the moon is bigger than any other moon in the world, it becomes a temporary bit of paradise. Then the wind comes back, after its brief rest, to surge wolfishly across the land, and from Fort Peck come such meteorological readings as: "July, Thursday, 114 degrees. January, Monday night, 66 degrees below zero."

On the exact site of Fort Peck the Assiniboines of old made sacrifices before crossing the Missouri. Here in 1867 Colonel Campbell Kennedy Peck of Iowa established a trading post in partnership with his brother-in-law, one Durfee from Kansas, and enjoyed a lucrative trade with the redskins until Orvil Grant, brother of President Grant, was given a bit of family aid in the form of a trade monopoly in the region.

Here in September, 1932, two U. S. Army engineers talked to the mayor of the dryland settlement of Glasgow and casually mentioned building a dam. "Why!" gasped the astounded mayor, "it would cost a million dollars!"

"Well—probably seventy-five millions!" said the engineers. By 1934 that sum had leaped to ninety millions. But it took more than one hundred millions before the dust settled. On October 14, 1933, President Franklin D. Roosevelt approved the dam as Project No. 30 under the Public Works Program, to be constructed under the direction of a corps of army engineers, Major T. B. Larkin in charge.

After the construction of the dam was approved and the preliminary stages were under way, there was a boom of major proportions, to match Montana's other boom-spasms. Around the site of Fort Peck towns sprang up overnight in the best boom tradition, named in honor of patron saints, Wheeler, Delano Heights, New Deal, Roosevelt.

They were peopled with a floating population that put
to shame the hell-roaring activities of frontier days—to such
an extent that the magazine *Life,* in its first issue, featured
the Fort Peck community.

This was another bonanza; a strange bonanza, true
enough, not from the earth like the bonanzas of metal
and grass and wheat, but from the Federal treasury. There
was hilarity all over Montana; weather-worn signs—PROS-
PERITY IS JUST AROUND THE CORNER—came down. Pros-
perity, after years of depression, had arrived. Montana
was in the money. Smoky days of the old West (except for
the gunplay) came to life anew around Fort Peck and the
gigantic pile of dirt began to take form. In July, 1936,
there were over ten thousand men employed at Fort Peck.
Four diversion tunnels, 24 feet in diameter and varying
in length from a mile to a mile and a half, swerved the
river from its course. The wild old Missouri, mistress of
the frontier, dark and bloody stream, had at last met a
master. Dredges and the Federal treasury tamed it.

In August, 1933, and again in October, 1937, Franklin
Delano Roosevelt, visualizing thousands of cultivated
acres in a country which had been supported by wheat al-
lotments; visualizing water conservation in a land where
the grass had been destroyed, visited the dam site. He grew
eloquent as he spoke:

"Before American men and women get through with
this job"—he said, amid cheers from Wayerski, O'Neill,
Lansetti, MacManus, von Lund, and thousands of others
—"we are going to make every ounce and every gallon
of water that flows from the heavens and the hills count
before it makes its way down to the Gulf of Mexico."

Fort Peck is built for posterity, which is only just according to the cynics who maintain that posterity will be paying for it. It is built solidly, with the best engineering plans known to man as well as the best credit on earth to back them up. Though humble dirt alone holds back what will in the last years of the 1940's amount to fifty billion gallons of water, the dam is solidly placed and without flaw, they say. The upstream face is protected against ice and wave action with a blanket of coarse gravel over which lies a rip-rap of stone cut from the sides of Snake Butte (where, say the Indians, lives a huge serpent with evil powers) 130 miles away. The billions of gallons of water will batter in vain against this face, against the solid base beneath. . . .

At 1:15 P.M., September 23, 1938, Jerry Mason, laborer, was working on the upstream face when he became aware of a strange tremor beneath his feet. Looking up, he saw huge blocks of rip-rap splitting away—"like when you knock over dominoes." Mason stretched his legs and managed to escape, but eight of his fellow workers were not so fortunate. When the dust cleared the engineers found that, though the wild Missouri was still throttled, some ten per cent of their dam—a section 200 feet deep by 2000 feet long, about 5,000,000 cubic yards of material— had slipped away into the water, taking railroad tracks, trestle, and dredge with it.

It was disconcerting but explicable, according to the engineers, who explained that this earth movement was "merely a local condition." Major Clark Kittrell, army engineer in charge since July, 1937, went on to say: "No basic engineering defects were found after the slide. . . . If we weren't sure the dam was solid in every way ready to stand forever, we wouldn't be finishing the job."

". . . ready to stand forever. . . ." Perhaps a new people, bred out of the chaos of a mad world, will in the future traverse this wilderness and gaze with awe upon the wreckage of what we completed away back in 1940 A.D., as we have looked upon the Great Wall of China or the Pyramids. The wild Missouri will not easily be tamed and turned from her course. The centuries come and go, but the Missouri goes on forever, treacherous queen of the prairies treacherously governing her kingdom.

11. Today

PARADE

THROUGHOUT the High Border Country but especially in the mountain region, there is a consciousness of the life of yesterday, a realization of the heritage of the pioneers. Days are set aside to celebrate the past: Vigilante Day, Pioneer Day, Early Settler Day, Days of '49, Helldorado, Last Chance Day—you find them everywhere. They are run for profit, but they are an instinctive tribute to the pioneers, a revival of things past which in reality were sordid and miserable but which in the neon lights of the twentieth century appear wholly glamorous.

Old-Timers' Day. You crowd towards the curb, breasting into the crowd, gaping down the street for a sight of the vanguard of the parade, which is always one of the main attractions. Behind you, beyond the settlement, lie the dusty reaches of the prairie or the upthrust of mountains. There is over all a smell of fresh crude oil which has been spread on the streets to lay the dust; if not, clinging alkali particles whip up into your nose and throat and you sneeze, watching the parade through tears.

The vanguard is civilized—usually it is the band of the local high school, blaring out *There'll Be a Hot Time in the Old Town Tonight* or *Springtime in the Rockies*.

288

There are gaudy uniforms and sometimes bare-kneed drum majorettes. They prance by followed by floats and cars and people in costume, more or less elaborate, more or less authentic—today's idea of life on the High Border of Yesterday. The marshal of the day is on horseback—with a silver-mounted saddle, of course, and fringed buckskin or Indian beaded vest, cowboy boots, Stetson hat. He may be the mayor, a local merchant, the banker, but today he is far from the prosaic world of commerce; he is the spirit of the old West.

In front of the floats come those for whom the parade has been created—the old-timers, the pioneers, the few remaining persons who actually lived through the old days, or at least some of them. These pioneers, old men and old women with seamed faces, leaning forward on their seats in modern, high-powered automobiles, have seen only the years since the '70's or '80's or '90's and the turn of the century. But they are pioneers, and today they are heroes as they wave to the crowd lining the street. Winners of the West.

Old women stolidly prim, old men solemn or hilarious. They pass in review, and then appears the parade proper —a dozen or a hundred horsemen, mostly younger people. There are horses—cayuses—of assorted shapes and sizes, good and bad; "forked"—ridden—by riders weirdly costumed in scraps and cast-offs of the past. Stetson hats and leather chaps, divided skirts, a few side-saddles, silver-mounted saddles, army saddles, bareback riders made up to represent Indians.

There follows a legion of people on foot—prospectors, priests, Indians, squaws, dandies of the 1890's, railroad workers, Chinese, dryland farmers, sheepherders. Then come the floats, and you watch eagerly if you are new to this; even if you have seen them before you watch with interest, for this is the panorama of the High Border. Most of the floats are built on truck bodies; some of them are horsedrawn. First is an elaborate group of black-robed priests and an Indian—a sign tells you this represents the conversion by Father De Smet of the Indians in Pierre's Hole. Then comes a slab shack, beside which is a section of narrow-gauge tracks with a dump cart on them: the shaft of a mine. Then a tableau of the Lewis and Clark expedition—several fur-hatted and buckskin-shouldered high-school boys carrying a canoe. There follow an old print shop, an ancient blacksmith shop, Indians lying in wait for whites, a bunch of lambs corralled around a slab hut, Indians in council, cowboys branding calves, rustlers overtaken in the act of blotting out brands—with one of them realistically dead on the rocky soil spread over the bed of the truck, prospectors attacked by Indians, miners attacked by Indians, pioneers attacked by Indians, a stuffed buffalo grazing on prairie grass while a hunter lurks in the background, drylanders burying one of their own, an emigrant burial, a miner's burial, an Indian burial, a Sunday in church, an 1890 hayride. This goes on and on and you begin to yawn a little, for either the sun is hot or the rain blows down or the wind hurls sand into your face. You yawn—and then you see a float that brings you back.

Nothing ornate—just a heap of sand on the bed of a V-8 Ford truck, a few sprigs of sagebrush, a couple of human bones, a brokendown and weatherbeaten buckboard. As simple as that, yet something catches you and you know that here you see something which might well

be called the spirit of the High Border—the strength and
the force of the land, of the men who came to do or
die—and died, of the vastness of this twentieth-century
wilderness that lies beyond the civilization along its
modern highways and its settled areas. You see a dream of
the pioneers and their sacrifice—their sweat, toil, fury,
cruelty.

The float passes on, and you watch the rest with renewed interest—a modern note intruding itself now, with
Vigilantes hanging outlaws and modern high-school boys
hanging Hitler, the scene captioned: "They did their part,
we'll do ours." There are hurdy-gurdy scenes, barroom
scenes, gambling scenes of a bloody nature. They are all
more or less authentic. But your mind goes back to that
simple float—the heap of sand, the bones, the decayed buckboard. And when the parade is finished and you find a
modern bar with its neon lights and its radio, you hook
the heel of your new high-heeled cowboy boot over the
rail and think of yesterday—of the mountain men gulping
their liquor, of cowboys painting the town.

The spirit of the past is strong in the High Border—
perhaps as a real, inner spirit, perhaps only as a red
bandanna around the neck of some business man. But it is
a definite spirit.

RODEO

Old-Timers' Day is merely one manifestation of the en-
during past—another sign of it are the rodeos staged an-
nually in Idaho, Montana, Wyoming, and to a lesser extent in Dakota. Usually they occur around the Fourth of
July. Even the largest communities of the High Border
have rodeos—Butte, for instance. Except in size and show,

Butte's rodeo does not differ from that of Gilford, Montana; or Goldstone, or other towns whose population is numbered in two and three or at the most four figures.

There are whiskered men everywhere, wearing high-heeled boots and red bandannas and sometimes chaps. Women wear divided denim skirts, fringed around the bottom—furnished by mail-order houses and very different from the divided buckskin riding skirts of pioneer women. Sometimes, to lend atmosphere, they string dummies up on posts. There are cowboys in from the range, professional rodeo-busters seeking prize money, cattlemen, sheepmen, wheat ranchers, and always gamblers, for though High Border states have all set up laws against gambling, there is too much of the gambling spirit of the past to permit their enforcement for more than a few days, or a few weeks, at a time.

Sometimes the rodeos challenge the past and are called fairs, the main attraction of which is horse racing. But even then it is the rodeo fundamentally, and the spirit is that of the rodeo. On the day, or two days, or week, of the rodeo most of the population gathers at the rodeo grounds in the afternoon or evening; by night gambling is wide open, dance halls do a boom business, juke boxes play into the dawn, the bars sell drinks to a motley crowd ranging all the way from sheepherders to tourists. There is fighting, liquor-inspired arguing—"augurin' " as an old-timer would say—name-calling, dancing—all the way from the square-dance to jive. A rodeo spirit, undiminished by the sweep of the prairie or the brooding immensity of mountains, dominates everyone.

Spectators crowd the grandstands at rodeo grounds, if there are grandstands; they swarm around the rodeo arena, around the bucking chutes and the corrals and the barns. You catch flashes of color, sights, sounds: a hot-dog man; two big-hatted cowboys in a corner tilting a black bottle of whiskey; conversation—"Rodeos? You oughta see Calgary (or Pendleton—or Miles City—or Cheyenne)"; dust; barn odor and sweat; dudes in fancy outfits; ranchers with brown faces under their beards; whiskers; a moving-picture cameraman; two girls eyeing a cowboy; an announcer bellowing inarticulate words; spectators screaming; a horse in mid-arena, prancing stiff-legged; a cowboy, number pinned on his back, flopping forward into the dust; another spectator screaming; a Brahma steer twisting viciously—

Then there is a bit of drama. The Brahma, which is a breed developed for bucking purposes, throws the rider and, as the man lies stunned, whirls to gore him. The crowd screams again, this time with another sound; the cameraman grinds away; other riders in the arena dash up to detract the attention of the killer. Friends lift the bloody man, carry him away. A spectator whispers in a shocked voice, "O-o-o, do you think he is dead?"

Then the rodeo is over and you go into town—into the restaurants or the bars or the moving-picture houses. You eat, you hook your heel in a rail, or you watch the shadowy cavortings of Gene Autry, or, if this is a pretentious rodeo and the manager of the show has resurrected an old Bill Hart picture, you watch Bill—a statue of whom, incidentally, broods over the land near Billings, Montana—ride in heroic splendor across a silent celluloid prairie that even today is only partially tamed by oiled highways and landing fields. You watch Bill fighting outlaws with thrilling nonchalance, you watch with interest because he is the epitome of the old-time cowboy, to whose spirit the rodeo is dedicated.

Cowboy. The word spells romance. As a matter of fact, his job was never romantic—it was too dirty, too dangerous, too low-paid. Old-timers of the country say that a cowboy's usefulness was ended after ten years in the saddle, a decade of badly cooked food, of rotgut liquor, of wind, blizzard, frost, and searing heat. There were other dangers, such as rattlesnakes and the semi-wild cayuses of the prairie. Doctors were scarce in the earlier days and medical attention almost non-existent. Primitive self-help meant, for all internal disturbances, the slapping of a hot stove-lid against the abdomen, and for any other injuries, crude splints and copious doses of whiskey.

They were a heroic tribe, those early-day cowboys. At least to hear the old-timers tell it. . . . Their stories are of a vanished race of horsemen that has been glorified out of all proportion by western pulp magazines and moving pictures; they are campfire sagas of the centaurs of the plains. They are tales of old, for the golden age of the cowboy, begun in the '70's, ended when the reign of the beef baron was over, around 1893, when the panic of that year swept across the land at the same time that drylanders, flooding in, began to break the feudal supremacy of the mighty owners of mighty herds—of men like Pierre Wibaux, whose bronze statue stands today in the town named after him on the Montana-Dakota border. Wibaux's herds, it is said, ran into the hundreds of thousands. And he was not the mightiest of the barons—others surpassed him. Their riders were centaurs of the golden age of the cowboy; when they began to pass, their men went with them.

The "skim-milk" and "mail-order" cowboy then began

to come into ascendancy, though Easterners doubt this.
He still rides the ranges, but he carries his horse in a
trailer behind his car until he reaches the country beyond
roads. He no longer packs a gun. He listens to the radio
and reads movie magazines.

Once he was the knight of the range. He is finished
now, and his obituary has nowhere been written more
vividly than in a letter to the editor of one of today's
great national magazines:

"SIRS: Few occupations are more over-rated and under-
paid than that of the cowboy.

"I know. I married one. . . . Not only is a cowboy's
bedroll crawling with fleas, but probably body lice and
bed bugs as well. No finicky soul, the cowboy never washes
his bedding, seldom hangs it on the line, usually doesn't
undress at all. However, he doesn't mind the crawl-
ers. . . ."

OIL SETTLEMENT

Crude oil makes the wheels go around, for from crude
oil—petroleum—come lubricating oils, gasoline, and a score
of other products. This black gold is generally found in
prairie country where hundreds of millions of years ago
a vast sea flowed—in one of a number of geologic epochs
which include the age of dinosaurs, whose remains are
found throughout the prairie regions of Montana, Wyoming and the Dakotas, and the age of ice, relatively recent—about 100,000 years ago. This ice sheet swept down
from the north and edged into Montana and the Dakotas;
it was so recent that traces of it still exist in Glacier
National Park and give that mountain playground one of
its main scenic attractions. The twentieth-century glaciers

are not diminishing, as logically they should; they rebuild themselves each winter from the snow that falls on them, and though Glacier's ice fields have existed for some time, there is no likelihood of their early destruction, not for several thousands of years.

It is geologically true that the Continental Divide did not always exist, that it was thrown up during a relatively short period and under conditions that are responsible for the rugged grandeur of the mountains today, especially in the region of the Lewis Overthrust, more commonly known as Glacier National Park. It is also geologically true that all the prairie country sweeping east from the Continental Divide was sea bed at one time, so that today bedrock is of a sedimentary type and water pressure has created vast coal beds underlying most of the Montana and Dakota prairies. One of the world's greatest open-pit coal mines lies near Colstrip, Montana. Every wheat rancher has his personal coal mine, generally one small shaft into the ground with a winch huddled over it, and here he digs his winter's coal if he has the time; however, if his crop has been good and he has extra money he buys his coal, for the coal under the High Border is none too good.

Dinosaur remains are plentiful in the Two Medicine country of Montana; along Two Medicine Creek they are of such quality as to attract both governmental and private expeditions. Hunting dinosaur bones is a sport of the elect and learned; you take a whisk broom, a light hand-pick such as geologists use, and in the spring just after run-off water has flooded down the coulees, you look for bones. If you are lucky—and usually you are—you find a section of bone embedded in rock, the overtrash having been swept away by the water. Then you whisk away and pick away to loosen the bone without destroying too much of it; if you are persistent you may find yourself the owner of a bit of dinosaur skeleton large enough to make lugging it over the prairie—for you have left your car four or five miles away where the thread of prairie road melted into badlands—a real task.

In this land there is oil—crude oil. There are a score of fields, most of them producing oil, some of them producing natural gas, which in Montana is piped hundreds of miles from the Cut Bank fields across bleak prairie and towering mountain range to the smelters of Butte and Anaconda. Sometimes as you drive along oiled highways stretching like dark lines into the prairie skyline you see slender spires beside the road. These are oil derricks, drilling for the black gold a thousand or five thousand feet beneath the surface. At other places you see little corrugated shelters where engines work the pump on a drilled-in well; sometimes one engine pumps five or six wells that stand at intervals of fifty or sixty yards from each other.

This is oil country, and the settlements that dot the country are oil towns—most of them small, all of them dirty, all prosperous, and all are twentieth-century replicas of the gold-boom camps of the '6o's and '70's, except that law and order reigns. The oil of the High Border does not compare with that of the Texas or California fields in quantity, since the great gushers of these fields are lacking; but the fields of the High Border generally have a thick, oil-bearing strata which will probably remain active for decades to come.

They say that a geologist, scouting in Teton County,

Montana, came across two cowboys cooking a meal over a small natural flame flickering from the earth—natural gas. This led to the discovery of crude oil and the pouring of millions of dollars into the pockets of dryland farmers who were almost broke.

Oil has made a tremendous change in the dryland settlement of a decade or two decades ago. The water tower is still there, the street is still there, but crude oil has been spread to lay the dust and the old school has been replaced by a new and larger building. The prairie spreads vast and remote as ever, dusty skyline to dusty skyline, but there are derricks dotting the land and roads run across the prairie where a few years ago cattle grazed undisturbed. The narrow street is crowded with traffic—big trucks, expensive cars. There's a rush and hurry, an air of strained excitement. Down there they're clearing out a lot for a possible well, and presently an ugly, pyramid-shaped derrick, enclosed in rusty tin to keep out the eternal wind, will rise and the engines will go to work, while the metal bit goes thumping down into the earth. No matter where you are you will hear that drill by day and by night: thump, thump—interminably.

There are strange men around, with soft Texas voices—for the men of the Texas fields head north to the oil strikes of Montana and Wyoming. There are new homes—with new trees, set by hand and nursed by hand. There is a consciousness of civic life that finds expression in service clubs and mayoralty elections. There is talk of zoning—to keep derricks away from certain parts of the town. There's talk of this and that, but always there's an underlying theme, and that is oil—oil, and the millions it will bring.

Any night, in the poolhalls, the saloons, or the hotel lobbies, you get the spirit. In hotel lobbies the men are of the promoter type, in the saloons and poolhalls they are the workers; but the theme is the same—oil. In the bars they stand four and five deep, kidding the barmaids or the bartender, whooping hilariously and dancing to the tune of a jangly orchestra. You call for a drink, elbowing your way through the mob to get it, spilling half of it before you maneuver the glass to your mouth. You turn to watch the space reserved for dancing; a couple has just taken a fall, the man sliding halfway across the floor. He lies there, whooping in whole-hearted enjoyment, then gets unsteadily to his feet. His partner, red-faced under her rouge, screams, "C'm' on, Charlie! Don't give up!"

The orchestra crashes into fresh boogie-woogie and the barmaid yells out, "This one's on me, hon!" and flourishes another glass. Again you spill half the contents. But you don't care. The stuff isn't very well mixed anyway.

Leather jackets are universally worn, or sheepskins if it is winter; heavy trousers and boots complete the dress. Even in hotel lobbies many of the geologists and promoters and oil barons wear boots and cannot be distinguished from the roustabouts and drillers and truckers who do the heavy work, except perhaps for a certain softness of feature. And day and night there is talk of oil—oil—oil. Occasionally you overhear, "Was that a binge I was on last night! Oh, man!" from oil baron and laborer alike.

Gordon Campbell, geologist, stood one day on the sandstone rim of a two-hundred-foot drop that winds interminably through north central Montana, giving to that section of the prairie the look of a gigantic shallow bowl, a downdrop known locally as the Rim. Gordon Campbell sensed oil; but he had no backing, nothing but his hunch and geological knowledge. He was then drilling a well near Roundup, Montana, which was a last hope for the state of Montana as far as concerned oil, for the geologist of one of the world' greatest oil companies had made the statement that he would drink all the oil ever produced in Montana. Campbell's well came in. Producing only a few hundred barrels a day, it was no gusher, but it opened the Cat Creek field which boomed during the '20's and then languished in the '30's.

Gordon Campbell remembered the Rim, the vast bowl of prairie, and when the dryland ranchers, on the point of catastrophe because of drought, sent for him and offered him a chance—and $250—he accepted. He scraped together enough to lease 100,000 acres—and in this region at the time a thousand acres was so small as to be scorned— and began to drill. The well came in; again no gusher, but it was all right. Gordon Campbell had discovered the Kevin-Sunburst oil field, in a land once crossed by the Whoop-up Trail. Here the most prominent settlement became Shelby, mentioned before.

A few years later, during the early 1930's, a new oil territory some few miles westward was opened up and developed into the Cut Bank field, said to be the largest oil area in the world. Here drilling goes on feverishly, surpassed in the High Border only by that of Wyoming fields. A newspaper, the *Pioneer Press,* in 1910 recorded such incidents as: "Dan Goff of Chester had an altercation with the town marshal. The marshal is a good shot. Mr. Goff is minus a finger." During Prohibition years it told the story of the man who trained ducks to carry liquor over the border: He tied bottles under the ducks' wings, released the birds north of the border, and called them to earth on the American side of the line. Today it prints such items as:

"Glacier Production—Fed. Land B. No. 2 C SE¼ SW¼ 30-34-5W, Oil 2834."

"Reagan-Tribal 194 No. 1 CEL SE¼ NE¼ 22-37-7W, Oil-Gas 3865."

Baffling information to the uninitiated, but to the oil fraternity it is the drilling log that keeps them posted concerning the progress and location of wells.

Bill Fulton, known at one time in his varied career as the "dry-hole king" because of the number of dry holes— "dusters"—he had drilled in search of oil, was originally a Wyoming man. He discovered signs of oil in a section to the south of the Cut Bank and Kevin-Sunburst areas. His first drilling rig caught fire and was destroyed; his second crumbled, breaking both his arms; fracturing his skull, nearly gouging out an eye. When he came out of the hospital, however, he did not hesitate; with the optimism of the old prospector or the miner of the '60's, he began to drill again—"wildcatting" for a million dollars.

He drilled twenty-seven dry holes in succession.

He was at the end of his rope. His credit had gone; he was as thoroughly broken financially as it is possible for a human being to be. But he persisted, deciding to cease wildcatting operations and settle down to something sure. He planned to lease a section of land in the Kevin-Sunburst field, drill a small well, and live beside it. He was through with the big money.

He drilled into country where wells had been pumping about ten barrels per day. His first well pumped 110 bar-

rels a day. He decided to drill a second. It came in 1600
barrels a day. His third well produced $1,000,000 worth of
oil in the first eighteen months.

Bill Fulton became a "wildcatter" again—in Colorado,
New Mexico, and other sections of Montana. In the midst
of his renewed activities, he was caught in an automobile
accident. No man could live in his condition, they said; yet
Bill Fulton, with doggedness that had enabled him to
endure disappointments, recovered. He lives today in
northern Montana, one of the oil barons whose tenacity
of purpose enabled him to became a baron after the most
utter failures.

Whetstone, Tarrant, Aaronson, Reagan, Cobb, and a
score of others, all the way from the border fields of
Montana to the Wyoming country, are the men around
whose names the sagas of the oil land are woven. They are
the oil pioneers, but the oil land is not yet old enough
to call them pioneers. The future will take care of that.

The future . . . when the oil runs out and the settlements resemble the ghost towns of gold which are everywhere in the mountain area. Nowhere have towns been
abandoned more quickly than in the gold country along
the Continental Divide. There are dozens of these ghost
towns, some large, some small; there is, for example, the
ghost town of Goldbutte.

GHOST TOWN

Back in the '60's an Indian discovered traces of gold in
a gulch along the western slope of the Sweetgrass Hills
in Montana. His discovery precipitated the usual stampede.
In the gulch Goldbutte sprang into existence. Miners'

shacks, stores, saloons came into existence. There was no
timber for construction except far up in the hills, and this
the miners dragged down with great difficulty. The camp
seems to have had both peaceful and smoky times; at all
events, the miners co-operated profitably by sharing the
little water that flowed through the gulch—water necessary
for the recovery of the gold. They profited; and, as long
as the golden sand held out, the settlement boomed.

Then the gold was no more and the town closed down
almost overnight. Miners emigrated to more profitable
gulches; saloonkeepers boarded up their windows; the
ladies departed. Silence fell over the land, except for
coyotes, an occasional Indian, and sometimes a rider from
the cattle ranches which had begun to flourish to the south
and west. In time, somebody opened a store, and the
ranchers began to make Goldbutte a provisioning center.
The cattle boom roused in earnest, and pilgrim cattle from
Texas came into the land, wading belly deep through buffalo grass and sweetgrass. Goldbutte drowsed, except for
its store and a hotel to provide a stopping place for ranchers riding scores of miles for supplies.

It is still a ghost town—below it spreads the dusty prairie.
To the west, dim in distance, lie the Rockies. To the north
the land breaks raggedly into Canada. To the east the hills
thrust up like cliffs, raggedly forested on the crown.

Unless there's a stray steer moving somewhere, your impression is one of silence—deep, thick, unfathomable silence. Up on the hillside there is a dreary heap of dirt
and the gaping mouth of a mine shaft abandoned years
ago. In the gulch, the stream flows, placidly muddy, pooled
here and there, for during the 1930's a gold-mining company put in a dragline outfit in an attempt to secure

the flour gold that had escaped the prospectors' pans and flumes. Draglines are steam shovels which lift the dirt, together with washing plants which extract the gold from the dirt—the whole representing an inexpensive and clumsy version of a gold dredge. Draglines are found everywhere in Montana and Wyoming and Idaho, recovering gold where the field is not large enough or rich enough to justify the installation of million-dollar dredges. The dragline at Goldbutte did not, evidently, prove profitable, for after a season or two it closed down.

Silence over a ghost town is so great that when a stone rattles underfoot you jump nervously. After you've been standing still for a spell, it takes minutes to adjust your ears again to the sound of your boots along the hillside. You stare at the sagging buildings, the false-fronted stores. One large building in particular fascinates you and you work a board off the paneless window and peer in, hesitantly, not knowing what may jump out at you. The place appears to be somewhat better preserved than other buildings—probably having been used recently. Dust covers the bar at one end of the room. An old gold scales stands on the bar. Behind, above a cracked mirror, hangs a picture —of Custer's Last Battle—distributed by a brewing company and once a fixture in every saloon. A rat scampers along the floor.

Down the gulch there is a rough log and board building, with roof fallen in, windows gone, and floor torn up —the remains of a hurdy-gurdy.

The sun is hot against the hills, and the sky is bright, and the horizon seems hazier than ever as you stumble down the slope to your car on the road at the bottom. From somewhere a gopher pipes shrilly, breaking the spell of the silence. From somewhere over the hills a steer bawls, the sound echoing up the gulch. Then the silence closes down again, and you get into your car, staring up at the bleak ruins against the gulch side, the rain-washed heaps of waste at the mouths of prospect holes, the dusty stretch of the gulch itself, the pools of unhealthy-looking water where mosquitoes breed by night and by day hot mirror-surfaces glare at you. This is Goldbutte, representative of the many ghost towns of the High Border mountains, settlements that will crumple year by year until the day comes when the expression "ghost town" will have no meaning at all. You step on the starter, your car bangs into life, and the hum of the motor is deafening. Then you move off down the narrow, rutted road, the ghosts dropping behind you.

WHEAT LAND

It's hot—so hot that when you sit on the metal seat of the tractor your sweat-soaked overalls hiss. There is a white flame of sun overhead and a yellow glare springs up from the prairie of wheat which stretches without break between skylines so level that Paul Bunyan might have smoothed them by hand. Up ahead of you a couple of hundred horses stampede in the engine block of the tractor, and behind—a monotone under the screech and bang and clash of loose-coupled pitments and concaves— the engine of the combine harvester echoes the rhythm.

A fifteen-foot, razor-toothed knife, flung back and forth until it is as invisible as the propeller of an airplane, chews into the wheat. An inferno of sound culminates in the stormy hiss of the yellow stream pouring from the elevators into a fifty-five-bushel bin hung on the side of the combine, and in the roar of chaff flung rearward by an artificial cyclone. Dust is everywhere, and so are the flies. The constant jarring of the tractor gives a man internal disorders so acute that they may mean permanent injury. And there's heat, heat, heat—heat of sun, reflected heat of the wheat fields, heat of the engine. You soak an old sheepskin in water, and you stand on it—you've got to stand, for no spine will endure that jouncing of the metal seat hour after hour without injury—but even then the heat burns through the soles of your boots and blisters your feet.

You're an engine man and behind your tractor you're dragging a combine harvester on which a combine tender rides. The wheat harvest of the High Border is on—has been on for ten days, will be in full rush for ten days more. Dark Hard Northern spring wheat—bread of the world; for Dark Hard Northern contains protein, and millers must have protein. You shift your burning feet, slap your ears, and wonder if silence still exists. Bread of the world—you're the magician responsible for it. The bin is almost full. You peer down the road that stretches like a hot, white ribbon towards the elevator and railroad twenty miles away. There's a small, black bug chased by a cloud of dust rolling along, and that will be Eddie, one of the truckmen. He bounces out into the field, under the bin, and you release the wheat into the truck. Then he's gone for town. Somewhere he'll pass the other two boys who are hauling. You have to sell the wheat as soon as you harvest it—whether the price is a dollar a bushel or twenty cents. There's money due on the combine, the tractors, the three trucks, the plows and discs. If luck holds, you'll have them all paid for next year, but they're worn out and you need new ones. And so it continues, year after year. Ole Gustaferson, who ranches a 640-acre plot over east, says, "Ya, we work for the machinery company all our life! Maybe the machinery company should bury us, ya?"

Heat—you sit on the steel seat to release the clutch, and jump up quickly. You'll not be sitting comfortably for a long time. You lean on the steering wheel and dream, for there is now no discord in this terrific clash of sound to keep you alert. It's a symphony of thunderous metal. You dream. Bread—you're the magician in overalls and sunglasses who is making it. You're the creator of the staff of life. You're responsible for women who worry about their figures. Without you men could not manipulate grain in Chicago and get rich—or go broke. Oh, you're a power, all right—and then a pitment screeches off key and, as you pause to grease it, you dream no more.

Then on again, with the bin filling steadily. Still the heat. Once more you dream—this time about heat. There's heat overhead and heat up in the engine—terrific heat in the engine: heat so intense that you pipe steam from the boiling radiator to cool it. Steam to cool steel.

But you wish you had something to cool you. Three times today you've emptied the canteen bag and still there's thirst raging through you. You wish there were plenty of water in this dry country—this dusty country, but there isn't. Rainfall is only a little more than that of desert regions and the creeks run full only in the spring, or at times of a flash flood in summer. On your ranch you haul drinking water from the hills twelve or twenty or thirty miles away; other water, for washing, for the radiators of the engines, you get from a cistern filled with melted snow and runoff from the roofs of buildings.

Water—it would be a salvation. Year by year the horizon grows dustier, the dust storms are bigger, darker, denser, and more and more fields are stripped of thin top soil down to the gravel a few inches below. The Great American Desert—creeping up out of the central states and Dakota into eastern and northern Montana. There is menace of a complete Dust Bowl—a menace lightened at intervals, during certain years, when rainfall is luckily heavy.

This land, once so fertile, is reaping the whirlwind. The wheat ranchers destroyed the prairie, tore out the grass roots in their need—and greed—for more acreage. Disaster lies ahead unless a series of wet years comes along to pack down what soil is left.

This land should never have been taken from the Indians, you say, cursing it; but as a wheat rancher, you know it's your living and any kind of a living is a good living. There's a discordant note and you drop out the clutch. This time it's a spark plug missing. You change hastily to a clean one. Plugs foul fast from the fuel the wheatland rancher uses—distillate.

Now, it's another day. No heat today. Last night a norther swooped down, right out of the Medicine Hat, and today the hot engine feels good. But there's still dust. And wind. Wind that moans, screeches, thrills; the wind that is the evil genius of this land, the master of the prairie. Today it's blowing hard—too hard for combining, really, but ripe wheat in the field is exposed to a hundred different forms of destruction, and you must harvest what you can before you lose it. You've got to have the money—got to put in another crop.

You'll put in a crop in the spring—on land mulched over this summer. Summer-fallowed, it's called, and it will always produce a crop of some sort, unless the wind strips it away. Some wheat you'll drill into the stubble. Shotgunning, that is called. There are shot-gun farmers who were lucky and had wet years and made thousands of dollars. Ranchers keep trying to diminish the odds in a game where chance is all powerful, where the odds are against them: the seeded wheat may blow out shortly after it's drilled in; if the spring is too wet, the seed will rot in the ground. During the growing season, a period of relative security, there are the ravages of rabbits and gophers and the wild horses that still range in the breaks. When the grain is heading, you must have rain or there will be no heads; hot winds may shrivel it; rust and smut will destroy it. Once the grain is ripe, rain a few days before combining will bleach it. But these are merely small hazards. There are the big ones, the all-devastating ones— hail, grasshoppers, Mormon crickets, wind that flails the heads clean, and sparks of fire which in the space of a minute can destroy a twenty-thousand-dollar field.

You think in thousands of dollars, deal in thousands of dollars, your debts are counted in thousands of dollars, and during harvest you carry wheat checks that run into four figures—but when it's all over and the interest is paid on the debts, or the debts are paid, you're lucky to have a few hundred dollars left to tide you over into next season. You live in tomorrow—next year; next year will be a bumper crop, next year you'll be out of debt.

Life to those who deal in wheat is a great gamble. They throw the dice with drought and dust and wind. Time is precious. No telling what tomorrow may bring—perhaps complete destruction.

The only thing any wheat rancher is sure about is that he'll go to bed dog-tired tonight with this year's cutting almost done. He'll dream of next year. There's a long winter between, but his next crop is the goal. In the long winter the desert of wheat becomes a white, frozen desert of silence. It's a sterile period, but an easy one, with nothing to do but play cards, get drunk, overhaul machinery, worry about debts—and hope.

FOREST

The forested wildernesses of the High Border are as vast and as deep as anything in the United States, or, for that matter, on the North American continent. It is a more inviting and picturesque land than the prairies, but there is danger in the forest, too, and the greatest danger is revealed by the vast scars in the green of mountain sides, by the tiny lookouts perched on every high pinnacle in the national forests—fire. Fire is the enemy of the forest. In summer a blue mist hangs all too often along the thousand miles or so of Continental Divide and spreads for hundreds of miles down on the prairie; by it you know that somewhere flames are leaping in the forest while men fight valiantly to save the trees that provide the High Border with one of its greatest natural resources. There are too few trees left, for the lumber barons swept the mountains clear and everywhere there is "stump land," waste land as desolate in its way as the dusty, worn-out fields of eastern Montana and Dakota.

Along U. S. Highway No. 10 through the Bitterroots of

eastern Montana, on the route to the Coeur d'Alene country of Idaho, there are fire meters to remind the traveler
that this region was at one time swept by a fire which in
the High Border—and perhaps in all the West, for that
matter—has no parallel:

It was in 1910 that the hills of the Coeur d'Alenes flamed
up in this greatest of conflagrations. Fire-fighters were at
work, and E. C. Pulaski, named by the forest supervisor
at Wallace to direct the men in one of the camps, was
supervising the building of breaks when on August 20 a
wind of hurricane proportions sprang up. The wind was
so strong that riders had difficulty remaining in their saddles and horses refused to face into it. That the forests
were doomed seemed certain; orders came for the men to
escape to Wallace, Idaho, a place of relative safety though
not wholly outside the danger zone, for timber extended
right down to the settlement. Pulaski and forty-five men
retreated and found themselves surrounded by flames and
falling trees. The heat peeled the skin off their faces and
the backs of their hands, and the flame-pressure was so
great that they could scarcely breathe.

The men were Pulaski's responsibility, and he determined to do what was possible for them. Soaked blankets,
the usual last recourse of fire-fighters, had to be discarded,
and the men were on the verge of panic. Pulaski kept his
head and led the crew in search of safety. By great, good
fortune, he discovered an old abandoned mine tunnel.
He ordered the men into this and forced them to lie face
down on the floor. Across the opening of the tunnel he
strung wet blankets that dried out and seared soon after
he had finished fitting them.

Smoke hung along the roof of the tunnel and the men's

hair curled—literally—in the heat. Outside the tunnel's entrance the flame lifted like that of a blacksmith's forge, a billion times expanded. Two horses were in with the men. The smoke thickened and lungs felt alternately filled and crushed.

"I can't stand it!" one of the crew screamed and, climbing to his feet, he made a rush for the entrance of the tunnel. Outside lay certain death, Pulaski knew; and though here inside the chances of living were slender enough, there was still a chance. He drew his gun and threatened the man.

"You come a step more this way and I'll kill you!"

The man came to his senses and lay down again sucking in the relatively fresher air along the floor of the tunnel. Pulaski himself remained upright, pouring water on the blankets and keeping them in place; his gun ready for any man who attempted a break. Men laughed uncontrollably; many of them dropped off into unconsciousness. Darkness was falling now—though darkness in the flame-light was something unreal. Darkness began to fall over Pulaski, too, and he dropped back against the side of the tunnel's mouth, his eyes closing.

"The boss's dead!" some man whispered.

Pulaski managed to pull himself together. His hair was gone now, his clothes were half gone, and his hands and cheeks and lips were seared of skin. The night hours swung by and the flames passed. By five in the morning ashes were cool enough for the men to wade through them. Pulaski let his charges emerge from the tunnel. The men ran here and there, seeking water; but the heat had dried up all the water and the watercourses were filled with ashes.

The men then set out for Wallace, not too far away. Most of them were clad in charred shreds, and they made a ghastly crew, reeling along a trail ankle-deep with white ashes, supporting each other but supporting most of all their boss, Pulaski. They stumbled into Wallace and collapsed on a street corner while townspeople rushed to care for them. A doctor bent over Pulaski, examined him, and then straightened somberly.

"Eyes burnt out. Blind!"

But E. C. Pulaski's eyes were not entirely gone, though he was blind for two months. For other months he struggled to recapture his health, hindered both by his blindness and by a severe attack of pneumonia. When he did recover, the marks of his afternoon and night in the red inferno remained upon him forever—poor eyes, weak lungs and throat, a general weakened condition that prevented any further hard work of the type demanded of forest workers.

Fire-fighting since 1910 has advanced almost as much as the art of warfare. Today fire lookouts stationed at lonely stations on lonelier peaks spot the first smoke and report instantly to the headquarters of fire-control units. If the threatened area is accessible, fast cars rush fighters to the scene of the flames. On the more difficult terrain parachutists can be dropped from airplanes to deal with a small blaze before it has had time to develop into a full-fledged inferno. This latter technique, developed during the seasons of 1939 and 1940 in the Missoula, Montana, forest district, may in the future be perfected to the point of complete fire control. Even when parachutists are not used today, the airplane plays its part—supplying fire-fighters with food and tools, in a few minutes achieving what ten or twenty years ago took days to do—and a few minutes may make a vast difference in forest fires.

Pulaski was a hero of 1910; a 1940 hero is Clarence B. Sutliffan, assistant national forest supervisor in the Bitterroot Mountains, those towering offshoots of the Continental Divide in the western section of the High Border Country. During the fire season of 1940—when the sun blazed all day long like a red flame and smoke hung over the mountains in a blue-black pall and every dry lightning storm brought new fears to the lookouts—flames raged along Roaring Lion Creek in the Bitterroot Mountains. This particular creek flows deep in a forested canyon and, in order to provide fire-fighters battling the blaze with supplies and equipment, airplanes were compelled to fly between mile-high crags. Dick Johnson, manager of a commercial flying service employed by the forestry authorities to fly men and supplies into the menaced area, and Clarence B. Sutliffan dropped along the gorge in a plane one day, carrying material for men on the ground. Beneath them a crown fire was sweeping along and the intense heat of flame created up- and down-drafts of force beyond the pilot's calculation. Original plans had been to parachute the supplies into an open camping spot, but smoke obliterated the site and the pilot was compelled to bank sharply in order to turn in the narrow space between the mountain walls. The bank was achieved without difficulty and the plane went roaring along the back route, headed out of the canyon, when an air current caught the light craft and tossed it about like a cork on a cascade.

"We're gonna crash!" Dick Johnson yelled.

Underbrush and jagged, rocky points leaped up at the fluttering plane. Sutliffan braced himself between two sleeping bags, hoping to cushion the shock of the crash. The pilot managed to throw the switch the instant before the plane went skidding into the brush, trees, and rocks, otherwise neither he nor Sutliffan would have lived to tell the story. There was no explosion when the plane hit, but the shock was terrific. A wing, sheared off, went hurtling dozens of yards away. What was left of the plane nosed over, clamped down on Sutliffan; something smashed against his head and knocked him unconscious.

This lasted for only a few minutes, however, and Sutliffan regained consciousness to hear a drip, drip of gasoline in the wreckage. At a considerable distance down the canyon but too close for comfort, the fire edged forward slowly. What would happen if the flames did reach the wreck was not difficult to imagine, and Sutliffan fought to free himself. It took time but at last he managed to make his way out of the wreckage and into the open. The first thing he saw was Johnson, the pilot.

Johnson hung head down, unconscious, his legs wedged in twisted metal crossbars. Sutliffan was injured, but not incapacitated; blood dripped from his fingers and spread over his chest and face from numerous cuts in cheeks and neck. He pried at the crossbars, but the steel, twisted into a trap around the pilot's legs, refused to budge. Sutliffan found a heavy, pointed rock and pounded at the metal.

It was no easy task. Sutliffan battered one point of granite to pieces and then picked up another. The fire had moved closer and though it traveled at a very leisurely pace it seemed to move with the speed of light. With a third rock Sutliffan managed to shock the metal apart;

Johnson dropped forward, falling onto a sleeping bag Sutliffan had spread out. The jar partly awakened him, and he groaned.

Sutliffan half dragged, half carried the pilot through the underbrush, searching for some place of safety. Several times he fell, but each time he forced himself up. At last he found a spot that seemed to offer a certain amount of safety—a sort of meadow, with rocks on three sides and, on the fourth, brush that was not so dry as to be easily inflammable. Here he dropped the pilot and sat down himself to rest.

What had happened behind him he could only guess, but the flames seemed to have ceased their forward movement. The thick crown growth appeared to thin out down the canyon, and the fire was dying from lack of fuel. Sutliffan remembered the radio in the plane. The plight of the still-unconscious Johnson, and of himself, was desperate. He must secure help. He forced himself into motion, retraced his steps, and found to his great joy that the fire had burnt out some distance from the plane, so that the wreckage was untouched. This joy was short-lived, however, for the radio was in no shape to be of use. Sutliffan then returned to Johnson, made him as comfortable as possible, and then decided to set out in search of some settler's home or a telephone.

Falling darkness made matters worse; what was more, Sutliffan feared that, once away from the pilot, he might not be able to find his way back. He got out his pocket knife to blaze trees as he moved on through the timber.

He was beginning to stiffen now from his wounds, and it was difficult for his injured hands even to hold the knife. But he persisted and covered a certain distance; was, indeed, congratulating himself that he did not do so badly when spasms of pain overtook him. He fell to the ground and lay there, wondering if this were the end. Sutliffan closed his eyes, and knew it would be impossible for him to go much further.

Just then he heard voices. He called out.

It was a party of C.C.C. boys, fighting the fire from below. They answered Sutliffan's hail, carried him to safety, followed his blazed trail to get the pilot. Both men recovered; and Sutliffan later received a medal from the American Fire Medal Board.

VELKOMMEN, OLAV, MARTHA!

As long as there are Norwegians on the High Border they will talk of the visit of Crown Prince Olav and Crown Princess Martha in the late spring of 1939. The country had just gone through a fairly disappointing winter financially, but the Norwegians bestirred themselves at news that Martha and Olav, currently touring America, were headed for Montana; they took up a subscription to make sure there would be adequate entertainment for the royal couple—some Norwegians subscribing as much as $100 to the fund. At the same time the King and Queen of England were touring the United States; they did not come to the High Border Country, but if they had their reception would have been mild compared to the one given to Olav and Martha. The High Border is Scandinavian country, even in the mountains. That fact is decisive.

Montanans collected their entertainment fund and with part of it purchased two riding outfits—chaps, hats, boots, saddles, bridles, and all the trimmings. Roy E. Ayers, Montana's current governor, proclaimed a Velkommen Day. Crown Prince Olav and Crown Princess Martha journeyed to the High Border with the usual fanfare of a royal visit —usual, until they reached Montana, where the celebration became intense and the Norwegians went wild, and never will these two personages encounter such a sincere welcome anywhere again.

Helena, capital of Montana, was chosen as center for festivities, and on the day Olav and Martha arrived some fifteen thousand people lined the narrow main street. (The entire population numbers about fifteen thousand.) Ranchers traveled for hundreds of miles—coming all the way from the Dakotas, some of them—to do the visitors honor.

Helena was also in the grip of another celebration—her Diamond Jubilee, celebrating the seventy-fifth year of her founding. For weeks display boards had bragged that Helena's Diamond Jubilee would be a Ring-tailed Caterwampus, and the town was dressed for the occasion. Business houses were false-fronted with logs and bark, whiskers, of course, were everywhere. A traveling salesman said, "This place must be prosperous. I've never seen so many well-dressed bums." "Is there a new religion around here?" asked another.

Velkommen! shouted the crowds at the railway stations along the line of travel. In Helena there was a dinner and reception in the civic center—an edifice formerly the Algeria Shrine temple, a building of Moorish design with a minaret, barrel-vaulted roof, grilled windows, and mosaic entrance. The surprise which this exotic temple gives visitors to Montana is sometimes very great. In this building the prince and princess sat down to a dinner introduced

by a musical program which included such numbers as
Dance of the Dwarfs and *Home on the Range.* The royal
pair were then given their riding outfits.

There were speeches, of course, and the prince talked,
first in the English tongue, then hesitantly in Norwegian,
whereupon a large part of the audience went berserk. Norwegians from the prairies, from the mountains, from Wyoming and Dakota, slapped each other across the back. The
impression the pair gave was wholly satisfactory, and when
they left everybody was on hand to see them off. The
crowd around the train was one of the largest ever seen
at the station. When the train pulled out, the Norwegians
went sadly back to their homes or their sheep or cattle
ranges, feeling that an old friend had come and gone.

Later the prince and princess visited Yellowstone and
Glacier National Parks. In Glacier the Blackfeet Tribe,
following its twentieth-century custom of adopting and
naming important persons, initiated the royal pair into
the tribe, giving to them the honorable names of Rising
Wolf and Flying Eagle.

Country Lore

Where there are mountains there are, inevitably, caverns. The hills of the High Border have their share of
such natural formations; two of them should be mentioned here—Morrison Cave in Montana, Shoshone Cavern
in Wyoming.

In 1902 Dan Morrison, prospector, camped in the vicinity of the cave named for him. At dusk one night, he
watched bats emerging from seemingly impenetrable rock;
next day he investigated—to discover, overlooking the Jef-

ferson River, a hole in the ground of such gloomy aspect
that he was a bit disconcerted. He was fascinated, however;
he tied a rope around his middle, lashed the loose end
to a rock, and descended. He did not have any exciting
adventures, but he saw enough to convince him that this
was more than an ordinary hole in the ground. He returned later and built steps and ladders which served
casual tourists until the year 1935 when the National Park
Service took a hand in the matter and annexed the area.
A C.C.C. group made the place presentable and assisted
in the installation of lights. Morrison Cave is one of the
scenic points of the High Border and is advertised, with
some truth, as the equal of the caverns of the East—Luray
and Mammoth.

The discovery of Shoshone involved a bit of drama. Ned
Frost, on a January day of 1909, in pursuit of a bobcat or
cougar, followed his hounds over the rim-rock. The beast
abruptly disappeared and Frost, seeking the solution, came
upon a great opening in the rock. That he had found a
cavern did not occur to him; he was more intent upon his
quarry, and without hesitation he plunged in after the
cat, his dogs crowding around his feet. Darkness struck
at him, and he drew matches from his pocket, lighting
them one after the other until it began to dawn upon him
that this was a full-fledged cavern. One did not travel
casually through caverns even in pursuit of cats, Mr. Frost
decided, and he began to retrace his steps—to find himself
faced by pitch-dark and the panicky certainty that he had
utterly lost himself.

His dogs, frightened, crowded around him and whim-
pered, which did not contribute to his peace of mind; for

if the animals could not find the way out, what chance had he?

He debated the situation for a time. He was down to four matches now. He discovered several old letters in his pocket, which he tore into strips and twisted into makeshift torches. He lighted one and went stumbling forward. Then he noticed that the dust of centuries lay thickly on the floor of the cavern, so thickly that his boots had made imprints. It was like a trail through snow. Mr. Frost's heart lightened and he hastily retraced his path. He passed through various vaulted chambers and was upon the point of losing himself in the dark again, his last torch turning black in his fingers, when he glimpsed a streak of light. Presently Mr. Frost hastened from the cavern, drew a deep breath, and blew the dust from his clothes.

Frost related his adventure in the settlement of Cody—named after Colonel William F. Cody, better known as Buffalo Bill. Bill was among those first to enter the cavern. The cavern itself was named after the Shoshone Indians, who also gave their name to counties, rivers, and many other natural formations of the Northwest. Shoshone is almost as familiar a name in the High Border as Sage—which at least two hundred creeks are called—or St. Mary's, which Father De Smet started.

The father had a distinct fondness for the name St. Mary's and today there are St. Mary's lakes, rivers, creeks, crossings, peaks, hills, without number. The miners were somewhat uncouth in their choice of place names, a cause of lament to a Blackrobe of a later era, Father Palladino, who wrote: ". . . St. Mary's river, St. Mary's peak, St. Mary's valley. What charms did not Our Lady's name lend at once to things and places. . . . Grasshopper, Boulder,

Horseshoe, Dry Gulch, Crow's Nest, Dead Horse. How
vulgar and how trivial are these when compared to the
noble and elevating appelations supplied by religions!"

The good father omitted Horse Heaven Hills, Butter-
milk Joe Creek, Dirty Ed Gulch, and the Sleeping Jesus
Hills—a name neglected by the Geological Survey which
later made names official. The Geological Survey sup-
pressed other local names, too; the three forks of the Jefferson River which Lewis and Clark in 1805 named Philosophy, Wisdom and Philanthropy (for President Jefferson's cardinal virtues) were generally known as Stinkin'
Water Forks. The Geological Survey decided that Stinking
Water should become a genteel Ruby.

Through Montana's biennial legislative session in 1941
stalked a feathered, beaded figure—Chief Enaes Granjo,
president of the Flathead Indian tribal council. Granjo,
moody, inscrutable, speaking through an interpreter,
sought from the white men certain rights given his tribe
years before—in a treaty made in 1855, principals to which
were the Blackfeet, other Indians, and the white men
represented by Isaac I. Stevens. By this treaty the Blackfeet not only agreed to remain north of the Sun and Missouri Rivers in Montana, but to cease warring upon the
Flatheads. The Flatheads were given the right to roam in
pursuit of fish and game to the Continental Divide, but
not beyond, this country being reserved for the Blackfeet
and other tribes of the plains.

It came about that the Flatheads were rounded up on
the Indian reservation of that name in western Montana;
they were given the right to hunt and fish on their tribal
lands but not elsewhere unless they purchased a white

man's hunting license. This was clearly in defiance of the treaty of 1855. The white man, however, has always made light of the treaty and has for many years derided suggestions that the treaty be honored. So it came about that Enaes Granjo, somber, not too optimistic, stalked the corridors of the capitol in Helena and did his best to secure treaty rights for his people. The chief was a picturesque figure, but was not taken too seriously. At the same time the redskins from another reservation were seeking legal rights to use the peyote bean in their religious ceremonies —a perennial issue in the state of Montana and to all intents a lost cause. Both Enaes Granjo and the peyote religionists were defeated.

The Flathead Reservation sprawls over some of the best duck and upland game bird hunting country in the High Border. Chief Enaes Granjo and his council took steps to bring this matter of treaty violation to the attention of the sportsmen of the country, if to nobody else. They threatened to close their reservation to all white hunters. The resulting howl was heard as far east as Washington, D. C.

Generally, redskins throughout the High Border are given the right to hunt and fish the year around on their reservations. Many Indian families are dependent upon game and fish for survival. Some years previously the Blackfeet Indians on their reservation up under Glacier National Park on the Canadian border had levied a special fee on white men using the reservation for sport; the grumbling was pitiful to hear.

SHEEPHERDER

Of High Border men—cowboy, miner, lumberjack, forest ranger, farmer, dude, drylander, baron—no one epitomizes the country better, perhaps than that individual so despised by the cattlemen, so untouched by any aura of heroism: the sheepherder.

The sheepherder is a sadly maligned figure, and this is not said in jest. It is true that the suicide rate among sheepherders is excessive, that many of them go out of their minds, that the sheepherder and his dog silhouetted against an evening skyline fills one with the ultimate in sadness. It is also true that sheepherders exist to help provide us with food and clothing.

Large sections of the High Border are sheep country. On the grasslands up under the Rockies, on prairie lands that have not been worn out by reckless greed for wheat, on barren hills and in national forests, you find sheep. You find cattle, also, remnants of the great herds and the mighty ranches of the old days; but sheep are there in greater numbers for sheep, while more trouble to care for than cattle, are far more profitable. Probably the nearest approach today to the livestock baron of the '80's and '90's is the sheepman with his thousands of acres and his huge bands of sheep—a thousand head to a band, his dozens of sheepherders, his home ranch and sub-ranches, his acres of pens, and his scores of sheep dogs.

The home sheep ranch may lie in the wilderness beyond the civilization of oiled roads, miles off the main highway; perhaps it is on one of the main arteries of traffic. There will be a squat huddle of buildings—cookshacks,

shelters, bunkhouses; another huddle of strange architecture—upright posts roofed over with grass or hay or weeds
supported on a framework of poles—is the sheep shelters
for lambing, for protection in winter against the bitter
north wind. There are sheep corrals and corrals for the
pack horses and pack mules employed in summer when the
bands of sheep go forth into the mountains. There are
dogs everywhere, charging out at you in packs—collies.
These are the guardians of the herds, in for a vacation—
for no sheep dog can labor the year around; he must be
sent to the home ranch at intervals, to loaf and stuff himself and recuperate after the difficult task of guarding
sheep. There are brown-faced men in boots and Levis and
woolen shirts—or Pendleton shirts if it is Sunday—lounging
or working on fences or in the cookhouse listening to the
latest war news from the cook's radio. Or they are mend-
ing equipment—saddles, pack saddles, tarps, tents, the
many necessities that the raising of sheep requires. Over
all lies a faint aroma unlike any other odor in the world
—the smell of sheep; it makes you want to curl up your
nose, yet, once you are accustomed to it, it is no more
revolting than, say, the smoke-and-beer odor of a High
Border night club.

It is a peculiarly pungent and clinging odor; when
sheep have grazed a range it clings for weeks. It permeates
the clothes of men; it saturates the atmosphere. It is totally
unlike the odor of cattle, the sweet odor of wheat, the
dank odor of a deep mine, the soft odor of wind over
the prairie in the spring, the acrid odor of burning forest.
Even in the larger communities—Butte, Helena, Great
Falls, Cody, Cheyenne—you catch a whiff of it now and
then.

In the late spring—May and June—that most important event in the life of the female sheep takes place—birth. The herds, hay-fed most of the winter, are corralled in canyons or sheds where the cold will not interfere with the lambing, which is not too complicated an operation. The expectant ewe throws up her head twice, whereupon the men on watch push a "baby buggy" toward her—an arrangement on wheels, into which the ewe and her lamb, or twin lambs, are placed, to be wheeled to shelter where all are crowded closely together so that the mother may become thoroughly acquainted with her offspring—a ewe cannot recognize her offspring until she has learned the smell of it beyond doubt, and when a lamb dies very often the sheepmen strip off the pelt and place it upon a lamb whose mother has been lost. Sometimes there are lambs for whom it is not possible to provide a foster mother; they are often fed by hand and are known as bum or bummers and become pets on the ranches or for children in nearby settlements. Most bum lambs are given away to any asker, and everywhere in the sheep country you see them wandering in yards, blatting at your heels, staring at you out of yellow eyes.

After lambing follows the task of docking, or emasculating, the male sheep. After lambing and docking comes shearing, generally during the latter part of June or July. Shearing is now done by power-driven sheep shears. The sheep for shearing are driven into a shed; shearers—one or two or a score—having ground their clippers, weight them with a leather thong and a bit of metal for better handling. An engine bangs into life, the clippers buzz. A shearer, a man in white overalls, reaches into a chute held shut simply by a strip of gunnysacking, pulls out a sheep, squats it on the floor, runs his shears over it quickly and efficiently—within a few minutes. The sheep huddles in blind terror, too paralyzed with fright to make a move. The shearer concludes his task with a flourish, wrestles the animal to its feet, sends it slipping down another chute into the open to a man who brands it—with tar against the white clipped coat. Inside, the shearer wipes his clippers, swabs his forehead—for this is hard work, one of the hardest tasks on the High Border—moves upon his heelless shoes to ease his back, and then reaches for another sheep. He receives, generally, around fifteen cents per sheep— double for the bigger, stronger bucks of which every rancher keeps a herd from which to breed the ewes. The dirty clipped fleece is tied up by another man; he throws it to still another man who drops it into a ten-foot long burlap sack and stomps it down tightly.

The shearer finishes another sheep. You can see his face glisten. His white overalls are already black from grease and dirt; tonight his wife, camped down by the creek as long as the shearing crew is working at this ranch, will wash them, for each morning they must be clean. If he works with sufficient speed he may make as much as twenty-five dollars today—and he has to work hard and fast, for his period of employment is brief and what he accumulates during the summer is his only stipend during the winter; High Border shearers generally spend their months of unemployment in California or Oregon.

Each rancher is responsible for the shearing crew during its stay on his ranch. Shearers' wives and families live in shacks on the ranch or in tents pitched in favorable locations; the ranch cook must feed the shearers but never the wives and family, though it is customary for the cook to invite all up for the last meal of the shearers' stay at a particular ranch.

Naked, hollow, looking like something out of a bad dream, the sheep are driven into the mountains—or into the national forests where permits are required so that the country will not become overgrazed. One herder and his dogs make up the personnel for each band of sheep that heads into the wilderness. The herder's home for the summer is a tent. He is kept in contact with the home ranch by a camp tender who visits him periodically, brings canned food, perhaps a bottle of whiskey, sometimes fresh meat, though the herder may have provided his own meat illegally. A ceaseless feud is waged between game wardens and sheepherders. In the autumn the sheep come down out of the mountains ahead of the snow, the lambs are sold, and the ewes bred for next spring's lambing. During the winter the herder's home is a sheep wagon—canvas stretched over a frame fitted into the bed of a wagon, much like the prairie schooner of pioneer days but smaller. Fitted with a stove, the sheep wagon furnishes comfortable enough quarters.

The sheep graze by summer in mountain country; dark timbered skylines, with clouds piled overhead. There are days when the herders lie on the hillsides, while the dogs dance importantly around with tongues out and the sheep scatter through the dark timber, leisurely, and there is over the land a laziness subtle as a drug. By night the sheep lie in shelter, the herder sleeps in his bedroll, the dogs alternately drowse and then wake to bark off some intruding coyote, and there are miraculous stars overhead.

The sheepherder's life is extremely lonely and under the strain of it—though dudes think it is wonderful—the sheepherder sometimes cracks. He is apt to be a Roumanian or Basque—"Bosko," a Turk, Russian, Spaniard, any of the dozen different nationalities that take to sheepherding. He thinks endlessly of his homeland, perhaps, and broods about the second World War, and the strain affects him. Many times he is unable to read, so that he cannot occupy his mind with books and magazines sent out to him. Often he becomes erratic, slovenly, dreaming only of his infrequent trips to town where for the space of a few hours or a few days he drinks liquor to his heart's and stomach's content and patronizes the red-light district, to resume his old life only when the money he has spent weary months in earning has been dissipated.

These trips to town are not, of course, his only celebrations—there is always the Fourth of July, when he visits the small backwoods communities where there is always a rodeo on the Fourth and people foregather hell-bent for a good time. Generally these small settlements far back in the mountains are of a type almost uninhabited in winter, only sparsely populated in summer, and have no jails. The sheriff solves his problems by handcuffing drunks and other wrongdoers around jackpine trees. When the handcuffs run out, the solution is not so simple and the lawman or lawmen are apt to depart from the scene quietly. And then there may be fighting. It is not, indeed, remarkable on a Fourth of July celebration to find the county sheriff fighting it out with a couple of drunken men, while an interested crowd roars on the sidelines—seldom with any sympathy for the lawman.

Sheepherders. There was Pete the Turk, an inveterate reader whose tastes ranged from the *Atlantic Monthly* to pulp romances. There was Jude: nobody knew his last name—who studied the dictionary and when in town experimented with his knowledge, with such amazing results as "The keyotes inhabitin' Lyons Crick are gettin' a multitude of sheep, damn 'em to hell!" There was Pete, who one day read a health magazine and learned about the beneficent effects of the sun's rays; there and then he became a nudist, and it was startling to see along the road the sunburnt person of Pete, with a cap on his head, his beard straggling to his chest, a rifle over one naked shoulder, boots on his feet—but otherwise as naked as the day he was born. There was the Rooshian, with hair down to his shoulders, who dreaded the sight of women; would, indeed, run when he saw one and when trapped in a room suddenly invaded by a woman would huddle in a corner, his back to her, while he trembled like a whipped sheep dog. There was Porky, of Austrian antecedents, who in the old country sold postcards hand-painted by a certain Adolf Hitler and, until the invasion of his native land, kept a picture of the dictator in his camp wagon and on the center pole of his tent. And there was Porrgeria, representative of too many of the clan, who one day took the lace out of one boot, looped it at both ends in the manner of the freighters of the old days, put his foot in one loop and hooked the other around the trigger of a rifle, clamped his teeth on the muzzle of the weapon—and stepped down hard. Silence and loneliness and the eternal blatting of sheep and the eternal smell of them were destroying his reason, and he defeated insanity with suicide.

No man has ever raised any monument to the guardians of the sheep, despised by so many yet as nearly representative of a land as anyone else. The statue of a cattle baron stands on the Montana-Dakota border; the statue of a cop-

per baron stands in Butte; a dozen monuments have been
erected in memory of the builder of roads, John Mullan;
in the Black Hills the giant granite faces of Washington,
Lincoln, Theodore Roosevelt, and Jefferson stare down
with imposing calm. The cowboy has been immortalized,
not always wisely or well, in fiction and moving picture.
The lumberman finds glory in his buildings and in sagas
of the forests. The pioneer has been remembered.

Only the sheepherder, of all people on the High Border,
has been ignored, though he has contributed as much as
any other to the building of the land as it stands today.

Index

333